SURVIV

your

HEALTH

CARE

Michael M. Warren, MD

This book and its contents are not intended to replace the patient physician relationship. Neither is it intended to be exhaustive but rather, to identify some problems you might have. If questions arise from the use of this book, it is essential that you discuss them with your physician.

Published by:

Ledero Press
U.T. Box 35099
Galveston, Texas   77555-5099

Library of Congress Catalog Card No: 93-91539
ISBN: 0-9627775-3-6

To
Dolly, my wife
Debora, Robert, and Leslie, my children
and especially TO YOU, THE PATIENT

Contents

Acknowledgement

This book would not have been possible without the moral and editorial support of Mr. Ron Gilmore, Ms. Shelagh Yospur, Ms. Becky Walsdorf and Mr. Robert Warren.   Their expertise and advice have made it intelligible and accurate.

Preface

A few words about the use of this book are in order. The format is somewhat unusual, but it has been designed to be extremely beneficial to you, the reader-patient.

First, it is not only permissible but important to write in your book. Several portions provide spaces for you to complete, with data about medical history, medications and so forth. This information is invaluable to you and your physician, and since it can change from time to time, it is important to update the material periodically. The book can then be saved as a permanent record of your medical history.

At the beginning of the book there is a "pre-test," including a series of true/false questions. Please write your answers in the space provided. The same list of questions is repeated near the end of the book; and again, there is space for your answers. Answering the same questions twice—once before you begin the book and once after you have read it—will indicate how you have benefited from reading all the material in between.

Also at the end of the book is a series of questions about your health care. These questions focus on potential medical problems. Again, answer the questions by writing in the book. Should you answer "yes" to one or more of these questions, it is advisable to visit your doctor. While a positive answer does not mean you necessarily have a problem, it does mean you should check out the possibility with your doctor.

And most important of all? Reading this book and completing the list of questions must never be a substitute for visiting your doctor should you suspect there is a need for such a visit.

Following several chapters is a series of items arranged in a "check list" fashion. These focus on selected items that were discussed in that particular section and can be used to make sure you haven't forgotten anything of importance. Reviewing this material can be helpful when questions arise or when you are about to become involved in the health care system. Referring to the table of contents will direct you quickly to the check off lists.

Finally, remember to keep this book in a safe place but one that is easily accessible. Refer to it often, and keep your medical history updated as changes occur. This should allow you to be fully prepared for visits to the doctor or to handle, with confidence, a lot of other health care related situations. Please remember, it's *your* health!

Pre-Test

1. Health care costs have levelled off in recent years thanks to intervention by the federal government.

    ❑ True   ❑ False

2. Depending on your medical problem, a small community hospital can be just as effective as a major teaching hospital in providing for your health needs.

    ❑ True   ❑ False

3. If a hospital has been approved by the Joint Commission on Accreditation of Health Organizations (JCAHO) it is equal to all other approved hospitals.

    ❑ True   ❑ False

4. If available hospitals are of equal quality in the care they provide, then it is appropriate to choose one based on amenities.

    ❑ True   ❑ False

5. Either your physician or the hospital administrator can grant your admission to the hospital.

    ❑ True   ❑ False

6. It is not necessary to notify your insurance company of your elective admission to the hospital, since they trust your doctor.

    ❑ True   ❑ False

7. Making a will before your hospitalization is a waste of time and money.

    ❑ True   ❑ False

8. It is important to bring large amounts of cash with you to the hospital so that you can buy extra food and clothing.

    ❑ True   ❑ False

9. Hospital security personnel perform the same sort of functions as other law enforcement individuals as well as many additional services for the patients.
   ❑ **True** ❑ **False**

10. Consent forms you will be asked to sign in the hospital are standard forms and don't require your careful attention.
   ❑ **True** ❑ **False**

11. You have every right to expect all health care workers and hospital employees to respect your right to keep your health care confidential.
   ❑ **True** ❑ **False**

12. Your insurance company has access to your medical information automatically, without your consent.
   ❑ **True** ❑ **False**

13. A private room is always preferable to a semi-private room, if you can afford the cost.
   ❑ **True** ❑ **False**

14. Hospital food should be appetizing as well as nutritious. You should expect your meals to provide both.
   ❑ **True** ❑ **False**

15. Since a hospital room is a bedroom, living room, dining room, bathroom and family room, it is natural to find a few insects and bugs now and then. Don't worry about them.
   ❑ **True** ❑ **False**

16. Hospitals take special precautions to ensure the operating rooms are insect free.
   ❑ **True** ❑ **False**

17. Some noise in a hospital is acceptable, but noise without good reason is not.
   ❑ **True** ❑ **False**

18. When you visit an emergency room you should be seen first by a health care worker before you are asked about your medical insurance.
   ❑ **True** ❑ **False**

19. Hospital employees wear name tags so you can tell who they are and what they do.

        ❑ **True**   ❑ **False**

20. Hospital volunteers provide many services to patients that would not be available without them.

        ❑ **True**   ❑ **False**

21. Private nurses are generally hospital employees and therefore they must be satisfactory or you can complain to the hospital administrator.

        ❑ **True**   ❑ **False**

22. Although private nurses are expensive, they are essential to good nursing care, particularly in the intensive care units.

        ❑ **True**   ❑ **False**

23. Hospital housekeepers' tasks are quite simple since they have all the most modern cleaning equipment available and since hospital construction is designed to maintain a clean environment.

        ❑ **True**   ❑ **False**

24. Hospital administrators are responsible for a smooth running, efficient business in the face of ever increasing costs.

        ❑ **True**   ❑ **False**

25. Hospital administrators are lucky to have many employees providing patient care and do not have to worry about day-to-day problems. They can sit in their offices and develop long-range plans.

        ❑ **True**   ❑ **False**

26. When choosing a gift to bring to a hospitalized friend or loved one, flowers, books and candy are always appropriate.

        ❑ **True**   ❑ **False**

27. Ambulance services are licensed by the state and are therefore equal in quality and service.

        ❑ **True**   ❑ **False**

28. You have the right to demand ambulance service to the hospital.

        ❑ **True**   ❑ **False**

29. Helicopter ambulances' main advantage is the speed with which you can be taken to the hospital.
    ❏ True ❏ False

30. Because they are small and light, helicopter ambulances cannot be as well equipped as ground ambulances.
    ❏ True ❏ False

31. Emergency rooms must provide you emergency care regardless of your ability to pay.
    ❏ True ❏ False

32. If the hospital emergency room cannot provide the level of care you need, they have to find you a place that does.
    ❏ True ❏ False

33. Emergency room care is provided on a first-come, first-served basis.
    ❏ True ❏ False

34. Depending on the nature of your problem, waiting in an emergency room even after you have been examined may be necessary, even though it is not busy.
    ❏ True ❏ False

35. The feasibility of day surgery for surgical operations is due to advances in medical science and cost containment needs.
    ❏ True ❏ False

36. There are a variety of anesthetics available for your surgical procedure. Trust your anesthesiologist to pick the best one for you.
    ❏ True ❏ False

37. Operating rooms are places of life and death decision making. They are usually full of tension.
    ❏ True ❏ False

38. There are many types of pain medication available, but your doctor may not want to give you any—for your own good.
    ❏ True ❏ False

39. You may be asked to do several things after your operation that may be uncomfortable. Understand why and do them anyway.
    ❏ True ❏ False

40. Donating blood is painful and dangerous even though it is important.

       ❑ True   ❑ False

41. If you are worried about receiving someone else's blood, there are still ways to use your own blood during surgery.

       ❑ True   ❑ False

42. X-rays are completely safe and can be used without fear of complications.

       ❑ True   ❑ False

43. Inserting needles into your body can be uncomfortable but information they provide about you is so important that it is worth the pain.

       ❑ True   ❑ False

44. Using needles can save you surgery, at times.

       ❑ True   ❑ False

45. Having your body invaded by tubes is uncomfortable and embarrassing. Know the reason why your doctor suggests it.

       ❑ True   ❑ False

46. The AIDS virus is an extremely fragile organism which is easily killed with common household bleach.

       ❑ True   ❑ False

47. Even if your hospital stay involves an unpleasant experience, don't bother complaining, it will do no good.

       ❑ True   ❑ False

48. You, the patient, have a right to refuse medical treatment.

       ❑ True   ❑ False

49. You have both the right to know the hospital rules and the responsibility to follow them.

       ❑ True   ❑ False

50. Prayer and faith can make a positive contribution to a patient's recovery.

       ❑ True   ❑ False

51. It is important for family members to participate in their loved one's care.
    ❑ **True**　❑ **False**

52. Extra time spent visiting patients in the hospital during holiday periods helps to diminish the depression often associated with illness during these times.
    ❑ **True**　❑ **False**

53. It is possible to be given the wrong medication in the hospital although great care is taken to avoid this.
    ❑ **True**　❑ **False**

54. Since hospitals are so clean and sterile, it is not possible to develop an infection while hospitalized.
    ❑ **True**　❑ **False**

55. Planning for your discharge from the hospital should begin even before you are admitted.
    ❑ **True**　❑ **False**

56. Medical care has become so sophisticated and complicated that it can only be done in a doctor's office or hospital. Care at home is impossible.
    ❑ **True**　❑ **False**

57. The best time to choose a physician is when you are well.
    ❑ **True**　❑ **False**

58. All doctors, who are licensed by the state, are pretty much the same so you might as well select any of them.
    ❑ **True**　❑ **False**

59. Your doctor needs an accurate description of your symptoms so he or she can make an accurate diagnosis.
    ❑ **True**　❑ **False**

60. You need to be careful about asking doctors for a "second opinion" so that they don't feel you don't trust them.
    ❑ **True**　❑ **False**

61. It's a physician's responsibility to stay up to date on all aspects of health care, regardless of his or her specialty. You should expect to pay for the latest and best care.
❑ True ❑ False

62. While it may be o.k. for a doctor to say "I don't know," it is essential that he or she help you find out or find someone who does know about your medical problem.
❑ True ❑ False

63. Medical students learn how to become physicians by participating in actual health care programs.
❑ True ❑ False

64. If you don't have an appointment, but you need to see your doctor, calling ahead will help minimize your wait.
❑ True ❑ False

65. You have every right to expect as much time as necessary with your physician but so do other patients, which may delay your care.
❑ True ❑ False

66. You can be sure that if you like your doctor you will also be satisfied with his or her associates who substitute when your doctor is away.
❑ True ❑ False

67. Medical conferences in exotic places allow the doctor to "refuel" both mind and body.
❑ True ❑ False

68. Physician's assistants allow the doctor to extend his or her health care activities.
❑ True ❑ False

69. All women in white uniforms are not nurses and all nurses are not alike in training and expertise.
❑ True ❑ False

70. Dental problems are limited to your mouth, so the dentist doesn't have to worry about the rest of your medical problems.
❑ True ❑ False

71. Appropriate tooth and gum care at home will help to decrease your chances of developing dental problems.
   ❑ True ❑ False

72. Medication bottles should be labeled with the name of the drug inside. This is helpful so that you can identify other peoples prescriptions to use for your medical problems.
   ❑ True ❑ False

73. The medications you take are expensive. One reason is that you are helping to pay for the development of new drugs by the drug manufacturers.
   ❑ True ❑ False

74. Generic drugs can be as safe and effective as non-generic drugs.
   ❑ True ❑ False

75. The main purpose of the Food and Drug Administration (FDA) is to delay drugs from being sold so that non-legitimate drugs will be kept off the market.
   ❑ True ❑ False

76. The new technology in diagnosis and treatment is very expensive and is the single biggest expense in a hospital.
   ❑ True ❑ False

77. Hospitals try to curtail costs but not at the expense of providing the best health care.
   ❑ True ❑ False

78. Health care is expensive and unfortunately beyond the ability of the patient to control.
   ❑ True ❑ False

79. Virtually all known illnesses can be diagnosed using laboratory or other tests. These tests are expensive but specific alternatives are generally not available.
   ❑ True ❑ False

80. The main value of health insurance is that the insurance company will pay for your medical bills.
   ❑ True ❑ False

1576

81. Hospital bills are done by a computer and are extremely accurate.
   ❑ True   ❑ False

82. Most hospital billing departments will be happy to work out a payment plan with you if you have difficulty paying your bill.
   ❑ True   ❑ False

83. "DRG" is a system the Medicare program uses to pay hospitals for medical care.
   ❑ True   ❑ False

84. Malpractice law suits are increasing in number and resulting in greater costs to patients as malpractice insurance premiums increase.
   ❑ True   ❑ False

85. Don't even try to understand what doctors tell you. They speak the way they write—in shorthand and abbreviations.
   ❑ True   ❑ False

86. Medications available from mail order companies may be effective but can't cure what your doctor cannot.
   ❑ True   ❑ False

87. Modern medical care uses computers in many areas. They are sophisticated and foolproof.
   ❑ True   ❑ False

88. Participating personally in your recovery may be painful but will help.
   ❑ True   ❑ False

89. Smiling and maintaining a positive attitude makes the medical staff feel good but really can't influence your recovery.
   ❑ True   ❑ False

90. Support groups are nice but your medical recovery really depends on you alone.
   ❑ True   ❑ False

91. Fortunately, all city, state and federal buildings are equipped for the handicapped.
   ❑ True   ❑ False

92. Planning ahead for health problems on your vacation is important, since you may find yourself in a part of the world without much medical support.
    ❏ True ❏ False

93. While traveling, make sure all your medications are in a single, safe place in your luggage to be certain you can find them easily.
    ❏ True ❏ False

94. Prevention of illness is good in theory, but humans can't really do much to control the development of illness or injury.
    ❏ True ❏ False

95. Mental illness should be treated just as seriously as any other disease.
    ❏ True ❏ False

96. Your doctor will ask you a multitude of questions during your visit, so you don't need to worry what to tell him or her.
    ❏ True ❏ False

97. Your doctor spent eight or more years getting an education. Don't try to learn about your illness. He or she will tell you what you need to know.
    ❏ True ❏ False

98. Learning CPR is difficult and requires extensive exertion. You will probably never need to use it, so knowing how to do it is not essential.
    ❏ True ❏ False

99. A well planned exercise program is essential to maintaining good health.
    ❏ True ❏ False

CHAPTER ONE

Introduction

The stakes are extremely high! And it's you against the world—at least, it is if you want to combat all those outside forces that seem determined to stand between you and your right to receive the best possible health care.

Who are these people, these forces that are threatening your survival?

For example, there's your insurance company. Advances in medical technology and increased costs in all areas for health care are forcing insurance companies to make a stand. Your premium payment has increased; benefits have been reduced; and you're still trying to figure out "preferred provider," "second opinion," and similar roadblocks.

Then, there's the government—which isn't without its own problems. Costs for federally-funded programs, such as Medicare for the elderly, have escalated to keep pace with the overall increase in health care costs. Again, reduced benefits and more financial liability to the patient have resulted.

There is no doubt that the average American is becoming "medically poor." Many of us simply can't afford to pay for the health care we need and which should be our right. Even the wealthiest would probably find it difficult to survive the financial burden of a major accident or illness.

But the health care industry cares. It is on your side—regardless of its own headaches with potential legal problems, staff shortages, increasing costs of equipment and the constant challenge to enhance technology and technique for the benefit of the health care consumer.

Unfortunately, there is no sign that things will improve: Your needs will not diminish, and there is every indication that health care costs will continue to increase. And you need all the help you can get.

This book does not discuss disease or injury; it is not a "do it yourself" medical textbook. It's purpose is twofold: To give you some understanding of the health care industry and to encourage you to take the steps necessary to ensure that you receive the finest possible health care.

This is your right. Remember, it's *your* health!

CHAPTER TWO

Hospitals Are Worth Considering When Planning To Move

You drive America's highways—to and from work; on vacation; and into the city for a ball game. Along the way, you see billboards, road signs, and warning notices of all different colors, shapes and sizes. Among them are the blue and white signs that tell you there is a hospital in the neighborhood.

And in an emergency situation, that's probably all you would want to know. But when you are planning a hospital stay, you should be aware of your choices: Not all hospitals are the same; and not all hospitals provide the services you might need.

Some hospitals are small community facilities with 20 to 40 beds; others are located at large institutions with over 1,000 beds. Each has its own specific advantages.

Hospital services vary both in quality and range because of size, the level of skill among employees and physicians, the equipment and finances available, and their "market" (many hospitals treat only certain ailments, such as cancer or burns).

Many people are born and live their entire lives in one town, where the majority of their health care needs are met by the local physicians and the town hospital. Although our society has become increasingly more mobile, many people faced with relocation never consider the available health care facilities in their new home town.

If you are about to move, add "hospitals" to your list of things to check—right alongside schools for the kids, golf clubs for your spouse, and housing for the entire family.

The fact that a hospital is small does not mean it can't provide quality care. But that care might involve fewer specialists and less high-tech or advanced drug treatment. Smaller hospitals are perfectly acceptable for an illness that doesn't require special knowledge or equipment; in fact, they might even be better for your recovery, since they are usually more personal and quiet.

In general, there are three types of hospitals.

Small community hospitals usually have less than 100 beds and are well qualified to care for uncomplicated illnesses. Most smaller hospitals do have (or have access to) the sophisticated equipment necessary for diagnostic and treatment purposes. And because specialization has become the norm in health care, smaller hospitals can often provide surprisingly diverse treatments. For example, twenty years ago, a town of 10,000 people probably would not have had a urologist, but today it probably would.

Larger community Hospitals have usually 200 to 500 beds and provide services similar to those of the smaller hospital. The larger hospital might have some additional equipment and procedures available; and some specialists have privileges at the larger hospital.

Before you make a choice, check out the differences between the small and large community hospitals. If the only difference is size and nurse to patient ratio, you might opt for the smaller. But your health needs should be the deciding factor—and your physician's advice should prevail.

Teaching medical centers offer a wide selection of specialists representing the majority of medical fields, and this is the major advantage of larger hospitals located in academic settings. Such facilities (and there could be several hospitals, each specializing in certain areas of care) range from 500 to over 1,000 beds. The very newest equipment, procedures and knowledge of medical care should be available. Of course, large medical complexes can be noisier and less personal—but at least, you do have a choice.

The next time you're driving along the highway you might not care whether you stop for a Big Mac or a Big Burger; but if you need a hospital and see that familiar blue and white sign, be prepared to make a serious choice.

CHAPTER THREE

Hospitals Are Different; Choose One With Care

Regardless of popular belief, hospitals are not all the same. And if you have to be hospitalized, you should be guided by the same sense of discrimination that guides you when you shop for anything else—a car, a pair of shoes, or a smoked turkey: Buyer beware!

While we would like to think that all hospitals are up-to-date, professionally staffed and equipped to provide top-notch health care, the truth is that hospitals are just like snowflakes—they're all different and some of them are prettier than others.

Hospitals can and do vary in quality, and if there is more than one hospital in your community, consult your physician; discuss which of the alternatives is the best one for you.

You can also do some checking on your own. Hospitals are inspected and accredited by a variety of local, state and national agencies, and they are expected to meet all designated requirements for safety and health codes.

Hospitals are inspected periodically by the Joint Commission on Accreditation of Health Organizations (JCAHO). This provides an in depth analysis of many of the factors that contribute to a good and safe institution. The inspections are voluntary, however, and a hospital is not required to participate in the accreditation program. But since it cannot receive federal funds for patient care (Medicare, for example) unless it is accredited, then most are eager to comply. If your hospital is accredited, there should be an appropriate certificate, prominently displayed in the lobby or similar public area.

At this time, inspections only deal with physical standards and such areas as proper medical record documentation. They don't determine whether or not the hospital really cures its patients or improves the health of the community. Still, these inspections do serve a purpose, since they indicate general compliance with national standards.

Assuming your choice can be made from a group of fully-accredited hospitals, you need to make further inquiries. The size, the quality of care, the availability of the latest medical equipment or treatments, type of hospital (private, non-profit, teaching, religion-associated), accessibility and affordability should all be considered.

Why are you going into the hospital? Are you in need of routine, uncomplicated surgery or treatment that requires basic medical knowledge and common equipment? Then a hospital near home might suit your needs. You would be close to your loved ones and could probably expect more personal care, especially if it is a smaller hospital.

Or have you been diagnosed with cancer or some other life-threatening disease that requires immediate or highly specialized treatment? In this situation, consult with your physician who will probably recommend that you take the fastest route to the closest major medical center that offers the most up-to-date treatment for your illness.

Your toughest decision is most likely to be if your condition requires an "average" hospital. (Larger than a dime; smaller than a breadbox?) In that situation, my advice is to seek and accept a recommendation from your physician.

If several local hospitals are equal in quality, then zero in on what is important to you. Do you want a private room, a varied menu, a high nurse-to-patient ratio (the impossible dream, these days!), a certain physician? Then make a list of your needs and choose the hospital that can come closest to satisfying them.

Think of hospitals as grocery stores. All stock food. But when you want that unusual cut of meat, an exotic selection of produce, you go to a specialty store. When you're just buying bargain milk and white bread, it's down to the "shop 'n' save." Determine your medical, personal and financial needs and proceed from there.

Checklist
Chapters 2-3

Choosing a Hospital

✓ How many hospitals are in your area?
✓ Determine the size and locations of the hospitals.
✓ Determine the type of hospitals.
>   Small community hospital
>   Large community hospital
>   Academic (teaching) hospital
✓ Is the hospital accredited by the JCAHO?
✓ Does the hospital have the staff and equipment you need?
✓ Is the governing body of the hospital satisfactory?
✓ Are the accommodations and food acceptable?
✓ Is your physician affiliated with the hospital?
✓ Have you sought out appropriate opinions?
>   Doctor
>   Clergyman
>   Friends
>   Local medical society

CHAPTER FOUR

Plan Ahead Before Entering the Hospital

It sounds like a bad joke: What do hospitals and prisons have in common? To be admitted to either, someone has to make a recommendation. And it's true. When you go to prison, you're sentenced by a judge; when you go to the hospital, you're "sentenced" by your physician! But let's get one thing straight—neither is a joke, either good or bad!

Usually, hospitals will accept patients only on request of a physician who initiates the process and who will take care of you in the hospital. But you can help to make the admitting process a little more efficient, if you make a few preparations ahead of time—discounting emergency situations, of course.

Make sure you have the answers to all the routine questions: Age, social security number, next-of-kin, mother's maiden name and all those other details that should already be on you medical record at your doctor's office.

Be able to provide the name of your insurance company and policy number, or proof of ability to pay the bill if you don't have insurance. If your insurance company requires a preapproval process, a second opinion or additional information, be sure to take the necessary action in advance of your hospitalization. If this is your company's policy, and you don't follow the rules, you'll probably find that the company will cover a smaller percentage of the cost; you'll be liable for the balance. In the past decade, the insurance companies have become increasingly more involved in your plans for a hospital stay. Sometimes, the insurance company attempts to dictate the nature of your medical treatment or decides to discuss your case directly with your physician. Their intent is to help contain costs, but such involvement can cause untold complications, a delay in your hospitalization and an immense amount of frustration both for you and your doctor.

However, unless you can afford to pay your own expenses, you must resolve any and all such problems with your insurance company, prior to hospitalization.

Assuming your insurance company gives you the "green light," there's a lot of other preparations to make. Have you arranged for someone to take care of your house? Canceled the newspapers? Made arrangements for Fido and your mail? Notified family members? And does your boss know you won't be at work for a while?

If you are anticipating a lengthy hospital stay, you might want to pay your bills in advance; cancel the utilities; or arrange for an alarm system on your house. You might want to handle some personal business—make a will; invest some money; make peace with an estranged family member.

Don't forget you need transportation to the hospital—and home again, when you're discharged. Are there other plans to be made in preparation for your return home?

Of course, the extent of your plans will depend largely upon the severity of your health problem; the anticipated length of your stay in the hospital; and whether you have an available support system—spouse, adult child or parent—who has offered to "take care of things while you're in the hospital."

But do take the time to plan ahead for your hospital stay. If you're very lucky, you might have nothing else to do but to remind your spouse to buy the bagels. Can there being anything worse than coming home from the hospital to a house without bagels?

CHAPTER FIVE

Finding the WILLpower to Get a Will

I know this book is supposed to be about health, but there are times when law and medicine cross paths. The need to make a will is one of those times, especially if you're anticipating a stay in the hospital.

No, I'm not trying to scare you! And I don't want you to leave me anything—not even that marvelous antique chair I've had my eye on for years!

But it makes sense. If you are entering a hospital, especially with a severe illness or for major surgery, the reality is that nothing is guaranteed. Agreed?

The whole idea of making a will is somewhat disturbing to most of us. There's an implication, a reminder of our mortality, that nobody wants to accept, and we tend to make excuses.

We have nothing to leave or no one to inherit our belongings; we're too young; we made a will 20 years ago; why tempt fate? We've got more important things to do.

But think of this: A positive attitude and peace of mind can speed recovery. Knowing that your legal matters have been handled is one less thing for you to worry about; one more contribution to your peace of mind.

Don't wait for an emergency and then decide to make your will. Do it now! Right after lunch; before the football game starts. And do it correctly. If you wouldn't try to remove your own appendix, don't try to draw up your own will. You're a specialist in neither; consult your attorney.

Wills can be very simple or highly complex. And it's always to your advantage to have one. You could save money for your family by considering such areas as estate taxes, annuities, trust funds and so forth. And you can make your own decisions about the disposition of those assets, of your body and about your funeral arrangements.

You have the right to determine what happens to you if you are well, profoundly ill and even dead. Through a will you can choose to donate vital organs so that others may benefit. You can choose to leave your body to medical science so that tomorrow's physicians may learn. You can opt for a regular funeral or a cremation. You have choices.

Today, more and more people are creating "living wills," so that they can dictate the measures they want their physician to take, when they can no longer communicate their desires—if they are in a coma or on a life-support system.

We hear such phrases as "death with dignity," and we read newspaper reports of families agonizing over the legal and ethical implications of removing someone from a life-support system. A living will allows you to relieve your family of that burden and allows you to make the choice.

Be sure that your family members know you have a living will or that you wish to donate your organs for transplantation. (You can indicate the latter on the back of your driver's license.) Also, tell your doctor that these documents exist and that your wishes are to be honored.

I've had patients who had no living will and who could not communicate with me. One was kept alive for more than two years on a respirator. The family refused to make a decision and no will could be found. The patient's wishes were never known. Alternately, I've witnessed several cases where patients refused heroic life-saving measures. Their wishes were honored.

Just as it's your right and duty to have a will, don't forget that wills can always be altered, if you have a change of heart.

Go now—pick up the phone—call your attorney.

CHAPTER SIX

Leave the Diamond Tiara At Home

I know you've probably heard this before, but the worst thing that has ever happened to men is that they have to shave! But the best thing is that they can shove all their stuff into their pockets; not like women—they have to carry purses.

"And what does this have to do with health care?" you ask. Well, regardless of whether you stuff your pockets or your purse, bringing valuables to the hospital could make you a target for a thief. And that you don't need under any circumstances, especially not when you're worried about your health and tomorrow's operation!

There's no question that hospitals are considered safe places. In general, you shouldn't need to worry about safety and security. But hospitals aren't immune to the problems that can arise when there's interaction among varied groups of people.

Crime can occur anywhere, but you can help to ensure that your hospital stay is safe by taking certain precautions.

First, never bring large amounts of money to the hospital. It's preferable to bring a small amount for the few items you might wish to purchase in the gift shop or cafeteria. If you feel you must have large sums of cash nearby, then check with the admitting office before you arrive. They usually have safe deposit boxes.

Also, there is no reason to wear or to bring jewelry or expensive watches. If you're lucky enough to own any, leave your gold, rubies and diamonds at home. Remember, there are many times, such as during operations, testing or x-rays when all your jewelry has to be removed, anyway.

Important papers and documents are best left in a secure place at home or in your bank's safe deposit box. There may be times at the hospital when you need an important document, but chances are good that a copy will suffice. Someone will provide that information prior to admission.

Most hospitals have security professionals who are trained to deal with a variety of crimes from theft and assault to excessive noise and other violations of hospital rules. The security team might wear easily identifiable uniforms or they may be in plain clothes.

The security force is there to protect and to serve. They usually have a great deal of pride in their work and consider themselves part of the health care team. If you have been a crime victim while at the hospital or on the hospital grounds, or if you simply need directions, security can assist.

Hospital police should always be identifiable by their name badges and you have a right to request identification should you have any doubts.

Access to most areas of a hospital is comparatively easy. And considering the multitude of people who are involved in the daily operation of such a facility, it's virtually impossible to safeguard the hospital from undesirable "visitors."

Not only do the patient's possessions attract thieves, but hospital equipment is often targeted. Monitors, syringes, catheters, are items that often are taken.

If you need a security person while at the hospital, either call the security department, dial the operator, or ask your nurse or doctor to get help. Police are usually on pagers or radios and can be easily dispatched.

When security arrives, don't be surprised if they act exactly like policemen, asking questions and initiating an investigation. In general, internal security forces at hospitals work closely with city and community police forces and will turn an investigation over when it's appropriate.

If you are the victim of a crime, remember to stay calm and try to recall everything that occurred, including descriptions of assailants, missing items, and so forth.

If security is important to your health care experience, then it is up to you to investigate prior to your hospital stay. Find a hospital that offers both top-notch health care and a safe, well-protected environment.

But be willing to contribute your share to a safe environment—please, leave the diamond tiara at home, will you?

Checklist
Chapters 4-6

Before Entering the Hospital

✓ Have you or your doctor made a reservation?
✓ Has the hospital contacted you to confirm?
✓ Have you received preapproval from your insurance company?
✓ Have you gotten a second opinion, if it is required?
✓ Have you gotten a second opinion, just because you wanted it?
✓ Have you collected up the necessary papers?
    Social Security (Medicare) information?
    Insurance information?
    Friend's telephone numbers?
✓ Have you paid outstanding bills?
✓ Have you made arrangements for your home, newspapers, mail?
✓ Have you arranged for transportation?
✓ Have you made a will?
✓ Have you packed appropriately?
    Pajamas
    Robe
    Slippers
    Toilet Articles
    Makeup
    Reading material
    Favorite toy or stuffed animal
✓ Have you left all valuables at home?
✓ Have you notified someone you trust of the location of your important papers?

CHAPTER SEVEN

It's Your Body—You Have To Give Permission

Many people thought that when computers came along, we'd be able to get rid of the file cabinets and mounds of paper that cluttered our offices. We'd just be able to store everything on computer discs or microfilm and the heck with paper. Not so, my friends.

There are times when it seems that a hospital couldn't get along without paper. It all begins with the appointment cards you receive for x-rays, laboratory tests or other similar necessities before you're even admitted. Later, you notice that the doctors and nurses maintain charts; the dietitians, physical therapists, blood bank technicians and a host of others make notes, keeping records on all their patients' needs.

When you enter the hospital, you have to read and sign a variety of forms, giving permission for the hospital staff to administer the appropriate treatment. And if you're going to have surgery, special permission for that procedure has to be given. Some of these forms are lengthy and complicated. They can be scary too, especially if you don't really understand the terminology.

You must always remember that many of these pieces of paper become legal documents once they are completed and contain your signature. With this in mind, I offer the following advice: Read the forms very carefully. Make sure they are intended for you—that it is your name at the top; and make sure your doctor's name is listed also. Check that the specific treatment or surgery is written on the form, so there's no chance of a mix up. If your doctor thinks there might be a chance of complications, these should be listed on the consent forms. If none appear, you might want to ask for assurance that none are anticipated. It is also advisable to share this information with a close relative, so that you are not the only person who is aware of the agreements you have made.

If there's something you don't understand, ask for an explanation. Don't assume that just because the words sound official, it doesn't matter if you don't understand them. And most importantly, don't sign anything, until you are satisfied.

Consent forms should be readable and easily understood by anyone without a medical education; in fact, they should be written with the user in mind. If this is not the case, you can request help. If the form is in English and a patient speaks another language, many hospitals offer a translation service to help. Some hospitals even have forms printed in those foreign languages that are predominant in its community.

This advice is not meant to scare you. As with any other phase of life, it is unwise to sign on the dotted line until you know exactly what you're getting into. You wouldn't sign for a car or an insurance policy without reading and understanding the agreement, would you? Giving your consent for any form of treatment in a hospital is even more important.

The bottom line of all this is, of course, that you are the only person who has the right to give permission for anyone to treat you. And if you are not satisfied, you have the right of refusal. Your signature on those forms is your permission for a doctor to act, albeit in your best interests.

Just know what you are signing. You might not have the expertise to treat yourself, but you have choices and can keep the control.

CHAPTER EIGHT

Mum's the Word—Patient Confidentiality Is A Right

We all have that one special friend or acquaintance. You know who I mean—the blabbermouth. If you want to spread a story or rumor, you tell it first to that special person—in confidence.

Unfortunately, hospitals employ hundreds of people; and though everyone is made acutely aware of the need for patient confidentiality, it's impossible to screen out all the blabbermouths. Let's face it: There are some people who simply can't keep a secret, regardless of the potential consequences.

But your illness is your business; you have every right to expect that your medical affairs are conducted in an environment that honors your need for confidentiality. But from the time you are admitted until the time you are discharged, there are many ways your confidentiality can be breached, either accidentally or deliberately.

A conversation between your doctor and nurse is overheard; the "wrong" person sees your chart; a neighbor works in the billing department; or you are simply the victim of someone who can't mind his or her own business.

There are some ways that you can help to ensure your privacy. When you are in conference or being examined by your doctor, insist that the door be kept shut. And if possible, close the door routinely at least to the point that you can't be seen by people walking around outside. Make sure that everyone who has access to the details of your case is entitled to that information.

Some hospitals post the names of patients outside their rooms. While this is intended for the convenience of the staff, it could also threaten your privacy. If this is important to you, request that your name be erased—or use a false name, as do some of the movie stars or other public figures, when they're hospitalized.

Your chances of privacy will be greatly increased if you go to a hospital in another town; but then, your family and friends might not be able to visit easily, so give some thought to such a drastic move before you make it.

If you are in a hospital or have gone to see a physician about a medical problem, your family, friends, co-workers and neighbors are not automatically entitled to know any or all the intimate details. This is your choice to make, and you must ask others to respect that decision. Those who continue to ask questions invite a firm (but polite) reminder that your health problem is your concern only and that you do not intend to share this information.

More difficult to control are medical and life insurance companies and governmental agencies that want to check up on you. A life insurance company has the right to turn you down for a policy for certain medical problems, or for failure to disclose your medical records. But the law requires your signature for release of all medical records, and no company or agency has a legal right to gain access to your records without your permission.

Unfortunately, once your confidentiality has been breached and private information has been disclosed, the damage is done—it cannot be reversed. Should this happen, complain loudly to the hospital administration. And if you feel that you have been harmed by this breach of confidentiality, you are free to seek legal guidance.

Be sure your doctor knows that your right to privacy is extremely important to you. And tell your family and friends, too. After all, if you want the whole world to know about your health problem, take out an ad in the newspaper; write to Ann Landers; hire a publicity company. But tell everyone else to mind their own business!

CHAPTER NINE

Your Biography Has Already Been Written

Do you use credit cards? Or own charge cards for your favorite departments stores or gas stations? Perhaps you have a mortgage that requires monthly payments and are surely responsible for utility and telephone bills on a regular basis. One way or another, there exists, somewhere, an extensive credit record of your financial history, available to others who need to "check you out." Indeed, we've all heard at least one or two horror stories about the dreaded credit bureau.

Similarly, as long as you were born in a hospital, your medical biography is already a matter of record—even if you've never been sick, never visited a doctor or never been hospitalized since mommy brought you home during the first few days of your life. And of course, if you have received health care from any source, then your medical record has expanded and is probably more detailed than you could imagine.

Medical records are vitally important, both to the doctor and the patient, if the best possible care is to be given and received. And for decades, they were closely guarded secrets, to be viewed only by your doctor or other legally-allowed health care professionals. But your health care records are exactly that: They are yours, and you have the right to see them, to request copies of them or to have the information they contain transferred from one health care provider to another.

Rarely do patients need to know every detail of their medical records; and to request so much information for no other reason than personal curiosity will cause extra work for someone in your doctor's office. Hopefully, you and your doctor have a trusting, honest relationship, such that you are confident that pertinent information will be shared with you.

Nevertheless, you do have a right to your medical records; and sometimes, access to that information is necessary. Usually, this situation will arise when you change doctors or seek treatment at a different clinic or hospital. For instance, when relocating to another town, it is extremely important for you to arrange for the transfer of your medical records to the new health care providers.

And be sure to take care of these arrangements prior to your move. Visit your doctor's office or hospital and request that the records be given to you or sent directly to your new physician. Certain forms will have to be signed, authorizing the release of these documents—which will not be released without the appropriate signatures. Your medical record is truly confidential, and only you can give permission for it to be shared with another party.

The transfer of records is an accepted practice in the medical profession. Physicians understand fully the to need to know their patients' medical biography and no-one will be offended by your request. Keep in mind, it is also your right, for whatever reason, to switch to an alternate health care provider, whose job should not be hampered by a lack of information.

CHAPTER TEN

You Can Get What You Want In A Hospital Room

We've all heard horror stories about hospital rooms: families of 12 visiting the patient in the next bed; mattresses that are too soft, pillows that are too hard; a nurse call button that doesn't seem to be connected to anything; a window that looks directly into another wing of the hospital. Nice. The sick looking at the sick.

But you can get the kind of room you want in the hospital, and although it won't be like a suite at the Ritz, your approach to securing a hospital room should be similar to that of making a hotel reservation.

It's your money. Why shouldn't you get a "room with a view?" Or at least a room that suits your personality.

If you're simply not a social person and your insurance or personal income can cover the extra costs, then insist on private accommodations. You deserve it.

Enjoy the advantage of a private room: You don't have to contend with the smoking, talking, snoring, or TV viewing of others. Just peace and quiet. And you can control your own family of 12 if everyone decides to drop by to wish you a speedy recovery.

But there are disadvantages of private accommodations. While solitude might be appealing, it can become boring, depressing, and lonely. Also, you could find yourself in trouble. If you require sudden and immediate assistance, you are responsible for summoning help; there's no friendly roommate to yell down the hallway on your behalf. And, there's a cost factor, since some insurance companies won't pay for private rooms.

The advantages of semi-private accommodations, are essentially the opposite of the advantages of a private room. You have company, someone with whom you can commiserate and who can perhaps provide assistance should you require it. And there's the best advantage of all. Your insurance company will probably pay for the room. If not, then a semi-private room is much less costly than a private room.

In the old days, hospital patients did not have the luxury of choosing their rooms. They were lumped together in large wards with rows of beds lined up against the walls. Later, wards were reduced to smaller units, and today it's rare to find them at all, except in older Veterans' hospitals or other military institutions. Even in these situations, patients find that the camaraderie can contribute to a speedier recovery. Sometimes helping others makes your own problems seem small in comparison.

When you check in, the admissions staff will usually ask if you have any preferences—and feel free to speak up if you're not offered a choice of rooms. You are paying the bill, and hospital rooms are expensive. Don't be shy. Make your wishes known. A good hospital room is a combination living room, dining room, bedroom and bathroom—a little like your first apartment.

Your room should have an adjustable bed, with multidirectional movement; a patient service module, including lighting above the bed, a call button, television controls, oxygen/air connectors, an outlet for electrical appliances, radio control, and special lighting used by the medical staff for examinations; storage space (closets and drawers); an over-the-bed table for meals, writing, and other activities that need an accessible, hard service; a window if that is the design of the hospital; chairs that make into cots for overnight guests (if permission is given); a bedside table with telephone; toilet and bathing facilities; a television; and other essential equipment for health care needs.

But when the bill arrives, remember that a hospital room is not just the bed and other visible facilities; your bill includes the services of nurses, dietitians, and housekeepers; it includes the use of up-to-date equipment and the food that was provided (and you were supposed to eat).

However, if your bill seems way out of proportion to your stay, or if it is not in line with other hospitals of similar quality, or if you are charged for services/items you did not receive—complain! That is your right.

CHAPTER ELEVEN

"Could You Make That A Hot Dog With Relish?"

To me, one of life's greatest mysteries is the hot dog. Not any old hot dog, you understand; but those assembly-line, two-dollar hot dogs they sell in the ball parks. Delicious! Fit for a king.

And then there's that other great mystery of life: Hospital food. How, I wonder, can food that is prepared in the ultimate of clean environments and to the exact specifications of dietary experts leave most patients drooling for an assembly-line hot dog? Let's look at this strange phenomenon!

At most hospitals, food preparation must meet guidelines that are set by accrediting agencies and rivals delicate surgery in its complexity and planning. When I cook, I use a pinch of this or a dab of that to get the taste right. But in the hospital, ingredients are measured to an extreme of accuracy; calories are counted and controlled; nothing is left to guesswork or chance.

Just as a pharmacist fills your prescriptions based on a doctor's instructions, the dietary department fills your food "prescriptions," geared to your specific medical needs. Nothing with cholesterol for Mr. Jones; no sugar for Ms. Smith; and absolutely no salt, fat or whatever else the doctor restricted.

Then why, you ask, did last night's steak, with no medical limitations, look and taste less appetizing than my old pair of Reeboks? Unfortunately, I can't answer that question—but I can give you some hints on how you might combat this potential abuse to your taste buds.

First of all, whether you believe it or not, all hospital food is nutritious. So how can you be assured that it will be attractive and appetizing as well?

If your hospital stay is preplanned (as opposed to an emergency), survey the various hospitals in your area. You'll surely be able to find a friend or neighbor who has been a patient in this or that hospital. Ask their opinions. Find out which hospital serves on fine china (some really do) and which use plastic "silverware" and paper trays. At least you'll have some information on which to base your decision.

On the day you check into the hospital, try to be patient and tolerant. Remember, food orders are placed in the morning—and since you were admitted after lunch, your menu has been chosen for you, with no knowledge of your preferences.

On subsequent days, you will have a choice (subject to limitations placed by your physician). But if there's nothing on the menu that appeals to you, ask if there are alternatives. Remember, you are paying the bill, and meals are very much part of that bill. Many hospitals will attempt to satisfy your request—but be reasonable. A scrambled egg might be a perfectly fair request; but a sudden taste for pheasant under glass or caviar would probably (and rightly) be considered unreasonable.

Appetizing food is an important ingredient for recovery, both in the hospital and after you are discharged. Discuss your needs with a dietitian—and follow the advice that is given. But while you are a patient, you have a right to certain expectations. Hot food should be hot; cold drinks should be cold. No, it is not fair that you should expect food prepared by the great chefs of Europe; but you do have a right to expect attractive food that is eaten because it is tasty—not because it's "better than nothing."

If your hospital food does not reach a reasonable level of expectation, complain. Complain to your doctor, to your nurse, to the hospital administration—and to your newspaper, if necessary.

There is one consolation, however. After you're fully recovered and all restrictions are lifted from your diet, you can always go to the ballpark and eat a hot dog. Or two. Or three!!

CHAPTER TWELVE

Roaches and Other Bugs Have No Place In A Hospital

Humans have been around for thousands of years. Trees, even longer. But in the beginning, there were roaches. And they will be here long after the last human vanishes.

Most people cringe, when they see a roach, feeling an immediate urge to crush this pesky creature. And everyone assumes that roaches are very dirty and carry dreadful diseases.

One thing is certain when it comes to roaches and all other bugs, they have no place in the hospital. But few things are more difficult to eliminate than bugs! Think about your hospital room: It is your bedroom, dining room, bathroom, and family room—a miniature house all crammed into a few square feet.

There's ongoing traffic bringing food, plants, flowers and other materials that are all havens for bugs. Yet you expect a clean room that is bug-free, and indeed, that is your right.

A patient's father complained to me once (after a heavy rain and during "ant" season) that there were ants in his daughter's hospital room. He wanted to know if there would be bugs in the operating room crawling on the scalpels, carrying dirt and bacteria. Of course, I assured the gentleman that this was most unlikely—and scurried off to check out the operating room.

I like to think that I've practiced medicine in the "modern era," but I do remember flies and other bugs entering operating rooms through open windows. That this was ever allowed to happen seems a bit ludicrous today, when such conditions are totally unacceptable. Have fly swatter, will travel?

Hospitals spend large amounts of money to control insects, rodents and other pests. Some larger hospitals hire in-house pest control professionals who follow a regular spraying schedule. Others contract with outside companies.

It's virtually impossible to eliminate all insects, even in hospitals. But if you do find bugs, you should stay calm and report the incident to your doctor, nurse or patient relations representative.

Express concern, and don't ignore the problem. Hospitals don't want bugs any more than you do. Expect reasonably prompt attention to the matter. A pest control professional should be called promptly, and if they are not available in a reasonable amount of time, you can request a room change.

Don't accept superficial or curt answers, as though the bugs were an insignificant problem; and don't accept reluctance or refusal to respond.

Hospitals should be responsible for maintaining proper bug extermination procedures, mainly because of the potential health problem, but also because they generally want to promote the image that hospitals are sterile, clean places.

Hospitals realize that you have choices. Few things will influence your choice of hospital more than a desire to avoid a dirty, insect-infested facility, even if it does have the best staff and the most sophisticated equipment.

Hospitals work constantly to find ways to "get the bugs out"; lend a hand; report the pesky creatures if you see them; the staff doesn't want them there any more than you do.

CHAPTER THIRTEEN

Some Hospital Noises Are Important, Most Are Unnecessary

The perfect hospital doesn't exist, any more than does the perfect child, spouse, or donut. Except, maybe, for chocolate-covered donuts filled with angel cream. They come real close!

If you could find one, the ideal hospital would be clean, comfortable and very, very quiet. Actually, it's reasonable to expect a hospital to be clean and comfortable. But quiet? In fact, "hospital" and "quiet" are contradictory terms. A bit like "teenager" and "reasonable."

There are two kinds of noise in a hospital: there's "good" noise and there's "bad" noise. For instance, there's a very sophisticated machine that emits a piercing alarm that signals you have a problem. And that's a "good" noise; it saved your life, didn't it?

But it's the "bad" noises that we should be considering in this chapter. If you've been hospitalized, you might well have experienced being awakened in the middle of the night, when someone entered your room to remove a piece of equipment; or to look for something that was mislaid earlier in the evening; or to check your I.V.

If you are disturbed for a seemingly inappropriate reason, you should ask for an explanation. The nurse might have been following the doctor's instructions; maybe your monitor at the nurses' station malfunctioned and someone wanted to make sure your were OK. Or perhaps a staff member was being thoughtless and insensitive to your needs. If you're disturbed unnecessarily, mention this to your doctor the next day. (No, don't call your doctor at home in the middle of the night; he or she might not be too sympathetic.)

If you are disturbed by another patient or that person's visitors, bring this to someone's attention. Noise at any time, even if you're not sleeping, can be annoying and unacceptable. Usually, if you're in the hospital, you need the rest and a chance to enjoy a peaceful environment. If such a situation becomes intolerable, request a change of room; that should be a viable alternative.

As a patient, you will have to tolerate some noise; and the larger the hospital, the noisier it will probably be. There will be more people; more phones ringing; more patients being wheeled through the hallways; more doctors and nurses conversing; and more machines clanking.

Be sure to figure out the difference between the "good" and "bad" noises; feel free to complain about the bad noises—but be grateful for the good ones.

Checklist
Chapters 7-13

Getting Settled in the Hospital

✓ Have you read and understood the admitting materials?

✓ Have you read and understood the admitting consent forms?

✓ Have you read and understood the surgical consent forms?

✓ Have you talked to your doctor about your impending operation?

✓ Have you discussed confidentiality with your doctor and hospital staff?

✓ Can you maintain your privacy in your assigned room?

✓ Is your room satisfactory?

✓ Is your room clean?

✓ Does the T.V. work?

✓ Do the bed, lighting, nurse call button all work?

✓ Have you determined if someone can stay with you?

✓ Have you talked with the nurses about special food needs?

CHAPTER FOURTEEN

Name That Uniform: Who's Who in the Hospital

Few of us get through life without ever having to walk into a hospital. Maybe as a patient; maybe as a visitor. But regardless, I've yet to find anyone who isn't thoroughly amazed at the apparent confusion that seems to greet them as they walk through those sliding doors for the first time. It doesn't seem to matter where you are—admitting area, patient finance, emergency room—there's always a lot of people scurrying around, sheets of paper in hand, and looking frazzled.

For many people, an emergency room is their first introduction to a hospital. Imagine: You are in pain or feel ill; you've been waiting for two hours; you wish the crying kids would shut up; you wish your spouse would shut up; you'd just like to take a nap; but most of all, you wish someone would come to take care of you and make the hurt go away.

I won't try to kid you: Knowing what is going on around you and knowing why all these people are scurrying around looking frazzled won't make the hurt (or the crying kids) go away; but it might make your situation a little more tolerable and a whole lot less frustrating.

The first person you see in an Emergency Room should be a medical person—a doctor or a nurse—and the first question you should be asked is: "What is wrong with you?" or "Why are you here?" And there's a good reason for this: In an emergency room, the most seriously ill or injured are seen first, so at least you know that if you are kept waiting, your ailment might not been considered too serious.

Usually, it is the triage nurse (triage is a French word meaning "sorting") who categorizes patients into groups, ranging from the most serious to the least serious cases. And once this stage is complete, you will have some idea whether your wait is going to be lengthy or not. (Long waits are never pleasant but knowing what to expect makes it easier to handle).

Keep in mind, too, that no one should be questioning you about such mundane things as method of payment or name of insurance company *before* you've seen a member of the medical team. If that happens, protest strongly and assert your right to be examined before dealing with anyone else. Only when the triage is complete, then it's OK for someone to ask you questions about insurability, next-of-kin and so forth. (Humor them; they need it "for the records.")

When it's your turn for treatment, a nurse, physician or medical student (in a teaching hospital only) should be next. After this and depending on the nature of your ailment, you might see one or several individuals, each with his or her own expertise: a phlebotomist draws blood; an x-ray technician, a social worker, a dietitian, or a medical specialist might be called to handle your case. And don't forget the cashier: Someone has to pay the bill!

If you're admitted to the hospital, the endless parade of people continues. More doctors, nurses, technicians, therapists, clerks, orderlies, clergymen, social workers, dietitians and many others, each expertly qualified to provide the treatment and care you need and deserve. (And if you're in a teaching hospital, don't forget the medical students who are trying to learn from your misfortune and probably look the most frazzled of all!)

Keep a few other things in mind, too: Know the identity of everyone who enters your room. Read their name tags; look at their "mug shots"; know where they work and their title. It's important that you feel secure about all the "players"; you are the patient, and it's your health that's at stake.

Let's face it. You're in the hospital. You don't need anything else to worry about!

CHAPTER FIFTEEN

Volunteers Are Essential to Health Care

Some things will always be in demand: A ticket to the Super Bowl; chocolate chip cookies; and hospital volunteers. Volunteers are among the unsung heroes of the entire health care system and without their hours of dedication, many patients would experience a sharp drop in the quality of their hospital stay.

Though volunteers are not directly involved in the patient's health care, hospitals depend on them greatly to provide a lot of services that might otherwise be nonexistent.

When you are hospitalized, you depend upon the nurses, doctors, and technicians for your health care; you assume that a variety of other needs will be provided by housekeepers, dietitians, transportation personnel, and so forth.

And just as you realize you're bored, and you've forgotten to bring along your favorite crossword puzzle book, in walks a smiling volunteer to see if there's anything you need.

Volunteers assist at information booths and hospital gift shops; they run errands; maintain library carts; make phone calls; help in the emergency room and other hospital areas; contribute time to administrative and clerical departments. Volunteers exist to serve the needs of the hospital; they are virtually indispensable.

And volunteers contribute much more than their hours. For instance, the money generated by their auxiliary services, such as bookstores, gift shops and snack bars, are usually donated to the hospital to purchase televisions for waiting rooms and similar items that hospitals might not be able to afford.

You can recognize the volunteers by their distinct uniforms. The famous "pink ladies" or their junior version, the "candy stripers" are ubiquitous in hospitals across the country. If not in uniform, then volunteers wear name tags identifying them and their role as volunteers.

Volunteers can be men or women; they can be 16 or 60; some give thousands of hours a year, others hundreds; and they all have one thing in common: they are dedicated individuals, committed to their "job" as a hospital volunteer.

It's not difficult to become a volunteer. Most hospitals have a volunteer office easily accessible to the public. When you find it, offer your unique expertise and describe your special interests. There are no minimum requirements for hours served, which are usually flexible and arranged to accommodate your personal schedule.

Also, volunteer groups are generally interested in new programs; make suggestions; bring along your ideas—especially if you have seen them work successfully at another hospital.

Be a volunteer; you'll never regret it. How could you? The reward of helping others can only add to the quality of your own life. What a way to live!

CHAPTER SIXTEEN

Do I Need A Private Nurse?

You probably don't need me to tell you that hospitals are expensive! And since health care costs don't tend to follow the old maxim that "what goes up must come down," there's little hope that hospital expenses will do anything but continue to rise.

The largest portion of a hospital's budget is dedicated to salaries, and a significant percentage of that amount is earmarked for maintaining a professional nursing staff.

Nurses are indispensable to every phase of your health care, ranging from the operating room to intensive care to the patient floors. But, traditionally, nurses have been underpaid, and this has contributed to the current, world-wide shortage of highly-trained professional nurses. In the United States, hospitals are now attempting to combat this situation by raising the salaries of their nursing staff.

While you are hospitalized, you will require nursing care, and your bill will reflect this aspect of your stay. But what if you decide you need (or want) more individual nursing attention than is usually available in an understaffed hospital?

Well, you can hire a private nurse, whose job it is to care for you and your needs exclusively. Doesn't that sound great? And there are advantages to hiring a private nurse—but there are disadvantages also. Let's look at both sides of the coin.

The obvious advantage is that your private nurse will focus his or her attention on you and no one else. You can be pampered and given moral support; your family can enjoy peace of mind, knowing that you are under constant observation, receiving individualized attention.

But private nursing care is expensive. Agencies that specialize in this service are listed in the yellow pages or can be on file with your local medical society. You can employ a private nurse for as few or as many hours as you wish—as long as you can afford the hourly rates.

Once you've decided to take this route, have received the relevant information from an agency and a nurse has been recommended, you should check credentials, work history, job performance, and if possible, references secured from someone other than the recommending agency.

You might like the idea of being pampered, but you only want to be pampered by a nurse who has maintained the appropriate levels of skill and is well-versed in current practices and procedures.

Remember, too, that a private nurse is not a hospital employee. You pay for this service personally, and payment is usually required "up front,"; it might not be covered by your insurance carrier, and you could be faced with a huge out-of-pocket expense. Also, if you are not happy with the service, it is your responsibility to resolve the problem—and you or a family member might have to hassle with the agency. The hospital will not do that for you. In fairness, however, you will usually get a satisfactory response from the agency; this is a service-oriented business which should want to keep the customer happy.

Consider, too, your need for privacy. Do you really want a nurse sitting in your room, hour after hour? Of course, you can always request that you be left alone—but if the nurse leaves at your request, the clock continues to run and the bill continues to mount.

There are situations when hiring a private nurse is inappropriate. For instance, if you are in an intensive care unit (ICU), you need the expertise of the specially-trained ICU nurses. A private nurse in such unfamiliar and highly-sophisticated settings would not be to your advantage.

Yes, the choice is yours. And the thought of all that special attention is very appealing. But please, do weigh the pros and the cons; it's important that you are completely comfortable with your final decision.

CHAPTER SEVENTEEN

Housekeepers: The Forgotten Heroes of Health Care

In any organization, there are the "invisible" heroes, whose efforts are virtually indispensable but rarely recognized: Maintenance personnel in the space program; equipment managers in pro football; and in the health industry, housekeepers in hospitals.

I've often thought that someone must have had hospitals in mind when they said that "Cleanliness is next to Godliness." I shudder at the unthinkable: A dirty hospital.

It takes talent and dedication to keep a hospital clean, and a difficult task in a small hospital becomes a monstrous challenge in a large one. Those of us who witness the daily determination of the specially-trained professional housekeepers applaud their contribution to your health care.

Keep in mind that hospitals have been closed by accrediting agencies, not because of the quality of treatment, but because they did not meet the required level of hygiene. Dirt can produce disease, and agencies, whose inspections can rival those of any U.S. Army sergeant, demand a squeaky clean environment. In other words, a clean hospital is more than just a pleasant place to recover. It's an accredited and therefore an "open" hospital.

Truthfully, my heart goes out to hospital housekeepers. Theirs is a never ending, thankless task. I've lost count of the number of times I've seen a housekeeper clean a floor to a brilliant shine, only to see someone track in mud or spill a cup of coffee. But the floor gets cleaned again— immediately. Granted, they have a lot of help: Self-propelled floor cleaners; top-of-the-line buffers; industrial strength products. But their most important tools haven't changed in decades: elbow grease and dedication.

The logistics of scheduling a housekeeping crew are similar to that of a super hotel. Rooms must be cleaned promptly and efficiently, either for the current patient or the one who might be brought in at any moment.

But the world around them does not stand still, and heavy traffic from staff and relatives add to the mayhem.

Long suspecting that no one really cares about hospital cleanliness except the housekeeper and the health inspector, I decided to test my theory. I dropped a piece of paper on the floor of a busy hospital corridor and settled in to observe the dozens of people walking by. Most ignored the paper, some stepped on it, and others even kicked it aside. Finally, a housekeeper picked it up.

Who are these housekeepers? They are caring men and women, professionally trained in both hospital cleaning techniques and in interpersonal skills. They understand a patient's right to confidentiality and privacy, and they know when NOT to clean a room.

But nothing's perfect, and you could see something that is not up to par in the cleanliness department. If this happens, bring it to someone's attention immediately. You have a right to expect the hygienic health care environment that is so important to your recovery. For the patient to settle for anything less than the best is unacceptable.

CHAPTER EIGHTEEN

Hospital Administrators: Multitalented Bureaucrats

Leadership! The United States has a President. Your local high school has a principal. IBM has a Chairman of the Board. And hospitals employ administrators!

Obviously, it takes more than doctors and nurses to run a hospital; housekeepers, food services, technicians, and accountants are but a few of the services that combine to become "the hospital."

But who is the unsung organizer? Who is responsible for coordinating the multitude of services and people, to ensure that the hospital runs efficiently and that you receive the best possible health care?

The hospital administrator is an integral part of the health care team. Though not necessarily medically trained, administrators are highly-educated experts, usually with many years of experience in health care administration. And simply stated, their job is to manage all services that are necessary to provide and implement health care programs prescribed by physicians.

In a sense, the hospital administrator is a hotelier, since patients are paying guests, and those guests have needs. Administrators have to be business experts, knowledgeable about purchasing goods and equipment, authorizing repairs, while balancing budgets so that the hospital doesn't run out of money.

As a troubleshooter and crisis manager, the administrator must make quick decisions when things go wrong. And in a hospital, mishaps are unpredictable and happen without warning. A cool head is always needed.

Since administrators must always be mindful of the patient, they are also part of and contributors to the health care team.

Finally, the administrator is a bureaucrat—not by choice, but as a result of overwhelming governmental regulations and restrictions, and part of the job is to keep up-to-date with these regulations and to make sure they are met.

Conversely, hospital administrators are not necessarily physicians, and they are not directly involved in medical care. A good administrator leaves medicine to the doctors and administrating to the administrators. They are not magicians either, although they are often required to make the impossible appear commonplace and relatively easy to achieve.

And what makes a good administrator? Well, good administrators don't sit in their offices all day; they are visible, walking through the hospital; talking to patients and staff; finding how things can be improved.

A good hospital administrator should be easily approachable and possess a ready ear for criticism and for praise and then act upon that information.

The administrator walks a tightrope between good business sense and providing quality health care. It is a constant juggle between expenses and fiscal integrity, and the need for keeping up with medical technology.

Hospital administrators have usually earned a business or hospital administration degree and then continued their education, acquiring expertise through the years of accepting positions with increasing amounts of responsibility.

When considering a hospital stay, don't underestimate the ability of the administrator to influence both the quality of the health care you receive and the ability to intervene if that care does not meet your needs.

Checklist
Chapters 14-18

Protecting Your Rights in the Hospital

✓ Do you want you name to appear on the door?
✓ Is you room maintained and cleaned well?
✓ Is the food served appropriately?
✓ Is the food palatable and what you ordered?
✓ Is your room and the hospital unit quiet and peaceful?
✓ Is the hospital staff courteous and caring?
✓ Have your needs for privacy been honored?
✓ Have your needs for volunteer services been met?
✓ Has the nursing care been adequate?
✓ Have you met the hospital administrator?

CHAPTER NINETEEN

Choose Gifts Carefully When Making Hospital Visits

Some people just don't know how to express their concern for hospitalized friends and relatives. Flowers, candy and books seem to be the traditional symbols of caring. And I'm not against giving gifts; I like my neighborhood florist; and I'm a regular customer at the bookstore in the mall; but there is such a thing as "gift overload."

This is especially true if the patient is to be in the hospital only for a day or two. And I really feel that the best gift you can offer to a hospital patient is yourself. Sick people want to know that their family or friends care. They want to hear a few comforting words or have the reassuring touch of a loved one's hand.

But if you really feel the need to bring a gift, choose wisely and try to find out whether there are any restrictions. Certain items might not be allowed. If the patient is on a strict diet, then candy and snacks could be inappropriate. Cigarettes and alcohol might be either harmful or contrary to hospital regulations.

Keep in mind that the patient will have many things to handle prior to discharge. It's difficult enough to remember all of the truly important items such as prescriptions, jewelry, toothbrush and clothes. So please consider the advantages and disadvantage to the patient, before you ask your florist to deliver the largest palm tree on the lot.

Your intent is to be generous and thoughtful; but your recuperating friend might not show the appropriate amount of gratitude as he or she struggles to pack everything in the trunk of the car.

Use common sense when visiting a patient! This should be a positive experience; and your presence (if the patient is well enough or wants company) can provide a much-needed lift. But keep the conversation light and cheery; don't bring tales of gloom and doom.

Most people feel awkward walking into a patient's room without a gift. But a handshake, a hug or a smile is just fine. Carefully selected (with the patient's condition in mind) get-well or "thinking of you" cards are sensible gifts. And take into account the patient's personality. Choose a card to suit the patient's preferences rather than your own sense of humor.

Other possible gifts include offering to shop, taking care of errands, or doing some house cleaning. Make a contribution, in your friend's name, to a charitable organization; say a prayer, if this is appropriate.

If you cannot visit due to schedules or distance, send a card, write a letter, or make a phone call. Send a family picture or ask your children to draw something. Most people who are hospitalized truly appreciate anything that is done especially for them. Little things mean a lot? Absolutely in this situation.

And if all else fails, you can always send flowers—as long as you use some common sense and don't get offended if the patient leaves them at the nurses' station rather than trying to pack them in the trunk of the car.

CHAPTER TWENTY

Be A Good Visitor

Here he comes! You know who I mean. He's wearing a loud sports shirt, a straw hat and is smoking a big, fat, smelly cigar. He's loud and boisterous and knows everything about everything—and his greatest pleasure is to bore you with his vast store of medical knowledge. He is the friendly visitor, determined to bring some cheer into the lives of sick patients—whether they want it or not.

Of course, visitors are important, but being a "good" visitor is even more important. In fact, it is not unusual for patients to recover more quickly as a result of "good" visits from relatives and friends, who provide a missing ingredient that encourages a speedier and more healthy recovery. But the opposite can apply also, and a thoughtless visitor who lacks common sense is worse than no visitor at all.

The first "good visitor" rule is to act as you would want others to act if you were the patient. This is especially true in sensitive areas, such as asking too many personal questions. If your friend wants you to know "all the details," the chances are you won't have to ask—the information will be given voluntarily.

Don't overstay your welcome. Observe posted visiting hours or try to sense when it is appropriate for you to leave. Several brief visits will usually be more appreciated and beneficial than one lengthy stay that requires the patient to be attentive for a long period of time.

Don't smoke in the patient's room or choose to visit after having a couple of drinks at your local bar. Avoid sitting on the bed (chairs are usually provided) and don't use the patient's personal possessions or toilet facilities. Keep in mind that the patient's room is his or her "home away from home," so treat it with care and respect.

Be careful to observe the hospital's rules—which are neither arbitrary nor designed simply to make your life uncomfortable. For instance, if the hospital does not allow visits from young children, leave your preschooler at home. If the hospital has "quiet" signs posted in the hallways, honor that request. Remember especially that the hospital's first responsibility is to its patients and the rules are for their benefit.

Some day, the tables might be turned, and you might be the patient, and you will understand the advantage of "good" visits. Then, you will ask loud, smelly friends to stay home but reap the rewards of thoughtful caring friends and relatives.

CHAPTER TWENTY-ONE

Someone Call 911—If It's There

Example 1: You're driving along and come across an accident. You pull over to help. Several people are attempting to assist the victim and someone tells you to get help. You call 911.

Example 2: You're mowing the lawn on a summer day. After about an hour, you feel tired and weak. You go inside for a cool drink, but now you begin to feel a gripping pain in your chest. You know you need help. You call 911.

Example 3: You walk into the kitchen and find your three-year-old child drinking from a bottle that she apparently retrieved from under the sink. The bottle is not labeled, but has a strong odor you recognize as cleaning fluid. You race to the phone to call the Poison Control Center, but can't find the telephone number. You call 911, instead.

Three different scenarios, each with the same solution—call 911. It's an easy thing to do, but did you ever stop to think about what happens when you make that 911 call? You never get put on hold or referred to someone else. You receive immediate attention from a highly trained individual who is prepared to help. A simple phone call puts you in touch with emergency personnel who can assist with every imaginable emergency situation and a few you could never have imagined.

But, what happens if you're home alone, you call 911 but for some reason you can't talk or you drop the phone. This situation really does happen and many 911 centers are equipped to deal with these emergencies, thanks to the development of new electronic devices. These devices allow 911 personnel to determine the caller's address and send help immediately.

Not all cities are equipped with this new service. While both of these services are more necessity than luxury (at least in my biased opinion), they are expensive to operate. But, they're well worth the price. If you live in a community that does not have 911, you must work to convince your elected officials of the importance of these services. The same holds true for the expanded 911 service. The peace of mind these services provide more than justifies their expense.

But, a word of caution to all 911 abusers. This is a sophisticated system only for use in case of an emergency. It does not exist for purposes of directory assistance, general information or conversation. Violators of the system should know that 911 personnel know the exact location of each incoming call and they take every call seriously—especially the prank ones.

As a citizen, I certainly want 911 personnel available when faced with an emergency. And, I don't want them wasting time with unnecessary calls. By the same token, it's better to be safe than sorry. If you're faced with a serious situation, but unsure of the need for 911, it's best to call and let the trained professionals make the determination.

CHAPTER TWENTY-TWO

Even In Emergencies You Have Choices

Emergencies usually involve panic, confusion, hubbub and fear, and one of the reasons the 911 system was developed was to aid people quickly and efficiently in such a time of need.

But if you think just punching those three numbers will bring you exactly the kind of care you need, be aware! There's more to ambulance service than meets the eye!

The informed patient should be knowledgeable about all facets of the health care experience. And this includes the ride to the hospital.

Ambulance service varies greatly and is often based on the community's size, the level of emergency services at the local hospital(s) and the support received from taxpayers. Some emergency services are privately owned and operated; others are governmental services; and still others are volunteer-based.

There are three levels of emergency transport: basic life support (BLS); advanced life support (ALS); and mobile intensive care units (MICU). All offer immediate service with qualified professionals who will transport you to the hospital promptly. But each is equipped to provide a different level of care and knowing these differences could impact the outcome of your health problem.

What do all of these acronyms mean? And what are the differences?

Basic life support services usually employs two emergency medical technicians (EMTs) who can provide first aid before transporting you to the hospital emergency room. Their knowledge of emergency care, while sufficient for many situations, is not geared toward severe trauma. Also, they do not normally have the sophisticated equipment on board that is necessary for major injuries and heart attacks.

Advance life support has an EMT and a paramedic who has had extensive training which includes the administration of I.V.'s and certain medications. The ALS crew can provide emergency care that would usually have to wait for the emergency room team, should you arrive by BLS.

The MICU ambulance brings the emergency room to you. Two highly trained paramedics use very sophisticated equipment that helps save lives en route to the hospital.

All emergency teams save lives. All provide a service. They just provide different levels of service and are capable of handling varied degrees of trauma.

Which of these services does your community offer? Request this information directly from the ambulance services, or contact your local medical society or city health office. Or simply take note next time you see an ambulance out in your community—there should be something printed on the side of the vehicle.

Just as important as knowing which services are available is understanding how to use them. By all means, call an ambulance if you truly believe one is needed. But should the ambulance team suggest that your condition does not warrant the use of their vehicle, don't argue. It might sound like fun to be whisked away in a speeding ambulance, knowing the siren is sounding just for you; but ambulances are like fire trucks—they must be immediately available to be used where they are most urgently needed.

Also, listen carefully to the 911 dispatchers when you call. They are professionals who will usually continue to talk with you while help is on its way, learning valuable information for the ambulance crew. They can also provide you with information to help yourself while waiting for the ambulance to arrive.

As with many aspects of health care, you have choices in emergency situations. But know about those choices, and be sufficiently interested to help your community to improve these resources.

Your actions in a time of crisis can make a difference to the outcome. Be informed. Cooperate with the 911 dispatcher; but choose your ambulance wisely—and know when to say "No."

CHAPTER TWENTY-THREE

Air Ambulances Help Save Lives in "Golden Hour"

You're driving along a country road, it's a beautiful day and the scenery is breathtaking. Suddenly, another car careens out of control and you're involved in a terrible accident.

Fortunately, your seatbelt has saved your life, but nevertheless, you're badly injured. It's miles to the nearest large town, but you breathe a sigh of relief as you hear the "thwup-thwup" of a chopper blade—a helicopter ambulance arrives and whisks you away to the closest trauma center.

People involved in emergency medicine talk of the "golden hour," the first hour between an accident until the time treatment is given. It's a crucial 60 minutes, which is why ambulances have sirens and flashing lights to help get you to an emergency room as quickly as possible. Statistics indicate that the survival rate is highest if treatment is delivered within that golden hour.

The importance of the golden hour became obvious during the Korean conflict, when helicopters were first used to transport the injured to hospitals. The concept was refined during the Vietnam War, when patients were carried inside the chopper and received medical treatment en route.

Today, many Americans benefit from helicopter ambulance service either directly or because a loved one was saved by air rescue.

You cannot call air ambulance service to your home. They are summoned by other health care services (such as ground ambulance crews, the fire or police department, or a 911 dispatcher) to accident sites, disasters, or when a major illness occurs; usually, the location is difficult to reach by conventional means or speed is the first priority.

The helicopters are flown by experienced pilots and carry a team of specially trained flight nurses and paramedics and/or doctors. The choppers vary in size and can carry two to four patients.

On board is equipment that rivals that of the highest level of ground emergency transportation, as the emergency room is literally brought to the patient. Sophisticated devices, oxygen, heart monitors, medications and I.V.'s plus a constant radio link allows the crew to work closely with the doctors based at the trauma center.

Besides emergencies, air ambulances are used to transport patients who need specialized care from one hospital to another.

The staff is highly trained, and a pilot must be available 24 hours a day. Special heliports must be constructed close to the hospital and the maintenance is ongoing requiring a full time mechanic. Thus, air ambulances are expensive to maintain and operate, but they add a much needed immediacy to delivering emergency care and save lives every day.

Just as ground ambulances have the authority to run red lights and exceed speed limits, air ambulances are given special authority by the Federal Aviation Administration providing them with priority in flight patterns and routing. They are in constant contact with air traffic controllers.

The pilots are a special breed and must be able to handle their craft in diverse places. They land on freeways at rush hour, on beaches at high tide, and on top of high-rise buildings.

There are risks for the crew. Helicopters don't glide. They are mechanical and can develop problems. But they are certainly no more dangerous than a ride in an ambulance through the city streets.

Unfortunately, not every community (or trauma center) is fortunate enough to have access to an air ambulance. Check out your local hospital—and feel lucky if you discover that this wonderful service is there—should you be unlucky enough to need it.

CHAPTER TWENTY-FOUR

Know Your Rights in an Emergency

You are a victim of the recession! You have no job and no health insurance. One evening, very late, you develop severe chest pains; you think you're having a heart attack. A family member drives you to the closest emergency room. And you're worried—you cannot pay for treatment. What can you do?

First, keep in mind that no emergency room has a right to refuse care, if it has the appropriate equipment and expertise. And if such care is not readily available, you can be transferred to an alternate facility. But the emergency room must make those arrangements; it is not your responsibility to find another, better equipped hospital.

However, there is an unfortunate reality to such a scenario. You have arrived at the emergency room, and the hospital begins to make plans to transfer you. It is inevitable that the second hospital will request information regarding your ability to pay health care costs. And it embarrasses me to admit that many hospitals, upon learning that you are neither independently wealthy nor covered by health insurance, suddenly realize that they cannot accept another patient: There's no room at the inn!

Sometimes, a hospital's inability to offer treatment is completely legitimate. Perhaps it is understaffed, or the specialist you need is not immediately available. But emergency rooms that base their decisions on a patient's inability to pay are somewhat beyond my comprehension (and tolerance level).

Of course, hospitals that depend solely upon patient fees for survival cannot give away their services consistently; they need income in order to exist, and that is understandable. But emergency situations should be considered on their individual merits; doctors are committed to saving lives.

Fortunately, new federal legislation has been passed that requires a hospital to accept a patient if that hospital's facilities exceed the capabilities of the referring hospital. Failure to do so invites the imposition of penalties. The legislation is new, however, and hospitals are struggling to incorporate these new rules and regulations into their existing operating structure.

As the patient, you have a right to emergency care, and if an emergency room refuses to provide treatment, you must complain, very loudly and until someone takes notice. Talk to politicians and legislators; to your doctor or clergyman; to someone at your local newspaper.

Don't be intimidated; know your rights; and act swiftly and decisively in your own behalf.

CHAPTER TWENTY-FIVE

Understanding Reasons For Emergency Room Wait

Chances are that when you visit the emergency room at your local hospital, you will have to wait. And you might have to wait a long time. So the next time you find yourself sitting on a hard wooden bench or an overly soft chair at 3:00 a.m. waiting for a doctor, work a crossword puzzle or take this book along to pass the time. And you might find out that you would have been smarter to have stayed home in bed.

It's not that your 99.6 degree temperature, your queasy stomach, or your swollen ankle are not important. Of course they are. Professionals in the emergency room care about all the patients and this is why they turn their attention first to those with the more serious injuries or ailments.

Your local E.R. does not work on the same principle as your friendly accountant: first in, first out. If this were the case, someone needing a refill for a prescription would be seen ahead of the patient with symptoms of a heart attack.

It's not easy, however, to keep things in perspective when you're the one who must wait two hours to see a physician. I know it's difficult to be understanding and generous when you're in pain and are absolutely sure that it would take just a few minutes to make you feel a whole lot better. But the emergency room personnel must weigh your pain and misery along with that of the other patients who need medical attention. In a well-organized emergency room, your throbbing ankle would be treated after the burn victim but before the insomniac.

So, when should you go to the emergency room? Usually, common sense should prevail. Of course, any time you need an ambulance (you fainted and someone called the paramedics, for instance), don't hesitate to take that ride to the emergency room. Major injuries or symptoms that suggest your life might be in danger, such as chest pains that could be the onslaught of a heart attack, are other times when the emergency room should be your next port of call.

Keep in mind that many conditions, such as cuts, bumps, nausea, and even broken bones can be treated at minor emergency medical centers and walk-in clinics available in most communities.

But once you're in the emergency room, be prepared to play the waiting game. It can be frustrating, especially when it appears that someone who looks perfectly qualified to tend to your needs seems to be ignoring you. Why is that guy reading the newspaper? He's a doctor. Why isn't he helping me?

You could be right. The guy reading the paper might be a doctor. So why isn't he helping you? Well, maybe he's qualified to deliver babies, and you've got a broken wrist. That's a bit like asking an auto mechanic to fix an airplane!

Also, many E.R. patients require tests, evaluations, x-rays, medications and various therapy and treatments that can take time. If the facility is smaller and a specialist must be called in, then the wait is longer. Didn't anyone ever tell you that patience is a virtue?

Emergency rooms are categorized by levels, with number 1 being the highest degree of sophistication. Your E.R's designation, the size of its staff, the number of patients in the waiting room, its ability to handle unforeseen disasters such as major fires or bus accidents, the time of day, and the day of the week can all impact the length of your wait.

Though you might never enjoy a long wait, understanding how emergency rooms prioritize patients can help your tolerance level; and knowing that if you were the one with the chest pains, you'd be seen ahead of the guy with the swollen ankle should make you a little more understanding and willing to be somewhat more patient.

It can also help you to decide whether or not to go to the emergency room in the first place. And that will always be your decision.

Checklist
Chapters 21-25

Preparing for Emergencies

✓ Does your area have public or private ambulance service?
✓ Does your area have basic, advanced or mobile intensive care service?
✓ Does your community have enhanced 911 service?
✓ Do you know how to call for ambulance service?
✓ Is helicopter ambulance service available?
✓ Do you know the telephone number of your emergency room?
✓ Do you know the route to the E.R.?
✓ Have you developed an understanding of waiting for assistance in the emergency room?

CHAPTER TWENTY-SIX

Costs Made New Surgery Options Necessary

In my career, I've seen amazing changes in the practice of surgery. In the old days, the removal of cataracts was considered major surgery. Patient were in bed for days, flat on their back with sandbags around their head to keep them immobile.

Now, one-day cataract surgery is common. You enter the hospital, have the surgery and go home. A hernia used to mean five to seven days in the hospital. Not any more—just one day is all it takes.

What's happening? How come these surgical procedures take less time? Well, they don't really—it's just that the patient gets to spend less time in the hospital. Day surgery has arrived!

As technology and medical advancement swept through the 20th century, perceptions of hospitalization failed to keep pace. Ten years ago, when it became obvious that escalating health care costs were bankrupting America, hospitals were still being viewed as a place to dally, a place to get some much-needed rest.

Eventually, it became abundantly clear to everyone—the U.S. government, surgeons, insurance companies—that ways had to be found to lower hospital costs to the consumer; one solution was to shorten the length of stay in hospitals.

The government restricted the amount it would pay for Medicare patients through the use of carefully regulated reimbursement rules. Insurance companies introduced preferred provider (PPO) arrangements and health maintenance organizations (HMO) (where they place restrictions on which doctors or clinics you can use) and through advance approval of elective hospitalization.

The medical community contributed by coming up with new techniques and treatments that speed up the hospital stay.

We used to think that the patient had to enter the day before surgery to settle in and to meet people and learn about their surroundings. While that was nice, it was actually unnecessary and now is considered an outmoded expense. Patients are encouraged to visit the hospital to ask questions and meet the staff—but prior to admission.

Certain procedures, of course, are more complicated and not every patient is a candidate for day surgery. But the list is growing. There are three basics choices for surgery today.

Day Surgery Units (DSU) allows the patient to check in, have surgery, and go home in one day; Day of Surgery Admission (DSA) allows the patient to be admitted on the day of surgery; and traditional surgery still calls for one or more days before surgery required and even several days after surgery.

However, there are some negative aspects to same day surgery. There is little time to get settled in or for the staff to get to know you. The increasing impersonal nature of hospitals can be a problem for some. But it's a trade-off that results in lower costs for all.

You do have rights. If your doctor suggests an operation and does not mention day surgery, you should inquire. Many operations can be done on a one-day basis but some still require the traditional stay.

If your hospital does not offer day surgery, perhaps another hospital or a freestanding day surgery clinic is more suitable to your needs. Also, if your doctor advises a traditional stay, it's best to follow the advice, though you should always feel free to seek a second opinion.

Procedures commonly performed on a one-day basis include hernia repair, cataracts, biopsies, breast surgery and plastic surgery. Those likely to be done on a DSA basis include prostate surgery and a variety of general and orthopedic surgeries. Traditional stays are for more serious surgical procedures like open heart surgery and kidney transplants.

In general, it's good practice to spend as little time as possible in the hospital. But ultimately, be sure to make your decision based on the most important consideration of all-the need to ensure the best quality care. You deserve it.

CHAPTER TWENTY-SEVEN

Questions For An Operation

So you're scheduled for surgery! So let's be realistic! Operations are like many other of life's adventures: Some are big and some are small; some are dangerous and some are not; but none are inexpensive and all have an element of risk. You should know what you're getting into before you take the first step.

Unless you are involved in an emergency or in a life-threatening situation that requires immediate attention, you should know the major details about your scheduled operation. It's *never* advisable to accept something you don't understand; that's why you're supposed to read the fine print before you sign a contract. Right?

Of course, your surgeon cannot provide so much information that you know as much about the operation as does the medical team and you don't need to know that much, anyway. But there are questions you should ask, if the doctor does not volunteer the information.

For instance, you should always know the purpose of the operation. Why do you need the surgery and what is the disease that is being treated? You should know what will be done during the surgery and whether the outcome will be a cure for your ailment. If the operation is exploratory in nature, you have a right to know what the surgeon is expecting to find.

And if the doctor does not provide an explanation in language that you understand, ask your questions again. Insist on receiving clear answers in understandable language.

You must keep in mind, also, that every type of surgery carries the potential for complications, even minor ones. Ask your surgeon about the possibility and probability of minor or major complications, and though most physicians will attempt to allay your fears, they must be honest with you. You are the patient, and you have choices. You certainly have the right to know what is to be done to you, as well as both the expected and unexpected results.

There are dozens of questions a patient might like to ask. Some of them, particularly those dealing with insurance coverage and other costs, will probably be asked and answered prior to hospitalization—and often while dealing with someone other than your doctor.

Many questions are important, however, simply for someone's peace of mind. How long will the operation last? How long will you be in the recovery room? Can your family visit you?

And what about information about that period of time immediately following the operation? Will you experience pain? What will be the treatment? How long will you have to stay in the hospital? Will you have a scar (to show to your friends!)? You should want to know (and you have the right to know) what you can expect.

Of course, it's virtually impossible to list all the questions that could be asked. Before you head into the operating room, make your own list of questions, and ask every one of them.

There's no such thing as a "dumb" question. If something concerns you enough to ask about it, then that's all that matters. Except, of course, for making sure you receive a satisfactory answer.

CHAPTER TWENTY-EIGHT

Putting the Fears About Anesthesia To Sleep

How many times have you said, "Nobody is indispensable"? And I agree, but I also feel that even in the medical profession, some are more indispensable than others. One area that comes to mind is anesthesiology, because without anesthesia, a great deal of modern surgery would be virtually impossible.

Centuries ago, anesthesia was unknown; four strong men held down the patient and that was that! Later, a steady supply of whiskey was provided to help the patient through the trauma. (I think about that whenever I see someone at a party who is "feeling no pain!") Then along came ether, true anesthesia was born, and today, pain-free surgery is taken for granted.

Once you know you are to undergo surgery, there are many things to consider. Who will be your surgeon? Do you have enough sick leave to cover time for recuperation? Who will take care of your dog while you're in the hospital? But I bet you never give much thought to anesthesia, a very important part of your upcoming surgery.

Not long ago, anesthesiologists—medical doctors who specialize in anesthesia—were considered the "phantoms" of medicine. Patients were barely aware of their presence, having only a vague memory of someone in a green cap saying: "Hi, I'm your anesthesiologist; you're going to sleep now."

Today, anesthesiologists are much more visible, and patients usually discuss the various options with them prior to surgery.

Sometimes, a general anesthetic (which puts you to sleep) is appropriate. A regional anesthetic (which numbs only a section of your body) might be recommended. And in some cases, a local anesthetic (which affects a much smaller area) is advisable.

There are advantages and disadvantages to each type and category of anesthetic. (You wouldn't want a general anesthetic to remove a wart from your finger, for example.)

However, you are the patient and have a right to explanations that will allow you to make intelligent choices about your anesthesiologist and the anesthetics. Usually, the anesthesiologist meets with the patient a short time prior to the surgery. But anesthesiologists are "real doctors," and you can request an office appointment, prior to being admitted to the hospital. Regardless of where or when you meet with the anesthesiologist, options should be offered (if possible), the type of anesthesia to be used and the procedure should be explained. You should be made aware of the risks associated with any anesthetic.

Remember, though, anesthesiologists usually work in teams, and the one you meet might not be the same one who administers the anesthetic at the time of your operation—but, of course your anesthesiologist's "order" will be followed.

A number of variables are considered when the type of anesthesia is chosen. Some operations take many hours, and usually a general anesthetic is preferred. The patient's general health can be a factor; and you, the patient, might be the ultimate decision maker. Some patients have a morbid fear of general anesthetics, feeling they might not wake up again. Conversely, others prefer to be "out for the count," not wanting to know what's happening either to them or around them. In such instances, the patient might be the decision maker if his or her choice was medically acceptable.

However, the anesthesiologist is the expert, and you will not be allowed to make a decision that is not in your own best interests. Both you and I can live with that, right?

CHAPTER TWENTY-NINE

Operating Room Secrets

Some people are really fascinated by operating rooms. I've never been able to figure out a reason; except of course, there's always a natural curiosity about the unknown. When I was a kid, I used to wonder what my mother did at the beauty shop; then I found out—and lost interest.

But operating rooms are not beauty shops; much more serious business. They're especially frightening for the patient's family members who have to stand by and watch their loved one disappear behind those mysterious swinging doors.

Movies and television don't help. Some portray the operating room as a place of great tension, where every decision has a life or death implication. Others portray them almost irreverently—a *MASH* setting with Hawkeye Pierce telling crude jokes while performing delicate surgery.

In truth, there is no single set of rules governing the atmosphere of operating rooms. You will not find a book that says they should be silent or noisy, cold or friendly, serious or lighthearted. Each is as different as the personality or the preferences of the surgeon in charge. Some prefer a light atmosphere with joking and chatter. Others insist on total silence and determination. Still others like a combination of the two, with no distractions during the more sensitive portions of surgery. Some like music and conversation to alleviate the tension. I have learned some of my favorite stories in the O.R. But at other times, I have asked everyone in the room to refrain from talking.

Perhaps the main reason that the operating room is such mystery is because it is off limits to the layman. And there are carefully defined guidelines and absolute justification for this isolation.

The operating room must be kept immaculately clean. All bacteria-laden clothing must be removed and replaced with "sterile" scrub suits which have been carefully laundered and stored separately, protected from the outside environment. The locker room is usually a physical barrier to the operating suites, the only entrance.

The operating rooms must be thoroughly cleaned after each surgery. A highly-trained staff of housekeeping personnel ensure that no dirt which could endanger the lives of patients is allowed to accumulate. Even the air is specially filtered. There are usually extra capacity ventilation systems that speed up the removal of used air.

Expensive, delicate and sophisticated equipment is used in operations, and every item must be kept both sterile and protected from theft or damage.

Are operating rooms places of high drama? There is no question that lives are saved daily by the extremely delicate procedures performed there. And I guess that could be called dramatic.

But are operating rooms the stuff of a John Wayne Oscar-winning movie? No, I don't think so. Just a place where a bunch of dedicated doctors and nurses set out to "do their thing." Does it really matter if someone tells a joke or plays country and western? No, not really—as long as the best interests of the patient are served. Ain't that the truth, Pilgrim!

CHAPTER THIRTY

"Button Hole" Surgery Returns

As times have changed, so has surgery. In the old days surgeons operated through tiny incisions, because many believed that large incisions put the patient at greater risk. The mark of a good surgeon was to make as small an incision as possible and surgeons prided themselves on having the smallest cut.

Then along came scientific advances that made surgery safe. Proper anesthetics, the recognition of the impact of infecting organisms, antibiotics, improved techniques and equipment; all made the size of the incision rather irrelevant. More important than the length of the incision was the technique of the surgeon. The popular saying among surgeons —"incisions heal from side to side, not end to end"— meant the length of the incision had little impact on the success of the operation.

Modern surgeons have a new ally that helps them to perform these surgeries successfully. Laparoscopic surgery, employs sophisticated optical instruments, or periscope devices that are inserted into the abdomen through small incisions, allowing the surgeon to view problems inside the body before cutting a patient open.

Moreover, by making a few additional small incisions, other instruments can be inserted into the abdomen and surgical procedures can be performed without ever having to make a large cut. This new technique is in its infancy, yet I predict that with additional experience and the development of new instruments, laparoscopic surgery could become more popular, and may some day completely replace surgery as we know it.

How should you, the patient, handle new developments like this? No one wants to be a "guinea pig" or the first person to have a new procedure performed. Don't worry about that. Surgeons are required to practice and even take additional training, before performing new procedures on patients. Even so, it is appropriate to question your surgeon and satisfy yourself that you are not his or her guinea pig.

Patients ask me all the time about my experience with certain procedures. I answer them frankly, explaining if a procedure is new to me. (Of course, the older I get the less often patients question my experience—I'm not sure whether or not to take that as a compliment.)

Don't forget to ask about the complications, both short and long term. And find out what the expected results will be. If your surgeon tells you this new procedure is replacing an old one, ask him or her to explain the differing results between the two methods. Make sure you are completely satisfied with the answers before undergoing the procedure.

CHAPTER THIRTY-ONE

A Healthy Recovery Means Dealing With Pain

I could never have been a professional athlete. Aside from the lack of talent, I cringe when the commentator says that this hockey player or that football lineman is playing with a broken bone or cracked ribs. But, as they say, "No pain, no gain."

In medical treatment, pain is sometimes unavoidable, although medical science has made great progress, finding ways to reduce the severity and duration of pain.

Today, there are dozens of drugs available that can effectively stop pain. But when your recovery depends largely upon your cooperation, your physician will insist that pain medication be kept to a minimum. For instance, if it's essential that you take a brief walk at regular intervals, your doctor will not prescribe pain medication that makes you sleep.

Telling your doctor that you are in pain might earn you some sympathy; but it won't earn you a reprieve if a speedier recovery is to your benefit. Sound harsh? Maybe. Your doctor's job is to make you healthy as quickly as possible; he or she knows that some pain now is actually beneficial to your health.

In fact, you might think your doctor doesn't even have any sympathy, especially if you're required to take action that makes you hurt even more!

For instance, you might be asked to cough, especially if you've had surgery. This is the best way to keep your lungs clear and minimize the risk of pulmonary infections, such as pneumonia. But, **ouch!** It helps to hold a pillow over the incision area and squeeze it while you're coughing.

Walking is also crucial after surgery. Many times, the doctor will ask you to take a walk the very next day, and help will be provided. Sitting up after surgery could be a chore in itself, so don't try to move too quickly. Sit up, ease out of bed, stand up, and then take the first step.

Good nutrition is essential to a speedy recovery; so eat the food that is brought to your room. (I didn't say enjoy it; I said eat it!) Your doctor will only prescribe the kind of food appropriate for your medical condition—so you know that it has been prepared with your well-being in mind. Using the bathroom can be painful, particularly following certain surgical procedures, or if walking is difficult and the bathroom is not within easy reach. Eliminating body wastes is absolutely essential to your recovery, and the chances are you might not be discharged from the hospital until your doctor knows that this particular part of your anatomy is in working order; if this becomes a major problem, your physician can help with medications—but the rest is up to you.

People who have had major surgery or who are seriously ill might have neither the energy nor the desire to hold a conversation. But it's important for you to communicate with your doctor and nurses. Talk to them! Tell them how you feel. If you don't tell them where it hurts, they can't help you.

The next time I have surgery, I'm going to pretend I'm a lineman for the Chicago Bears. It won't make the pain go away—but it might make it easier to "bear." **Ouch!**

CHAPTER THIRTY-TWO

Blood Banks Are Not Really Frightening Places

Many people break into a sweat just at the thought of donating blood; in fact, if you want to hear some of the most original and inventive excuses, circulate a sign up sheet for a blood drive.

Granted, donating blood isn't anywhere near as much fun as a candlelight dinner for two; but trust me—it's a whole lot more rewarding and a lot less expensive. This is one time that there is truth to the expression: It's better to give than to receive. Blood is one of the world's most precious commodities: it is perishable and its only source is another human being; its supply is limited by the number of people willing to be donors; and no amount of money in the world can buy blood if a donor is not available.

So why don't people stand in line to replenish the blood bank's supply? After all, transfusion technology is highly sophisticated and very safe. All donations are tested for hepatitis and the AIDS antibody—even yours.

But none of this seems to alleviate the fear of having a needle inserted into your arm; watching your blood flow into a plastic container; and the possibility of feeling light-headed after it's all over.

Let's put this into perspective and pretend that you are the one badly in need of blood during an emergency situation. Not only is your life in danger, but consider the emotional pain that is being felt by your wife, children or parents. And you're afraid of a needle stick? Shame on you!

While blood banks resemble regular banks in that both allow for deposits and withdrawals, there is one major difference. If you deposit your money in a bank, it can stay there forever, earning interest. But the deposit you make in the blood bank must be used quickly, before it spoils. Consequently, blood banks must constantly face the challenge of replenishing their assets.

Certain times of the year are more critical than others. After holidays, supplies are often reduced due to an increase in holiday-related injuries and postponed elective surgeries.

Also, some blood types are more in demand than others, regardless of the season. AB Negative, a rare blood type, is always in short supply. If you are AB Negative and have healthy blood (the blood bank determines this through pre-testing), then you are a particularly valuable customer.

The most common blood type is O Positive. But because it is the largest blood group, the blood bank must have a generous supply on hand.

If your major fear of the blood bank is its inability to monitor its own supply, you can consider "autologous transfusion," if faced with elective surgery. This simply means that you donate to yourself in advance of the operation. The blood can be kept for only a limited time. You cannot store your own blood for future use indefinitely.

Today, blood banks can divide the donation into various component parts, so that each component can be used for a different reason. This allows for better storage and a longer shelf life. Storing donor blood in freezers has also increased the length of time that it can be used.

Sometimes, as human beings, we must do things that we don't really want to do. We go to funerals; have cavities filled; refuse to give more money to our children. But when we find ourselves in such a position, we know we are making a decision based on one very simple belief: It's the right thing to do.

If you have resisted donating blood, then such a thought probably ranks right up there with having a cavity filled. But if you are concerned about your own health, and if you care just a little bit about your fellow human beings, it would seem that you can't help but consider the possibility of visiting your local blood bank.

CHAPTER THIRTY-THREE

All About Dr. Roentgen and His Magical X-Ray Machine

The x-ray machine. Most of us have had an x-ray at some time in our lives; yet it's probably true to say that few of us understand its amazing contribution to medicine—and our health.

You might think that x-ray machines have been around for ever, but in fact, they have been around for less than 100 years. The x-ray machine was invented by a German physician, Dr. Roentgen, and was at first considered a mysterious and magical device.

The original machine was simple: a glass tube with an electrical current passing through that produced invisible rays that could penetrate human tissue. Of course, this was long before any of the dangers were recognized, and x-ray machines were used with little caution in the doctor's office; they were even demonstrated at carnivals, and I remember going to a shoe store as a child where I would place my feet in a fluoroscope (an x-ray machine) to have my size "read."

Safety measures were introduced from the 1930s to 1950s when the dangers were understood. Today, a tremendous emphasis is placed on safety and protection both for the patient and the health care workers.

Lead offers the best protection, and medical professionals use plastic identification badges that contains a photofilm sensitive to x-rays. The film is checked regularly to test for over-exposure.

There is little danger of overexposure for the patient. A minimal amount of x-rays are used—only the amount necessary to focus on a particular body area, and computers are used to enhance the image. It is virtually impossible to get overexposed to x-rays in a routine medical setting.

Of course, if x-rays are used for treatment (as opposed to diagnosis), a much higher dosage is used, because the whole purpose of using radiation therapy is to destroy such things as malignant cancer cells.

If you require an x-ray—either for a routine diagnosis or for treatment—you could meet one or more specialists. Radiologists are medical doctors who specialize in radiology; they supervise and interpret the films taken during each procedure. A radiation therapist specializes in cancer treatment. The specially trained individual who actually takes the x-rays is the radiologic technician; and the radiation physicist ensures that the equipment is safe and in working order.

The radiologist has many tools available to ensure that x-rays are used to your benefit. In addition, there are several newer techniques that allow the same benefits without the need for x-rays at all.

The fluoroscopy is similar to a movie, a continuous x-ray that is usually "directed" by a radiologist. This procedure is especially helpful for determining the function of internal organs. Barium enemas are used to examine the lower gastrointestinal tract. For upper gastrointestinal tract examinations, the patient swallows barium which is then tracked by the use of fluoroscopy. Fluoroscopy can also be used to look at blood vessels, the heart, kidneys and the urinary tract.

The CT scan (cat scan) uses a computer to enhance the action of the x-rays, thus reducing the amount of x-rays needed.

Ultrasound, like the sonar of submarines, uses sound waves to bounce off the internal walls of the body. There is no risk in this non-x-ray procedure, which has many uses, including the evaluation of developing babies while still in the mother's womb.

Magnetic resonance imaging (MRI) also does not use x-rays, but produces excellent pictures of the brain and internal organs with little or no risk to the patient.

Although the basic x-ray machine has been fine-tuned since Roentgen's day, both the way in which it works and its usefulness in the diagnosis and treatment of illness has not changed. While its workings may remain a mystery to you, there is no need to fear it. Be grateful it exists; and of course, respect for any complicated piece of equipment is always to your advantage.

CHAPTER THIRTY-FOUR

Needles Hurt, But They Also Can Save a Life

I have a confession. I'm scared of needles. It's true. After spending eight years getting an undergraduate degree and a medical degree and then another five years in a residency program, I've finally made it to the "right" side of the needle!

It's not an uncommon fear. Most people don't like having sharp objects stuck into them, regardless of the payoff. It's a bit like telling kids that spinach is "good for you"—doesn't make it any easier to take.

But, as they say, no one promised us that life would be a rose garden, so maybe we have to think of the occasional needle as the thorn in our side!

As with so many other areas of medicine, it might help to alleviate some of your fears if you understand just what needles can do for you.

Doctors do not enjoy giving shots to patients, but the information and results that can be gained through their use are invaluable. For example, needles inserted into the veins can remove blood to be tested for hundreds of conditions, from AIDS to zinc levels. And just as things can be taken out of the body, others can be injected, such as antibiotics, lifesaving plasma, medications and water.

Arteries are major blood vessels that carry blood from the heart to the rest of the body. A needle can be used to draw blood from the arteries, providing information on oxygen levels and other critical readings.

Through arteries, needles can even be used to place small, sophisticated tubes directly into the heart to measure function, to take x-rays of vessels, and to perform angioplasties, a form of "plastic surgery" to open diseased or injured vessels.

Similarly, tubes can be inserted through needles into the kidneys, the brain—anywhere there are blood vessels, for testing of blood, to take tissue specimens, remove growths, for treatment and for x-rays.

Needles can be stuck directly into the liver, kidney, brain, lymph nodes and other areas for biopsies, to drain abscesses, to perform tests and to determine if all is working normally.

Larger instruments the size of a pencil or small cigar can also be inserted through the skin for a variety of purposes including the removal of kidney stones, gall bladders and to perform tubal ligations. Large needles inserted into the joints can help observe and treat cartilage problems, including arthritis.

There is virtually no place in the body that a needle cannot be used. What a dreadful thought, you say?

But because this simple instrument is so effective, doctors are able to help you avoid many types of major (and expensive) medical procedures including some surgery. The bad news is that you get the needle.

However, just as you must take charge of other aspects of your health care, it's important to question any procedure, including the use of needles. Just because you have a vein, doesn't mean it needs to be stuck. Exercise your right to be informed.

CHAPTER THIRTY-FIVE

The "Totally Tubular" Approach To Medicine

There's no question that medical care has become very sophisticated. In the 1990s, doctors have clever, exact instruments, computers, lasers— and we're very proud of the advances that have been made. The trouble is, that in the 1890s, the doctors were saying the same thing. They looked back to the 1790s as the "simpler times." What will the physicians of 2093 think of our abilities?

One advance unique to the 20th century is the ability to study patients from the inside as well as the outside for examinations, diagnoses and treatment. Much of this is done with the use of tubes. Bluntly put, if you have an opening, then doctors have something to put into it.

Having tubes inserted into your body orifices is usually indelicate, immodest, uncomfortable and embarrassing, but in most cases, absolutely necessary. But you have every right to ask for explanations of and reasons for such a procedure. Of course, if it's a lifesaving maneuver, such as an emergency trachea tube that allows you to breathe, waiting to seek your permission would be ludicrous, particularly since the chances are you would be unconscious.

Virtually every body orifice can be examined. Perhaps the discomfort and embarrassment might be easier to tolerate if you have a better understanding of some of the various procedures.

Nose: Nasal tracheal tubes are placed through the nose into the lungs to allow you to breathe, by forcing air or oxygen with the use of a respirator. Nasal gastric tubes are used to empty the stomach of its contents (stomach pumping) or for examination. Still another special device can measure the body's temperature from the inside.

Mouth: Endotracheal tubes are used to provide air and oxygen. Through special tubes and instrumentation, physicians can perform surgery, biopsies, close open parts and open closed parts, stop bleeding and deliver medication to the upper gastrointestinal tract and lungs.

Rectum: Colonoscopes are used to explore the large bowel, and tubes are used for biopsies, to stop bleeding, remove growths, treat excess gas and to look for problem areas. And then there's the infamous enema. It can even be a lifesaving procedure, despite its much maligned reputation.

Urethra: Tubes (catheters) inserted in this sensitive area drain urine from the bladder when the patient cannot urinate naturally. They are also used to examine the interior surface area of the urinary tract, to examine the kidneys, bladder and ureter. Moreover, surgery can be performed through these tubes.

None of these procedures are comfortable. Many (especially those used for examination) require a high degree of experience in use, but all can be valuable.

Although one of the earliest medical instruments (discovered in ancient Egyptian tombs) was a urinary catheter composed of hollow river reeds or silver, most of these procedures were impossible just 100 years ago—many even 20 years ago. For example, the miniaturization of tubes for kidney exams was introduced only about 10 years ago.

Despite the growing sophistication, one thing remains constant—you have the right to require an explanation of what is being done to you. With this knowledge, you can make the intelligent decision to pursue successful treatment through such procedures.

Consider the amount of time you spent grilling the salesman the last time you bought a car. Don't hesitate to be equally interested in matters that concern your health.

CHAPTER THIRTY-SIX

"Doctor, Will I Get AIDS In The Hospital?"

Recently, a patient told me that she didn't want to check into the hospital. Her reason? A fear of contracting AIDS. My first reaction was to make light of her concern, but then I realized she was sincerely worried and that her fear was probably representative of many people's concern about this still misunderstood disease.

Can you get AIDS while in the hospital? I suppose it depends on your behavior; if you're foolish enough to have careless, unprotected sex or use a contaminated needle—and can get away with it while you're in the hospital—there's a possibility that you could contract AIDS. However, since there's not much of a chance that you'd get away with that kind of behavior in the hospital, then—well, you figure it out!!

But let's get serious and look at the facts. Indeed, hospitals are admitting more and more AIDS patients and the number of cases increases. But elaborate precautions are taken to prevent the spread of the human immunodeficiency virus (HIV virus) and the chances of you contracting AIDS while in the hospital is virtually zero.

The HIV virus is an extremely fragile organism which is difficult to pass along through casual contact and is easily killed with common household bleach.

Medical instruments such as syringes, scalpels and other items that may come into contact with blood are disposable. The needle that draws blood from your arm is thrown out, and nondisposable items are carefully sterilized.

Besides, for their own protection, AIDS patients are normally placed in an isolation area, away from other patients. Employees take special precautions by wearing gloves, masks, eye protection, and gowns; spills of blood or bodily fluids are quickly removed.

Expensive and well-planned employee education programs keep hospital workers up to date on the AIDS situation. Those isolated needle-stick AIDS cases that make national headlines are rare indeed. Although employees are at slightly greater risk than are the patients, even their chances of contracting AIDS are minuscule.

Rather than worrying about contracting AIDS while hospitalized, individuals should be more alert to protecting themselves in the general conduct of their daily lives. The United States Surgeon General's Office warns that risky behavior incudes sharing drug needles and syringes; anal sex, with or without a condom; vaginal or oral sex with someone who takes drugs intravenously or who engages in anal sex; sex with someone you don't know well or with someone who has known several partners; and unprotected sex (without a condom) with an infected partner.

However, there is no risk of contracting AIDS through everyday contact with people around you in school, at work, in the stores, or at the swimming pool; from mosquito or other insect bites; through saliva, sweat, tears, or urine; by kissing; or from clothes, a telephone, a toilet seat, or eating utensils; or by being on a bus, train or elevator with someone who is HIV positive.

If you are not infected with AIDs, then do not fear those who are, even in the hospital; unless of course, you intend to engage in risky sex or share a contaminated needle to satisfy your drug problem. But then, that's not the hospital; that's your stupidity, right?

CHAPTER THIRTY-SEVEN

"The Customer Is Always Right" Applies To Health Care

You've probably been on a flight that took off two hours late; dinner was a tiny bag of peanuts and you flew through a thunderstorm. The plane circled above your destination for an hour, and you waited for an eternity on the tarmac before the pilot was allowed to "park."

And as you left the plane, the captain added insult to injury by telling you he hoped you'd had a good flight and would use this same airline again. Obviously, this captain understands the need for good public relations; at least you might remember the friendly send-off (as well as the lousy trip) when you go to make your next flight reservation.

Hospital administrators could learn from the airline captain. Since a hospital stay can be either a smooth or a bumpy flight—administrators should take a moment to communicate with the patients just before they are discharged.

Your hospital stay might be very comfortable, if the patient census is low and you have sufficient nursing care, a private room, and a health problem that does not require uncomfortable treatment.

But when you must survive an unpleasant experience, you should inform the hospital staff—especially the administrative staff. There's nothing wrong with legitimate complaints and constructive criticism; reputable hospitals welcome the comments of patients who provide information that allows the hospital to improve its service. Some hospitals provide comment cards—use them if they're available.

Your happiness is important to those who run the hospitals, clinics and agencies that cater to sound health. You will tell your family, friends and co-workers about your experience; and one of them might have to choose a hospital some time soon.

But if you have a complaint, approach the situation calmly; a few, well-spoken words can be much more effective than an obnoxious tirade; few people really listen to temper tantrums or angry words.

Be sure your complaint is well-founded and be prepared to supply details and specific information so that administrators can take action.

If you wish to complain, start with those who are attending to you—your nurse or doctor. If you don't get satisfaction at that point, ask to talk to a higher authority. Eventually, you should reach someone who can resolve the problem. Also, many hospitals have patient relations departments whose purpose is to investigate and take care of patient problems.

A few months ago, I took a trip. The plane was delayed for two hours in Detroit, and when we reached our final destination, the airline had lost *everyone's* luggage. Do you think I'll ever use that airline again?

And the administrator of Hospital XYZ knows that if his hospital provides similar service to the patients, there's a good chance that many of them would go elsewhere for hospital care. I know I would.

CHAPTER THIRTY-EIGHT

Doctors Questions May Seem Strange, But Are Important

I agree, doctors are strange people. They ask many unusual things of their patients and at times it is difficult to see the relevance. Often however, essential information necessary for the doctor to diagnose and treat your illness, appears unwarranted to the lay person.

Why, for example, would the doctor want to look into your eyes if he or she suspects you have hypertension? What do eyes have to do with elevated blood pressure? Plenty! Inside your eye are many blood vessels that become easily visible with the help of a special instrument. The blood vessels are affected by hypertension and physicians can study them to learn more about your problem.

And why would the doctor examine your neck if he or she were worried about kidney stones? It's possible to develop kidney stones as a result of a tumor in one or your parathyroid glands that are located in the neck. There are many examples of seemingly unrelated facts that together make up a disease, and the doctor, like any good detective, must gather the facts to make a diagnosis. It is in your best interest to ask questions. If you don't understand what is happening or why examinations or tests are necessary, your doctor can explain the relationship to you. It is essential that you understand.

One of the greatest areas of confusion occurs when the physician discusses seemingly unrelated sexual matters that the patient thinks are inappropriate. What could the timing of your menstrual periods have to do with your headaches? Why does the pattern of your sexual habits relate to the burning sensation you experience when urinating?

Yet, these are relevant questions and the answers can go a long way in helping your doctor to help you. Sometimes the questions are detailed and delicate. If you are unsure of the relationship between the questions and your problem, then ask. Satisfy yourself that the information is necessary before answering the question.

And, it is important to answer your doctor's questions honestly. Don't exaggerate some details while omitting others that seem embarrassing. Hopefully, you and your doctor have a relationship that allows frank and open discussions. Accurate answers are essential and rest assured your doctor will keep the information confidential. It's difficult to make a correct diagnosis. You can help by providing us with the facts.

CHAPTER THIRTY-NINE

Read What's Hanging On the Hospital Wall

When you walk into most hospitals you will find a variety of signs and messages hanging on the wall. If you stop to read them, and you should, you will find important facts about the hospital.

For example, you should find a certificate of accreditation from the Joint Commission on Accreditation of Health Organizations (JCAHO). If the hospital requests accreditation (and all should since payment of funds by the various federal programs depend on accreditation), it will be visited and inspected by this national organization. After a rather in depth inspection process the hospital may receive accreditation for up to three years. It is a measure of the hospitals quality and should not be ignored.

You might also see a statement that the hospital will provide a portion of its resources for care of indigent patients. Also, perhaps, a certificate stating that the hospital provides appropriate access and aids for handicapped patients.

Some hospitals also display the "Patient's Bill of Rights," which explain the rights and responsibilities of the patient. This is a very interesting document and I think appropriate to quote it in its entirety here.

The Patient's Bill of Rights

1. The Patient has the right to considerate and respectful care.
2. The Patient has the right to an explanation in terms the patient can understand of all information concerning diagnosis, treatment and prognosis. The Patient is responsible for giving accurate and complete information regarding health and medical care.
3. The Patient has the right to receive full information about all procedures and treatments and to proceed with them only if he or she gives informed consent. Informed consent is consent in the

light of full information concerning risks and medical alternatives. It is the Patient's duty to tell the health care provider if he or she does not understand the information given about the procedures or treatment.

4. The Patient has the right to refuse treatment to the extent permitted by law. The Patient has the right to be informed of the medical consequences of that refusal. The Patient becomes responsible for the outcome if treatment is refused or instructions not followed.

5. The Patient has the right to privacy concerning medical care. Such discussion, examination, and treatment shall be conducted discreetly.

6. The Patient has the right to confidentiality regarding all records and communications concerning the patient's care.

7. The Patient has the right to reasonable responses to requests for service. The hospital provides evaluation, service and/or referral as appropriate to the patient's needs. When transfer to another facility is indicated, a complete explanation, including alternatives will be given. Before transfer, the receiving institution must first have accepted the patient.

8. The Patient has the right to know who is involved in his or her care and their relationship to the hospital.

9. The Patient has the right to be advised of medical research affecting care or treatment, and to refuse to participate in such research.

10. The Patient has the right to be informed of any continuing health care requirements. The hospital shall maintain the patient's medical record and transfer it upon request by the patient.

11. The Patient has the right to receive an explanation of hospital charges. The Patient has the duty to arrange for payment of those charges.

12. The Patient has the right to know the hospital rules and regulations that apply to patient conduct. The Patient is responsible for following hospital rules and regulations affecting patient care, patient and visitor conduct, and payment of services.

Please notice that several of these rights are also followed by responsibilities. Your health care is a mutual affair and you as well as the health care providers play a role in its conduct. It pays to do your fair share.

CHAPTER FORTY

Religion Often Plays An Important Role In Medicine

My father was a wise man who used to say "Never discuss religion or politics." Well, let's leave politics out of this, but since religion and medicine tend to co-exist in a hospital setting and often complement each other, a few observations seem to be in order.

When you check into the hospital, the admission form usually asks you to identify your religious affiliation. No, the hospital is not being nosey, and you don't even have to answer the question. But if you think you might want to talk to a minister (or if you want to make it clear that you don't want a visit from a clergyman), this is the time to make your feelings known.

Most hospitals have a chaplaincy program. Usually it is composed of a few dedicated individuals who are available for the patient's spiritual needs, or simply just to talk and provide company. Also, if you're lucky, the chaplain might be your own clergyman, since most departments of ministry are staffed by volunteers from the local community. Chaplains can bring serenity to a stressful experience, provide reassurance to worried families, or perform certain religious rites or traditions, if required.

In my mind, there is no doubt that faith and prayer can make positive contribution to a patient's recovery. Most doctors have witnessed a minister's influence that has resulted in a resurgence of hope and eventual recovery in patients who had virtually lost the will to live.

I have seen clergymen involved in almost every aspect of patient care. They bring people to the hospital, take them home, or stay up all night holding a patient's hand. I've even seen them spend their own money to supply the patient with something they require. And most doctors will be eternally grateful to the clergymen for their dedication and the accompanying extraordinary results.

Many hospitals provide chapels where patients and families can seek solitude for meditation and prayer. It can be a quiet refuge from the clatter of the sterile hospital hallways, the buzzing of the intensive care unit.

Regardless of your ailment or anticipated length of stay, a visit from a clergyman is available for all patients. You can request a minister who represents your personal religious affiliation; and if you have indicated a desire for a visit from a clergyman and this does not materialize, don't hesitate to bring this to someone's attention. Tell your doctor or nurse; contact a patient relations representative.

The clergy is there to comfort, not preach, and the doctors are there to heal. Together, we can provide the physical, mental and emotional support that can help to speed your recovery. What a partnership!

CHAPTER FORTY-ONE

How You Can Overcome the "Hospital Blues"

No one enjoys being sick or hospitalized. It isn't bad enough that you're in pain or feeling awful; but now you're in a strange bed, in a strange environment, sharing a room with a stranger who snores, and the TV doesn't even carry your favorite channel. Who can blame you for feeling just a bit sorry for yourself?

But wait! What about your family? Not only do they feel somewhat lonely and abandoned—*now* who's going to fix the dripping faucet?—But they feel helpless, too. How can they help? Contribute to your recovery? Do something? Anything?

Family members should talk to your doctor or nurse; they can visit the patient relations department; and by asking the right people the right questions, family members can discover many ways they can help to make your hospital stay more comfortable and less traumatic.

For instance, some hospitals allow family members to stay overnight. Accommodations might not rival those of a fancy hotel, but they are adequate. If the patient's spirits are given a boost, just by knowing that a family member is there at all times, what more could you want? However, if the patient doesn't want such arrangements to be made, this decision should also be honored. Always remember, it's the patient's well-being that must be the primary consideration.

Restrictions on visiting hours should be honored. There has to be certain times when members of the medical team can be alone with the patient to administer prescribed treatment. There is no patient in the world who wants an audience while an enema is being given. Family members—please respect those moments of privacy. Similarly, there could be strict rules regarding visiting hours, if the patient is in intensive care or suffering from a contagious disease. Please do cooperate when faced with such circumstances.

Long hospital stays (either as a visitor or a patient) can be boring. Many hospitals have lending libraries or gift shops with magazines and books. Bring your needlepoint, write the Great American novel—bring things to do. Show your loved one that the hospital stay can be a productive experience. (But again, if the patient needs to take a nap or simply requires some solitude, be understanding.)

Lift the spirits of your family member by being happy and supportive. Don't bring your problems (or your bills) to the hospital room. Maintaining a cheerful demeanor is one of the most important and valuable contributions you can make.

Ask your family member's doctor for explanations. If you understand the illness or operation that your relative is facing, you know how to act and react so that you can maintain a positive attitude. Know the facts, but keep in mind that there is such a thing as patient confidentiality, and the doctor might not be ethically free to divulge everything.

If the hospital allows family members to participate in some aspects of patient care such as occupational therapy or music therapy, grab the opportunity with open arms. Your family member will then be able to experience, first hand, your sincere desire to contribute toward his or her recovery.

One important thing to remember is that a distressed family member can have a negative impact on a patient's potential recovery. If you realize that you are emotionally or physically overwhelmed (and this is nothing to be ashamed of), take a break! Ask other relatives to take your place while you take a rest, bask in a hot bath, watch a movie or just take time to regroup. Stress can be devastating, and many hospitals can offer support, arranging for counseling with psychologists, psychiatrists or chaplains, depending upon your needs.

Knowing the "don'ts" is also important. Generally it is advisable to leave children at home; refrain from smoking; and resist the temptation to supplement hospital food (unless the doctor says it's OK to do so). Regardless of how humane it might seem, it can be devastating to give chocolate candy to a diabetic or a bottle of beer to a heavily-medicated patient. Occasionally, you have to be "cruel to be kind."

CHAPTER FORTY-TWO

Holiday In the Hospital Can Be Hard

I once played Santa Claus, which is hard to believe, especially if you know me. The physique is about right, but I don't have a beard, I'm not overly jolly, and I'm Jewish. But nevertheless, I was Santa.

One year, as part of a planned program, I dressed up in a red suit and white beard and visited every patient in the hospital, giving them small presents, with a "ho-ho-ho" and a "Merry Christmas." And you want to know something? It was one of the singularly most rewarding experiences of my life. The reaction of the patients was extremely touching.

It's amazing how fast a hospital empties out during the holidays. Those who are able, go home to be with their families; but for the patients who must stay, the Season of Good Cheer can be terribly depressing.

To complicate matters, these patients are often lost in the hustle and bustle of the holidays. All around them, trees are being decorated, people are humming carols, and exchanging gifts. Visits from family and friends are often filled with talk of Christmas shopping, elaborate dinner plans, and exciting parties. Meanwhile, the patient looks forward to a change of I.V. and some infamous hospital food.

What can you do to help? Well, you too can play Santa Claus by donating gifts or time to your local hospital volunteer office. You can take a few extra minutes to visit a friend or loved one in the hospital. Be generous with your time. Who knows, it could be you that gets to spend Christmas in the hospital some year.

Believe it or not, there are some benefits for patients who spend the holidays in the hospital. For some, empty hospitals are happy hospitals. If you are seeking peace and quiet and don't mind being in bed while the rest of the world looks for parking spaces at the mall, then perhaps you should consider having your elective surgery at Christmas. Another bonus is that since there are fewer patients, you stand a better chance of having more personal care since hospitals remain staffed and ready even during Christmas. If you would like a certain surgeon or physician, however, plan ahead. Your doctor might have scheduled time off and not be available.

For the majority, however, home is where the heart is at special times of the year. The sad fact is that most patients who must remain hospitalized at this time of year are the sickest: chronically ill, accident victims, burns patients and others requiring careful monitoring.

Of course, the most heartbreaking of all are children. The holidays are particularly difficult for pediatric patients, but most children's care units are well aware of the need to brighten up the rooms and hallways with decorations. Most take special pains to ensure that the children don't miss out on Christmas. Parties, presents, visits from Santa Claus and carolers are often included.

Ensuring that patients get excellent health care and to lift the spirits of hospitalized patients during the holidays requires a dependable and unselfish staff who would rather be home stringing popcorn for the tree. If you have family members who must work at Christmas, take extra time to ensure they don't miss out on the fun. Plan gift exchanges around their schedule, or give them a basket of goodies to take to the hospital.

You don't even have to rent a Santa suit and practice shaking your belly like a bowlful of jelly (easier for some than others), to help make Christmas a happier time for loved ones in the hospital. It can be simple things. A phone call to say "I love you;" a basket of (physician-approved) homemade baked goods; a miniature artificial tree near the bedside; a poinsettia plant; and most of all—you. Visit them. Be there, and give your time and/or money to help those you don't know, but for whom you have compassion. That's what it's all about. That's the spirit of Christmas.

CHAPTER FORTY-THREE

Fear Of Hospitals Is Unfounded

My uncle says he gets sick to his stomach just at the thought of hospitals; he says they "smell funny." Actually, I know lots of people who hate hospitals. Not me. I spend half my life in a hospital. I'm glad I'm a doctor.

Of course, hospitals have not always enjoyed the best of reputations. A long time ago, they were places where people went only if they could not afford a doctor at home, or if they were about to die. The sad truth is that before modern sterile procedures and antibiotics, it was often safer to be treated at home. There was less chance of infection and maybe even a better chance of recovery!

Things are vastly different today. And if you're about to be hospitalized, you have enough on your mind; the last thing you need is to be stressed out simply at the thought of going to the hospital. Maybe a few words from me could help dispel those fears. At least, let me try, will you?

I've heard people express various concerns about hospitals (other than my uncle's "funny smell" that is most likely nothing more than cleaning solutions!).

"I'll catch something" is one frequently heard comment. It's possible, but it's highly unlikely. Thorough cleaning, staff trained in minimizing risk of transferring infections, and "compartmentalization" of infectious diseases, have made hospitals extraordinarily safe places to be treated.

Once a patient asked me to wash my hands, right there in her room, so she could be sure I'd taken the necessary precautions. I admired the fact that she cared about good health care procedures, and of course, I respected her request, washing my hands thoroughly. Besides, if this made the patient feel more comfortable and have more confidence in me—what the heck! We both win, right?

Another concern seems to be, *"I'll receive contaminated blood or medication."* Great care and expense is given to ensure that this does not happen. Blood is collected under very strictly monitored conditions and tested before it is accepted. Medications are prepared in special rooms with vented hoods that prevent even airborne contaminants from reaching them.

"I'll receive the wrong medication" appears to be another worry. While I hate to admit that this could happen, the chance is slight. In a large hospital, there are thousands of doses of medicine dispensed daily. But the risk of error is greatly reduced by procedures for double checking and the number of staff that must witness the order throughout the process greatly reduce mistakes. However, as a patient, you can help by asking about your medication. If it looks or smells different, ask for an explanation. Or if it is the first time, then ask the nurse or doctor to explain the medicine to you. This involves you in your own recovery and serves as another check point for accuracy.

Another fear is, *"I'll have the wrong operation."* I've had patients who have written special instructions on their own skin (Take out the left kidney, doc, not the right one). While "many a true word is spoken in jest," this is a real fear for some patients.

Again, the number of staff involved throughout the surgery process from admitting to recovery, provide built-in double, triple and even quadruple checkpoints. Your hospital identification tag also minimizes risk—it is checked continuously. But if you feel that an error might be made—make a pest of yourself. Ask about the procedure or tell the surgeon of your concerns. And a family member can check with the surgeon near the time of surgery as a final precaution.

If you're worried about confidentiality (*"The whole world will know."*), your privacy and records are protected by law. This is a basic right, and if you feel that your patient confidentiality has been breached, yell "loud and clear."

One patient told me, *"I won't be a guinea pig."* No medical treatments that are considered experimental can be done without your consent. All procedures should be explained in detail, and if you are not comfortable with the nature of the treatment, then ask questions until you are satisfied; and of course, feel free to get a second (or third) opinion.

One of the best ways to overcome your fear of hospitals is to spend some time in one. But don't wait until you are sick; join the ranks of volunteers or ask for a tour, if one is available. Many hospitals now offer tours for children, and even for adults, to offset such fears and to explain how the hospital works. Talk to knowledgeable and informed hospital personnel. Read this book!

Now that I have convinced you that there is nothing to fear in a hospital stay, please read the next chapter carefully.

CHAPTER FORTY-FOUR

A Hospital Stay Can Be Hazardous To Your Health

Believe it or not, people used to think of the hospital as a kind of "resort"—a place to rest and get some badly needed peace and quiet.

Indeed, many people checked in for ailments such as "nervous exhaustion" and "insomnia" and went home a couple of weeks later, ready to face the world again.

Today, smart health consumers do not treat hospitals like *Club Med.* For many reasons including the cost, decreased reimbursement from insurance companies and governmental agencies and increased technology, hospital stays are becoming shorter. But there is another reason to avoid an unnecessary stay in the hospital. They can be dangerous places!

Nosocomial (hospital-acquired) infections have evolved over time to be resistant to many antibiotics. They are usually caused by bacteria that are found everywhere. Telephones, light switches, door handles, your skin—all are potential harborers of disease. Most are harmless unless you have a predisposition to them or have not previously been in contact with them. If your immune system is compromised and you meet up with a "new bug," then infection could occur.

While it's impossible to eradicate all bacteria from the hospital, the greatest efforts are taken to win this uphill battle. Hospitals invest large sums of money to ensure that the environment is as clean as possible. But, once one organism is under control, a new one often appears. Why take a chance? Who wants to go to the hospital for a minor problem and end up getting *really* sick? Hospitalization is serious business and should be undertaken only if necessary.

Why are infection-related diseases on the increase? Simple evolution. When antibiotics were introduced as "miracle drugs," a relatively small amount was effective in fighting disease-causing organisms. Today, because the germs' resistance has grown, there has been a ten-fold increase in the dosage required. New antibiotics have been developed as old ones become useless, but they also lose power.

Infections are not the only dangers facing hospital patients. Increasingly complex instrumentation such as magnetic resonance imaging, x-rays, and testing procedures that use radioactive material can pose a threat even while offering extremely valuable benefits. Patients should ask for information. How much radiation is involved? Are there any potential risks with these tests? What are the estimated costs? Is there a possibility for an allergic reaction to certain medications? (You should know your allergy history and always provide this to the physician.)

Still another strike against unnecessary hospitalization is the cost. Due to cutbacks in governmental insurance reimbursement and similar policies adopted by private insurers, it's no longer financially intelligent (or feasible) to check into the hospital for a long rest. Don't expect Uncle Sam or Mutual of Centerville to foot the bill for a couple of weeks of sleeping and reading! Times have changed.

Don't misunderstand me! It's not all doom and gloom at your local hospital. Hospitals are still safer than ever. Before, there was the risk of contamination from a non-sterile needle. Today they are disposable, as are many instruments. Powerful air conditioning units that do not recirculate contaminated air add to a healthy environment.

Also, most hospitals have an infection control department to monitor the processes leading to infection, to educate the staff and to help ward off potential epidemics. And watching over the hospitals of America is the Joint Commission on Accreditation of Health Organizations (JCAHO) which regularly inspects and accredits hospitals. Look for the JCAHO plaque in a prominent location at the hospital, usually in the lobby area.

While it's often prudent to bypass the hospital for non-urgent medical problems, *never* put off hospitalization if your physician suggests it. Go to the emergency room, when you feel you have an urgent medical need. Always consult your physician.

While hospitals can be dangerous places, they are still havens of health at the appropriate time. Millions of lives are saved, because individuals recognized the need to be hospitalized.

But be cautious! Ask questions! And take your vacation in Hawaii!

CHAPTER FORTY-FIVE

Getting Out Of the Hospital Takes Planning

Whenever I travel, I buy a round trip ticket. Not only is it less expensive that way, but I know that my return flight is already planned, even before I've packed by bags and left home. Now that's peace of mind!

So how does this relate to your health care? Well, when you're scheduled to be hospitalized, buy a round trip ticket! Make sure you have planned for your return home well before the day arrives—either before or very soon after you've been admitted.

Hospital stays are getting briefer; patients are no longer invited to stay for a day or two longer but are encouraged to begin their recuperation at home.

Unless your problem is unusually severe and will require an extended stay in the hospital, it's generally possible for the doctor to predict your approximate discharge date. And regardless of whether you will be returning to your own home or spending time at a convalescent facility, you will need to make the appropriate arrangements: travel, special needs (crutches, maybe?) or special arrangements, such as a private nurse.

The discharge process begins when the doctor writes an order for you to go home (paperwork). Then the nurse acknowledges the order (more paperwork), medication is obtained (more paperwork), the admitting office is notified (more paperwork), and the financial office clears you for discharge (lots more paperwork). Finally, someone arrives to escort you to your vehicle.

You can help the process by requesting certain information be processed ahead of your discharge date. For instance, if you are going home tomorrow, perhaps the paperwork could be done today. Perhaps medications could be ordered a little earlier; and you'd actually enjoy listening to the special instructions while you're eating supper, the night before going home.

Know whether there's a specific checkout time—you don't want to be charged for an extra day—and ask your personal chauffeur (parent, spouse, or friend) to arrive before the designated deadline.

It's possible that a variety of hospital personnel are involved in your discharge including nurses, social workers, chaplains, and transportation orderlies. When it is time to leave, thank everyone if they deserve it, however, offering tips is never appropriate—and it's usually against hospital policy. However, it's an appreciated gesture to leave your flowers at the nurses station (or send them to another patient's room); and if someone has been particularly helpful, a note to his or her supervisor will be more than welcome.

And don't forget anything. Look around, items lost in a busy hospital can be difficult to find. If you left valuables in the hospital safe, don't forget to retrieve them.

Never leave the hospital without being escorted by a staff member. Hospitals want to ensure that you reach your car safely and provide an escort service for this purpose. And don't forget your prescriptions, special instructions—or crutches.

The ride home is important too. Make sure that you have a friend or relative who can give you a ride and who can assist you if you need help walking or climbing the stairs. Use a taxi if you have no other way to get home—but if you need assistance, talk to a social worker before your discharge. Help can be arranged.

Once home, make sure there are no surprises. Furniture might need rearranging; a bedroom on the ground floor could be a temporary solution; medication should be within easy reach; and appropriate arrangements for trips to the pharmacy or to the doctors office must be a consideration. Hopefully, your family will have made all the necessary arrangements to ensure your pleasant return to the comforts of home. But don't you make the mistake of forgetting about "life after hospitalization." Make sure everyone has rallied around to make you happy to be home; this is one time when it's perfectly OK to think of yourself first.

Checklist
Chapter 45

Leaving the Hospital

✓ Have you talked to your doctor about when you will be discharged from the hospital?

✓ Have you talked to the nurse about your discharge?

✓ Have you arranged to have your medication delivered to you before you leave the hospital?

✓ Have you made arrangements for transportation home?

✓ Have you official papers to sign before you leave?

✓ Have you left anything in the room or in the cashier's office?

✓ Have you made arrangements for follow up visits to your doctor?

CHAPTER FORTY-SIX

Select A Nursing Home With Care

Nursing homes: Dreadful places where grown kids bring their elderly, burdensome parents; where the food is barely edible; and where the infirm are tied to wheelchairs and virtually ignored by the staff. Well, isn't that the truth? Isn't that what the investigative reporters and supermarket tabloids say?

While there are occasions when such a description could be applicable, more frequently this stereotype belongs only in a bad movie. Unfortunately, however, the reputation of the entire nursing home industry has suffered because of the sensational stories generated by the few proverbial bad apples.

It is a reality of the 20th century that we are living longer—though not always blessed by good health. Also a reality is the fact that it might not be possible to depend upon our children to provide care in our later years. Careers can scatter families across the country and the world; financial constraints can take a major toll on the younger generation striving to build its own future; and truthfully, it might be just plain unfair to ask our kids to put their lives "on hold" to take care of an aging or infirm parent, suffering from Alzheimer's disease or some other debilitating, long-term illness.

So, what are the alternatives? Badly needed care can be provided in the parent's own home by hiring appropriate nursing care and other help. But this can be expensive as well as emotionally taxing on the rest of the family. Elderly people need affection, attention, and love from other family members; hiring help and paying the bills just might not be enough.

Moving your parents into your own home is seldom the answer. Often, parents feel they are imposing and are uncomfortable with such an arrangement, especially if they are aware that their presence is causing some financial hardship or placing constraints on their children's lives.

But a good, reputable nursing home is a viable option, though research is needed to find the one the appropriate for any specific individual.

There are nursing homes that offer every imaginable amenity, including constant attention from a full staff and the atmosphere of a luxury hotel. (Of course, these are expensive.) Some have religious affiliations; others are nonprofit organizations; and others are bona fide businesses, where profit is a major consideration.

The answer is to visit several different facilities—just as you visit college campuses with your teenager. Interview the staff and, if possible, some of the patients. Try to get personal recommendations; evaluate the medical care and activities available for the residents; and try to get a general feel for the atmosphere and the environment. Also, be sure you can afford the price, keeping in mind any possible cost increases in the future.

Your decision will not be easy; indeed, it might well be the most difficult decision you have ever had to make. But make your decision wisely so that there is no need to make a switch to another nursing home at a later date. As with most things in life, it's better to do it right the first time.

CHAPTER FORTY-SEVEN

Hospice Represents A Caring Alternative

"Hospice" brings to mind words like dedication, sensitivity, caring and experience. But many Americans are unfamiliar with the hospice concept, an idea that has in fact been in existence for many centuries.

Consider, for example, that a loved one has been diagnosed with an incurable disease. Your doctors have explained that there is no life-saving treatment and even those physicians you consulted for a second opinion agree.

You accept that death is inevitable for all of us, but you have heard stories about dying in the hospital and have decided that home is the best place for your loved one. You and your family want to be with your loved one as long as possible and to provide a comfortable and calm environment for their final days—this is where hospice can help.

What will happen once you contact your local hospice? You will meet a group of the most caring and considerate people you can imagine. Not only do they possess the skills necessary to provide for your loved one's needs, but they understand and share your desire to make your loved one's final days comfortable and of significance.

Hospice workers not only care for the terminally ill patient, but also provide for the patient's family and friends. Dying is not an individual event. The death of a loved one affects the many relatives and friends who know and care for the person. They each require the comfort and sympathy that a skilled hospice worker is ready and willing to provide.

Hospice also can help with the myriad of details associated with terminal illness and death. They have access to nurses, social workers, doctors and many, many talented individuals trained to provide for the physical, social and psychological needs of everyone involved. But most important is their attitude. And, I can vouch for this personally. My family recently had occasion to use hospice care. (In fact, we probably overused their services.) Our experience gave me a chance to observe the workers' activities closely. And, I can assure you that throughout the working day, at night, in emergency situations—from beginning to end of their entire relationship with our family—we received the finest care I could imagine.

Remember, these will be trying times. They will not be easy, happy or joyous. But, hospice care can help make this time comfortable and as relaxed as possible. These caring individuals can provide education, as well as health care and solace to the patient and the patient's family.

As I review this chapter, I find that I might have overused all the "caring" adjectives, but there are no better words to describe hospice. If this sounds like a commercial for them, I don't apologize—they deserve it. In sum, I recommend hospice care without hesitation.

Furthermore, if you are not in need of their services, but you are looking for a way to help your fellow man, consider becoming a hospice volunteer. These organizations are always in need of volunteers and working with a hospice can be one of the most satisfying experiences in your life.

CHAPTER FORTY-EIGHT

The Return Of the House Call

House calls are back! In fact, the whole idea of home care is becoming more and more popular.

In the old days (and I mean the *very* old days), hospitals had somewhat unhealthy reputations. Only poor people went to hospitals which were generally avoided by anyone who could afford to seek treatment elsewhere. While that image no longer prevails there is a very definite movement toward avoiding hospitals and seeking health care surrounded by the comforts of home.

It would be great to be able say that this renaissance of home care resulted from revolutionary medical research reported in the *Journal of the American Medical Association* or some other learned publication. But unfortunately, this is not the case.

The impetus for the resurgence of home care is two-fold: First, the insurance companies and other third party payers have realized that home care is far less expensive than a lengthy (or any) hospital stay. Second, the health care industry, albeit a bit slower to accept change, has acknowledged that in many cases, patients benefit from home care and might even recuperate faster.

For decades, it was thought that the hospital was the only place anyone could administer treatment to a patient. But today, it is recognized that there are many areas of treatment that can be handled at home by a visiting nurse. A hospital room or clinic is not an essential setting for drawing blood, taking urine samples, or giving shots, for example. As long as the person giving the shot or drawing the blood is qualified and competent, it can be done just as easily in your own home as in a hospital room. And of course, most of us are much more comfortable and relaxed at home, surrounded by our family, sitting in our favorite chair and being pampered just a bit because we're sick!

Of course, home care is not always appropriate; whether or not home care is the route to take can depend largely on the nature of your ailment and on your doctor's judgment call. Your preference will seldom be the deciding factor. And this is true regarding your need or desire to be admitted to a hospital, as well.

Third party payers, especially insurance companies, have become very involved in the decision-making process regarding where you should be admitted or even whether you should be hospitalized at all. Second opinions are usually required, especially for elective surgery; preregistration is virtually mandatory and a failure to follow the required steps can result in a large portion of the hospital cost being your responsibility, not that of your insurance company. (I suppose you could get around the whole system simply by offering to foot the bill yourself for your entire hospital stay; but for most of us, that's beyond even the realm of our wildest dream!)

Regardless, you should remember that under some circumstance, home health care is a viable and appropriate alternative, to say nothing of less expensive! Keep in mind, too, that your physician would not even suggest this route if he or she didn't think it would be in your best interests.

I don't know about you, but I'm a firm believer in the fact that there's no place like home. And I'm not adverse to a bit of pampering either.

CHAPTER FORTY-NINE

Choosing the Right Doctor Is Essential To Good Health

My neighbor was complaining to me about how long it takes his wife to choose a cantaloupe at the grocery store; lamb chops, too. I offered my neighbor the correct amount of sympathy, but the conversation set me wondering about why so many people can spend virtually hours picking out just the right cantaloupe or lamb chop—but when it comes to choosing a doctor? Well, into the basket without a thought—just like a can of creamed corn.

And even though I'm obviously biased, I can't help but think that there's more value to choosing a doctor than to choosing a can of creamed corn—or a cantaloupe, for that matter.

As a "health consumer," you should know that choosing a physician could be one of the most important steps you can take toward obtaining the best possible health care.

It is also a difficult decision, and some people never do get around to making a choice. Then an emergency strikes, perhaps a sudden illness, and someone else selects a physician—or they are treated by a total stranger, who just happens to be on duty that day.

Don't let that happen to you. Find a doctor while you are well, one with whom you are comfortable, one who will listen to you and who will be there when needed. Take the time to find a doctor who is "just right" for you. (You don't go to any old beautician, do you? Then why go to any old doctor?)

Just remember that doctors are individuals with their own personalities, educational backgrounds, and specialty training. Some have the classic bedside manner; others are seemingly brusque or impatient. It's up to you to do the research and find a doctor who suits your needs, both in medical training and personality.

There was a time when you didn't really have to choose a physician. Everyone in town went to the same doctor, who was perfectly willing to ride out to your house in his buggy, if necessary. Health care wasn't too sophisticated then, but at least your friendly doctor was intimately familiar with every aspect of your family's health.

Today, the familiar buggy doctor has been replaced by the high-tech, sterile environment of "group" medicine. Many patients feel uncomfortable in the hubbub of a seemingly impersonal, modern hospital, battling the rules and regulations of HMOs, PPOs, DRGs, and a lot of other obstacles that sound as if they were invented by NASA. Little wonder so many people avoid the issue—and never choose a personal physician. Take heart, patient! It's still possible to have your very own doctor. You should expect a physician who will take the time to know your unique medical needs and attend to them with compassion and expertise.

There are many ways to ease your search without resorting to the "hit and miss" method. While the phone book is a good starting place (doctors are listed alphabetically and by specialty in the yellow pages), seek input from other, more informed sources, such as your clergyman who probably spends a good amount of time visiting ill congregants and might have a valuable opinion.

Friends and neighbors can help, but be careful. You are looking for objective opinions—and your neighbor's judgment might not be based on the same measures that you will use. You are, perhaps, more interested in medical qualifications whereas your neighbor might be more interested in personality.

The local county medical society can tell you about a doctor's training and whether that doctor is "board certified," an examination required of all specialties. Perhaps you have a friend or relative who is a physician; that would be an excellent source for information.

OK—so why is this so important? Well, it might not be, if you don't mind being treated by a doctor who doesn't know your medical history, who is a total stranger, who might not possess the qualifications to treat your specific ailment, and one in whom you have absolutely no confidence—mainly because you don't know him or her.

Yes, excellent health care is your right, regardless of whether your doctor is a total stranger or has been with the family for years. But having your own physician gives you one less thing to worry about should you find yourself hospitalized suddenly. At least, you won't lie in that strange bed wondering who on earth is prodding and poking your body.

Of course, if that's OK with you, then fine. But you might as well be a cantaloupe. Or a can of creamed corn, for that matter.

CHAPTER FIFTY

Too Many Doctors Could Spoil The Broth

Walking through a medical professional building the other day, I saw a friend. He was copying down all the names and office numbers of the doctors listed on the directory posted by the ground floor elevator. Curiosity got the better of me! My friend explained that he wanted to visit at least one doctor in each specialty, just to make sure he was getting the best possible information about his medical problems and health needs.

OK! Yes—good health is definitely your most valuable possession. But visiting 15 or 20 different physicians guarantees only that you will spend a great deal of time and money; it certainly does not guarantee that you will achieve and maintain good health.

The first step toward better health care is to create a satisfactory patient-doctor relationship with a general or primary care physician—and you will not reach even this stage if you "shop around," forever trying to find either the "best" doctor or the one who will tell you exactly what you want to hear.

Of course, you must be comfortable with your primary care physician; the basis of a good doctor-patient relationship is honesty and open communication between the two parties. But the trust must work in both directions. Indeed, a patient must have faith in the doctor—but the physician cannot provide the best treatment, if he or she receives either inaccurate answers to questions or only a part of the necessary information.

At the same time, the physician must be totally honest, discussing the patient's needs and problems so that the explanation is fully understood. Physicians must be caring, tactful and compassionate; but they must also be frank and truthful, constantly reinforcing the trust and faith of their patients.

Choosing a particular physician for primary health care does not exclude the need to seek second or third opinions. In fact, most insurance carriers require at least second opinions, especially when surgery or other extensive treatment is prescribed. And most physicians understand that some patients have an emotional need to seek another opinion, especially when the ailment is particularly severe. Indeed, many doctors welcome this kind of affirmation of their own conclusions and help the patient to secure the second opinion.

Fortunately, my friend was happy to listen to some advice; he abandoned his plan to visit 10 or 12 physicians and settled, instead, for a reputable family practitioner.

And guess what? Last night, my friend asked me out for dinner; he'd saved so much money, he even picked up the check.

CHAPTER FIFTY-ONE

It's Impossible For Any One Doctor To Know It All

Perhaps you've heard the story. A man dies and goes to Heaven where St. Peter tells him that everyone is of equal status. The man sees someone cut into the front of the line at the cafeteria dressed in a mask and a green suit.

"I thought you said everyone was equal. Why is he so different?" asks the man. St. Peter replies: "Oh, that's God. He likes to play doctor now and then."

If you think that many doctors find it very difficult to admit there's something they don't know, well you're probably right. Instead, some physicians use medical jargon to hide their inability to answer your question or the fact that they haven't been able to figure out what's causing your ailment.

Physicians—it's time to accept one basic, undeniable fact: We're only human, and it's virtually impossible for any single individual to "know it all."

We can blame the age of specialization for much of the frustration that doctors feel when we realize that we can't answer every question. The body of knowledge in medicine is now so enormous that physicians and other professionals have been forced to focus on specific areas of their profession.

And specialization is getting narrower and narrower. Now, there are orthopedic surgeons who only operate on knees, hands, or shoulders. There are urologists who treat only kidney stones, cancer or infections.

For the patient, the advantages are great. A physician who devotes his or her entire professional life toward treating kidney stones will certainly understand virtually any problem that arises. But don't ask that same specialist about your orthopedic concerns!

Even in the doctor's own area of expertise, there might be a time when he or she simply does not know the answer. Many physicians think that to admit this is a sign of weakness, but realistically, if a doctor does not know the answer, you should hear: "I don't know, but I'll find out," or "I know another physician who should be able to help you," or "I'm mystified. Let's get input from another source." Your doctor might also need to run tests, take x-rays, go to the medical library, call fellow physicians for advice—whatever it takes to get an answer.

You should never be dismissed with a litany of medical terminology that leaves your head spinning and your questions unanswered. And if you suspect that your doctor is not being completely honest with you, seek another opinion. You have a right to an accurate evaluation of your medical condition, even if the answers to your questions are "I don't know, but I'll find out."

Once the physician has an answer, it should be explained in plain English. If you don't understand, ask again. And never leave a doctor's office until you understand your medical problem completely.

Your primary care physician can legitimately say "I don't know" and refer you to a specialist. The specialist can say "I don't know" and either find the answer, or refer you to another specialist.

"I don't know" should be one of the most important phrases in any physician's vocabulary and should be used without shame or embarrassment. The patient should be able to expect and be thankful for such honesty.

CHAPTER FIFTY-TWO

What The Age Of Specialization Means To You

The other day, my brother-in-law was complaining about the terrible time he had finding an attorney who was willing to handle his will. Jake had just moved to a small town and apparently, there are only three attorneys: One of them handles divorces: another is a tax attorney: and the third takes only criminal cases. And Jake learned something I've known for years: Law, just like medicine, is a profession of specialists.

You have a headache, and the neurologist says it's not a brain tumor—more likely hypertension, and you need to see an internist. It's a relief when the urologist says your kidney is fine—but you might have an ulcer and someone else will have to take care of that. And a rheumatologist is just what the doctor ordered, if you have arthritis in your knee; but an orthopedic surgeon might be needed to take care of the old football injury in that same part of your anatomy.

So how do you avoid wasting hours of time and a great deal of hard earned dollars by making your appointment with the right specialist in the first place?

Of course, there are several types of doctors who are trained to care for the "whole patient" and to make sure that you visit the appropriate specialist when those services are required. These groups—primary care physicians—include doctors who specialize in family medicine, general medicine, internal medicine, pediatrics (for children) and gynecology.

From this point, life actually gets much easier. Establish a good relationship with a "primary care" physician. Try to create this relationship while you are healthy—don't wait until you are sick to choose a doctor from the yellow pages of your telephone directory. Visit your doctor when you need basic health care, such as annual physical exams, shots and so forth.

At a later time, should you find you need medical treatment that is more specialized than your primary care physician is trained to provide, he or she will refer you to the appropriate specialist—and this is one less thing for you to worry about.

In the past 30 years, specialization has become a dominant characteristic of the medical profession, much to the benefit of the patient. The volume of knowledge has expanded to such an extent that physicians must specialize, if they are to master their own particular corner of medicine.

Think of it this way: Your primary care physician is like the conductor of a symphony orchestra, who should know something (but not everything) about each instrument. But the individual musicians are the soloists; they are the specialists.

While the primary care physician is knowledgeable about all the parts of your body, he or she has not mastered the fine details to perform intricate surgery or to recognize a rare disorder. This must be left to the specialists.

I have to admit that I sympathized with Jake, my brother-in-law. It would be terrible to move to a town that had only three doctors and to find that one specialized in heart surgery; another in sports injuries; and the third in diseases of the skin. Because with my luck, I'd probably come down with a sore throat.

CHAPTER FIFTY-THREE

Medical Ethics: A Contradiction In Terms?

It seems that I spend half my time these days grumbling and grouching about people who let me down or don't keep their promises; about people whose word I have trusted, to no avail. My favorite politician voted for more taxes, after he'd said he wouldn't; the Savings and Loan fiasco was depressing; and just last month, my son bought a used car that turned out to be a lemon.

Few things make me madder than poor ethics, and though I hate to acknowledge it, there are even times when unethical conduct is found in the medical profession. It's one thing to be stuck with a lemon of a car— it can be replaced; but poor ethics in medicine can threaten a person's health, or even cost a life.

Ethical issues abound in the practice of medicine. Today, most medical schools have incorporated this particular aspect of medicine into their curricula, trying to prepare students to deal with the ethical problems they are likely to meet as practicing physicians. Often, physicians are called upon to make decisions or give advice that is far from "cut and dried."

Interpreting the concepts of "right" and "wrong" can be especially challenging when the health and lives of others are at stake. And of course, something that is "right" for one person might well be "wrong" for someone else. On a daily basis, newspapers report stories about the ethics of abortion, prolonging life for the terminally ill, the right to die with dignity, euthanasia, and similar emotional topics. And physicians are faced with difficult decisions constantly; regardless of personal opinions, they must be guided by the ethical standards of their profession.

In the past decade, physicians have also been tainted with stories of fraud regarding their handling of Medicare (Federal support for senior citizens) and Medicaid (support for the medically indigent) payments. It truly saddens me, as a doctor, to know that fellow physicians were tempted to misrepresent charges for their services, on the rationale that because individual patients were not paying the bills and since no one would check the billing carefully, then it was acceptable to overcharge or fictionalize services rendered.

Drug and alcohol abuse are also ethical problems, and doctors must deal with a variety of associated issues. For instance, if a physician knows that a patient is an addict but needs a particular narcotic drug for a specific ailment, should the doctor continue to prescribe something that helps one sickness but perpetuates another? And how should the physician react to a patient who might be faking an illness to acquire narcotics?

Physicians do not have any special insight or magical powers when decisions must be based on ethical judgement, rather than objective fact. It's much easier to recommend surgery than to know whether something is "right" or "wrong" for an individual patient, given an individual set of circumstances. But doctors must reach deeply into their hearts and minds and make the best possible decisions, based on experience, expertise and ethical standards.

As the patient, you have the right to question the doctor's decisions regarding your health problems. When ethical issues are involved, it is especially important for you to be knowledgeable about all aspects of any situation, so that you can participate in determining the appropriate and ethical course to follow.

CHAPTER FIFTY-FOUR

You Be The Patient and I'll Be the Doctor

If you're a mechanic, I bet you sometimes feel that everyone's a mechanic. They're always telling you what's wrong with their cars. Well, you have my sympathy—because there are many times that it seems like everyone's a doctor, too.

As soon as I graduated from medical school, my mother became a doctor, and through the years, my wife and kids have displayed their instant medical expertise. Even my patients tell me what's wrong with them and how to fix their problems. Let's make a deal, guys—you be the patient and I'll be the doctor, OK?

So now you're wondering why it's so bad to tell the doctor what's wrong with you, right? Well, you could have made a mistake; maybe the familiar sinus headache isn't really a sinus headache this time. And then what happens if your busy doctor accepts your "diagnosis," prescribes an appropriate medicine and you have an allergic reaction?

Rather than attempting to diagnose an illness, describe the symptoms and answer your physician's questions. Let your doctor be the doctor and figure out the nature of your problem.

Smart patients take the time to write down everything about their health problem before they get to the doctor's office. Make sure your notes include a description of your chief complaint and how long you have been feeling sick. What makes you feel worse or better? Is this the first time you've experienced these symptoms? Have any members of your family experienced similar symptoms?

Know which medications you have taken and bring a list showing medication name, dosage, amount and schedule. If you have a long, complicated medical history with many surgeries and medications, then bring a list of those as well. And if you've had x-rays or other tests during previous health problems, try to get copies of test results or even the x-rays; the more you can provide, the easier it is for your doctor to reach a conclusion.

Many people would never dream of entering a grocery store without a shopping list. So why wander into the doctor's office completely oblivious to your medical background, vaguely aware of what is troubling you, but being prepared to offer your own answers to the problem? Strange, very strange!

Sometimes, your doctor will ask questions that seem totally unrelated to your problem. For example, you have a sharp pain in your back, and the doctor wants to know if you eat a lot of ice cream—because the excess calcium can lead to the development of kidney stones, which produce back pain. You didn't know that, did you? You thought it was that old aching muscle acting up again, right?

Using the information you provide and adding a touch of medical knowledge, the doctor should be able to reach a valid conclusion and diagnose the cause of your problem. And you can still be an aggressive participant in your own health care *without* playing doctor. Of course you can be part of the team. But, we do have a deal, don't we? You be the patient; I'll be the doctor, OK?

CHAPTER FIFTY-FIVE

Rich and Poor Look Alike With Their Clothes Off

When I was a student, I learned many important things from my professors—and some had nothing to do with the mysteries of medical practice. In fact, one of those lessons has stayed with me forever and has become an important part of my personal philosophy as a doctor.

I remember it as if it were yesterday. I was ill and went to see this particular professor in his role as a physician. During the visit, he gave me a one-on-one lecture about how to deal with "special" patients—meaning doctors, medical students and VIPs. Of course, I was young and somewhat unsophisticated, so at first, I was a bit flattered at being included in this elite group of special patients.

But this glimpse of my own self-importance was fleeting, as the professor reached the point of his story: He had no intention of treating me, or anyone else, differently. He didn't care if I was a millionaire or a pauper; a good doctor treats everyone the same.

The doctor explained his reasons this way: When dealing with special patients, the physician might be tempted to take short cuts, or at least try to make the diagnostic evaluation and treatment as special as the patient. Senator Jones or Great Uncle Charlie are busy people; they don't have time to waste, waiting around for lengthy tests. So Senator Jones and Great Uncle Charlie get "shortchanged" as the physician attempts to inconvenience their lives as little as possible. And of course, this kind of special attention can be dangerous since the patient might not receive the correct or appropriate treatment—with potentially disastrous results.

When "special" patients come to see me, I make sure I treat them the same as everyone else. And if you want the best possible treatment and your physician is a friend or a relative, insist on being seen as "just another patient."

Don't allow your physician to delay tests, x-rays or the need for a second opinion, simply because he or she does not want to inconvenience you. Try to resist tempting favors, such as being seen without an appointment or (even worse) being treated at no cost. The doctor-patient relationship is very special; excessive favors tend to tarnish that relationship and can be detrimental to the patient.

Now, don't get me wrong. I'm not trying to eliminate your friendships with members of the medical profession. But I am trying to emphasize the need to maintain separate relationships: Your doctor can be your friend; but your doctor can be your physician, also. And "ne'er the twain should meet."

I like to tell the story about a very rich lady I met at a party. When the lady started to ask me medical questions, I told her I'd be delighted to answer her questions, but she'd have to take off all her clothes so I could examine her first. She changed the subject very quickly!

Checklist
Chapters 49-55

Choosing A Doctor

✓ Are you happy with your doctor?
✓ Have you decided to find a different doctor?
✓ Have you decided to find a different doctor when you are well?
✓ Do you know what kind of primary care doctor you need?
Family practitioner
Internal Medicine
Pediatrician
Obstetrics and Gynecology
✓ Have you decided if you want a male or female doctor?
✓ Have you considered the personality of the doctor you want?
✓ Have you consulted with appropriate referral sources?
Clergyman
Hospital administration
County Medical Society
Friends, neighbors, relatives
Yellow pages
Other physicians

CHAPTER FIFTY-SIX

What's Up Doc? (Only Medical Lingo Spoken Here)

Every field enjoys its own special language or slang. In the space shuttle, astronauts can converse for weeks and never utter one word that sounds like English. And maybe that's okay in space; as long as they understand each other, maybe it's just as well that no one else knows what they're talking about!

But people who work in the health care profession must be able to communicate with patients who often don't understand medical jargon.

When health care professionals talk to patients, it's not unreasonable to expect them to use the language of the country in which you all live; and in the United States, that's generally considered to be English. (Although I know a few Britishers who might disagree with that statement!) Regardless, explanations of diagnoses and procedures should not sound as if they are being quoted directly from a medical dictionary. You have a right to understand.

Often, members of the medical profession forget that not everyone understands the terminology, and they ramble on using long, complicated words that end in "itis," "ectomy," and "oxide." Also, lots of abbreviations.

Doctors love abbreviations. I think abbreviations are great. They simplify life, making it possible to say more in less time. Not that they help much if no one (except the doctor) understands what they mean.

It doesn't do Mrs. Jones the slightest bit of good if she doesn't know that taking her medicine "per os Q.D." means that she should swallow a pill once a day. Neither would it mean anything to Mrs. Jones to tell her to take her medicine "PRN" (as needed), "IM" (through intramuscular injection), "TID" (three time a day) or "Q4H (every four hours) and "HS" (before bedtime).

While reading the doctor's prescription is the domain of the pharmacist, understanding his or her oral instructions are the sole responsibility of the patient. Therefore, it's important to ask if you are unsure.

Likewise if you are in the hospital and your nurse rushes out of the room after hearing "Code Red, Blue or 99" over the loudspeaker, it's not a nuclear attack. It simply means a patient requires immediate (and emergency) medical attention.

You might be admitted into the hospital, but you might wind up in the ER (emergency room), OR (operating room), ICU (intensive care unit), CCU (coronary care unit), PICU (pediatric intensive care unit), BICU (burns intensive care unit) or the RR (recovery room).

Your doctor might need to see you ASAP (as soon as possible, but not right away) or STAT (immediately). They might have to hook you up to an EEG (a machine that records brain wave patterns) or an ECG or EKG (records heart rhythms).

If you are really sick or having surgery, your doctor might leave instructions that you should be NPO (non per os, Latin for no food allowed). In this case, you will probably receive nourishment through an I.V. (intravenous tube).

There are hundreds of abbreviations, and it seems that new ones are invented every day. Abbreviations and jargon are so important to the medical profession that hospitals adopt official lists so that everyone speaks the same language.

While you will probably never stop your health professionals from using weird words and abbreviations, it's up to you to stop them when you don't understand. Otherwise, how will you know that everything is "A-OK?"

And there's no truth to the rumor that medical students graduate as M.D.s, because after four expensive years of study it's an appropriate abbreviation for "much debt."

CHAPTER FIFTY-SEVEN

What Do All The Doctor's Certificates Mean?

Visit just about any doctor's office and somewhere, usually in the waiting room or the consultation area, you'll see a number of certificates prominently hung on the wall. All too often, you have plenty of time to read these certificates, but what do they mean?

In most cases, the certificates relay the physician's education and specialty training. However, they can sometimes be misleading. Let me explain what I mean.

Diplomas are important. Spend a few minutes to learn where your doctor received his or her education. You may find diplomas from your doctor's medical school, college—even high school (depending on wall space and level of fanaticism). But, no diploma is more important than the one received most recently.

Some diplomas will be written in Latin or Greek. These universities must feel this gives their diplomas more credibility. I believe they're simply harder to read. To decipher the name of the issuing university, look for the largest type on the page and for a word that begins with a familiar sequence of letters, but may end differently.

One of the certificates hanging on your physician's wall should be from a medical school. Locate your doctor's name and note the M.D. (Doctor of Medicine), or similar degree following it. There may also be certificates stating that your doctor successfully completed internship, residency or advanced fellowship training. In the old days, additional training following medical school was not required. Today's physicians are mandated to take some additional training.

Following residency, many physicians take a competitive exam to become certified by the specialty board in his or her field of training. Another certificate will be issued by that board. Newer versions of these certificates may include an expiration date if certification must be renewed periodically. However, this new practice is not followed universally.

Your doctor may be a member of several medical societies, both within his or her specialty training and within the field of medicine in general (i.e., the American Medical Association). These societies also issue certificates of membership. Your doctor may have attended continuing education courses. Some of the more in-depth courses will issue certificates of participation. In addition, your physician may have received honorary degrees, awards, honors and other documents that are proudly displayed.

But, buyer beware. There are some physicians who acquire certificates without earning them and you may have difficulty determining which, if any, are false. I know of a physician who obtained a large picture post card of the famous Mayo Clinic in Minnesota. The card was designed for visitors to purchase and mail to friends and family back home. But, this doctor framed the card and hung it in his office. He never made any claims about the photo, he just let it hang there—but, the message was inescapable. He wanted his patients to believe he had studied at the Mayo Clinic, when in fact he was simply a visitor to the prestigious clinic.

Fortunately, this is the exception, rather than the rule. Your doctor is proud of his or her achievements and wants you to take note. On the other hand, there are some physicians who have no certificates on display. If this is the case with your doctor and you want to know more about his or her education and training, then ask.

Chapter Fifty-Eight

"Just Making Sure"....The Second Opinion Dilemma

There's something about getting a second opinion for a medical problem that challenges our sense of trust in doctors. For centuries, doctors held a near-magical spell over those they treated, and it was as though once the doctor had spoken, everyone listened. Almost biblical!

And while some physicians might still subscribe to this theory, most will agree that it's foolish for consumers NOT to seek as much advice and wisdom as they can, when it comes to their health.

But will my doctor get angry, you wonder? Will that unspoken pact of trust be broken if I want a second opinion? If your doctor reacts in this manner, then it's definitely time to consider getting a new doctor.

Doctors know that they're not infallible, and besides, many third-party payers now require a second opinion.

Of course, second opinions can be misleading. You've heard the old story about the doctor who tells the patient, "You're overweight and need to go on a diet." The patient says "I would like to get a second opinion." So the doctor says, "Okay, you're ugly too."

But let's get serious about second opinions! When is it appropriate to get another opinion? Second opinions should be considered when you are having elective surgery or some type of major medical treatment. However, emergency situations, when time is of the essence and lives are at stake, do not lend themselves to second opinion status.

Because of changing insurance requirements, it's extremely important for you, the patient, to take an active role in your health care decisions. Know your insurance company's policy regarding second opinions or you could be held financially responsible for your medical expenses. Remember that many third-party payers will not reimburse if a second opinion is not obtained.

Definitely get another opinion if treatment involves a risk or great expense; if there is some confusion in the diagnosis or when you simply do not understand your medical problem; when your physician admits he or she is unsure; or at any time you wish. It's a free country.

How do you get a second opinion? You can ask your doctor to recommend someone. And don't be afraid that he or she will only pick someone who agrees with him or her. He or she knows that such an action would be unethical.

Ask your insurance company. Many times, they might even specify who you should see or supply a list of preferred physicians, depending upon your insurance plan. You can also contact your local medical society to check credentials.

Physicians who provide a second opinion generally agree not to "steal" the patient, but you have the right to choose any doctor you want.

Who pays for the second opinion? Many times your insurance company will pay if it is their requirement that you seek another opinion. If you have to pay, it's probably worth the extra money, just to have peace of mind that you have aggressively sought the best solution to your health problem.

What do you do when the second opinion differs from the first. There is something called a third opinion, but that's another story.

CHAPTER FIFTY-NINE

When Medical Opinions Differ

Here's the scene. You become ill and visit the doctor. Your physician performs a thorough examination, including tests and x-rays; makes a diagnosis; and discusses a treatment plan with you. Because you are a concerned and intelligent patient, you have some natural anxiety. So, you ask for a second opinion.

Your doctor understands your concern and arranges for the second opinion. You visit the second physician and after careful evaluation of your problem, he or she gives you an opinion that is significantly different from the first. What do you do?

This is not an easy question. One option that is often appropriate is to get a third opinion. Many insurance companies are requesting a third opinion, and like the second, they will usually pay for the entire visit. The third opinion may, of course, agree with one of the first two, or you could receive a different view. Now you're faced with three contrasting approaches to your problem.

The point is that there is often more than one acceptable solution to a problem. We doctors like to think we know everything about health and disease, but this is not always the case. Sometimes we know a lot about a disease and have developed an ideal way to treat it. However, sometimes we know little about a disease and therefore have several treatments, because we are not certain which is the best method. And, each of us doctors have developed "favorite" ways to treat some diseases. These methods become our recommendations to our patients.

Each time your doctor recommends a treatment, you have the option of asking about other ways to treat the problem. Never accept the statement that treatments are "too complicated" for you to understand. It's your physician's responsibility to explain your options in language you can understand. If you do not understand, keep asking for the explanation in simpler terms.

Once your doctor has explained the options and you understand them, ask him or her why a particular treatment is favored. Has past experience with this treatment been successful? What about the cost of this treatment versus others viewed as equally good? These are valid questions to ask and you should not be afraid to discuss them.

By the way, explaining the things in uncomplicated terms is not only a medical dilemma. Every profession has its own language. Try talking to computer experts, pilots, accountants, lawyers or just about any other professional, about their area of expertise. I become as frustrated as you when I don't understand the language. It may not be essential that you understand the intricacies of a computer in order to operate it, but it is essential that you understand your options to make informed decisions about your health.

CHAPTER SIXTY

Who Says Doctors Are So Smart?

Doctors love to use long, mysterious, or complicated words; maybe they think it makes all the money spent on their education seem more worthwhile. Take "prognosis," for instance. Doesn't that sound great? Wouldn't you have to be well educated to use and understand a word like that?

Of course, the answer to both these questions is "No," because prognosis simply means a prediction of an end result, given a certain set of circumstances; and in medicine, a prognosis is an attempt to predict the outcome (or end result) of an illness. Will the patient survive? How long will it take for him or her to recover?

For many diseases, especially those that have been known and treated for decades or centuries, doctors can often predict the course of events. Studies have gathered data and statistics, and "survival rates" or "probability of survival" can be discussed with some degree of accuracy.

But individual patients are neither statistics nor data, and they don't always follow a convenient set of rules. Patients have been known to "beat the odds" such as when a seemingly terminal condition has mysteriously gone into remission. Some might say simply that "miracles can happen."

Most doctors are well aware of the pitfalls involved in predictions, and the experienced physicians avoid making them, especially distant ones. My style is to offer an accurate appraisal of the patient's current status, a description of the general course of the disease, and a disclaimer that it's impossible to be completely certain regarding the outcome, for any specific patient.

Unfortunately, some patients and their family members feel uncomfortable with uncertainty and actually prefer a prediction—even if the doctor suspects the patient might not recover or that death is imminent. And sometimes, patients truly want to know what the future holds for them and whether they need to "put their house in order."

Thus a compromise might be in order. If the disease is life threatening with a predictably poor outcome, I share this information with the patient. And I offer some suggestions: Live one day at a time, as if each is your last and enjoy each waking hour; seek peace of mind by "mending fences" with former friends or alienated family members; travel, take art classes, learn to be a gourmet cook or whatever it is you've always wanted to do but never had the chance.

Most people faced with terminal situations choose to continue their familiar life style, seeking comfort from relatives, friends and clergymen. Often, they see the world around them through "different eyes," appreciating each flower, bird, tree and sunset. And they try to pass along to others this new-found appreciation, knowing it will be their legacy to humanity.

CHAPTER SIXTY-ONE

Being Caught In The Middle Makes Doctors Uncomfortable

The other day, my son told me he was "between a rock and a hard place." He didn't want to miss Joe's party, but a former girlfriend would be there, and he didn't want to face her either. Unfortunately, my son got mad at me—and all I said was that I thought he'd get over it. Besides, many physicians find themselves in similar situations—but with far more serious implications or consequences.

Sometimes, when a disease is serious, and it seems likely that the patient will not recover, family members request that this information be withheld from the patient, feeling there is little to be gained by upsetting the patient with such grim news. On the other hand, many patients, upon hearing the same news, ask that it not be shared with family and friends— for the same reason. And the doctor is caught right in the middle! A physician knows that everyone involved in this kind of situation will eventually learn the truth, and those who have been deceived will usually react with anger toward the doctor. The physician knows, also, that his or her actions must be guided by the patient-physician relationship, with its accompanying primary obligation to the patient.

One solution is to tell each party separately—and ask everyone to keep the information confidential. But let's face it: A secret is *only* a secret until you tell someone! Ultimately, the truth "will out," and then everyone will be furious with the doctor for taking this approach.

If the physician has created a trusting relationship both with the patient and the family, it is fairly easy to explain the value to sharing all the available information. Emotional support and mutual understanding will emerge, making the burden much easier for everyone to handle.

In most cases, however, the patient is the final decision maker, and his or her wishes must prevail. But if the patient, the family and the doctor enjoy a sound relationship, frank and open discussion will usually be the best route to take.

I do admit, though, that when I'm faced with a dilemma of this nature, I'd probably prefer to go Joe's party—and take the chance of bumping into my son's old girl friend!

CHAPTER SIXTY-TWO

Your Doctor Was Once A Student Too

I cannot tell a lie! It's true—many years ago, I was a medical student. Today, I like to think I'm pretty good at what I do but getting there didn't happen by magic. I had to learn how to be a doctor; more importantly, I had to learn how to be a good doctor.

As I get older, I accept that eventually I'll retire, and someone will have to take my place. But make no mistake; I know my successor will be someone knowledgeable and experienced. I know also, without a shadow of doubt, that my successor will be a former medical student.

Medical students are considered by some to be the "lowest of the low"—they get the worst assignments and the least recognition. Yet the truth is that medical students are a vital part of your health care, because without medical students, there would be no doctors. We've all gotta start some place, right? And to put it another way, just as the kids in boot camp become seasoned soldiers, so medical students are the future doctors of the world.

"That's fine doc," you say, "but I don't want them practicing on me or my family. I want a 'real doctor.'"

Well, let me assure you, I don't want them practicing on you or your family either! Not until medical students have completed their entire program, have received their M.D. degrees and have become "real doctors" are they allowed to "practice" on anyone!

Medical students learn from and contribute greatly to a medical institution. They do the "scutwork"—a hallowed term to describe the support they provide: running errands, picking up x-rays and lab results, changing dressings. Medical students are supervised closely, and though they are allowed to take medical histories, examine patients, and perform various menial tasks, medical students are not allowed to treat patients or perform surgery.

After graduation from medical school, the former students will become fully licensed physicians, certified by the state. They enter residency programs which are designed to train them in their chosen specialties—pediatrics, surgery, psychiatry, and so forth. Residency programs take from three to seven years to complete depending on the specialty, and yes, residents are allowed to "practice" on you!

But don't get nervous! Residents are closely supervised both by their faculty advisors and by a chief resident (a resident in his or her final year of the program). And even then, residents perform duties only according to the level of training they have received. They might assist in surgery (but not "go it alone"); they might contribute to a diagnosis; or they could aid with the postoperative care of a patient.

Some patients in my practice insist that they do not want to be seen by a resident. This is a major problem for me for a number of reasons. First, I depend on residents. They provide a great service, and their enthusiasm is often a benefit to the patient as well as to me. They keep me on my toes by asking difficult questions, and this forces me to keep up to date (who wants to be outsmarted by the kids, anyway?). Second, I would not allow a resident to see a patient, if I was not perfectly confident in the resident's ability; and finally, I was a resident once, and I know it's impossible for a resident even to begin to become a seasoned doctor without the appropriate access to patients.

So if my patients insist on not being seen by a resident, I explain their role and their importance to the medical profession. Understanding the role of medical students and residents can make you more receptive to being seen by them, thus ensuring top-notch care more quickly and efficiently than if you always insist on seeing the "top guy." Besides, the "top guy" is never far away and always committed to closely watching everything the resident does.

As always, it's good to ask questions when your health is involved; but it's also good to recognize quality; and in this case, it's even good to trust the system. Medical students and residents are *your* future doctors. Don't be afraid of them.

CHAPTER SIXTY-THREE

It Really Is Possible To Minimize "The Wait"

I bet you've often wondered why most doctors are no longer willing to make house calls. Actually, it makes a good topic of conversation at dinner time, and regardless of the many opinions (honestly, we're not just lazy), let me offer an explanation. And don't panic—you don't have to invite me to dinner!

In the old days, the doctor came to your home in a horse and buggy or the Model T. Often it was easier for the physician to get to your house than it was for you to go to the doctor's office; and everything necessary to treat your ailment was in the little black bag stashed on the back seat.

Today, even the most routine examination for the most minor complaint requires far more equipment than a doctor could transport in his or her little black bag. Indeed, the doctor could come to your home, listen to your heart beat, take your temperature and blood pressure—and then advise you to come into the office (or hospital) for a more complete set of tests. Do you really want to waste your money by paying for a house call and for an office visit?

However, as the consumer of health care, you do have choices. You can go to your doctor's office; if your problem seems sufficiently serious, you can go to the emergency room at the hospital; for minor illnesses and injuries, you can visit a neighborhood clinic.

If you choose to visit the doctor's office or the emergency room, you're already dreading "the wait." But there are ways to minimize the time you spend waiting for health care.

Call before you leave home. If you walk into your doctor's office without an appointment, you can expect to wait. You wouldn't show up at the theater without tickets and expect to be seated, would you? Explain your problem to the doctor or nurse. This will allow the office time to find your records, before you arrive. It could also provide some insight into how serious a problem you have. (Your doctor might advise you to call an ambulance and go directly to the hospital if the symptoms you describe sound serious or life threatening.)

For emergency care, call ahead. This might sounds ridiculous, but if you are being taken to the ER by someone other than your local emergency team, then do take the time to let them know the nature of your problem and when you will be arriving. You'll be surprised at the warmer reception you will receive. If your physician will call the emergency room for you, that's even better!

Pick the time you go. For a sudden emergency, this is simply not possible. But for lesser illnesses or problems, you will receive more prompt attention if you avoid peak emergency hours. Usually, the slowest times at an ER are in the mornings from around 8:00 a.m. to 11:00 a.m., on weekdays. But since emergency situations are unpredictable, that telephone call can save you hours of waiting and untold frustration.

Regardless of how hard you try to do the "right" thing, there will be times when you have to wait. Your doctor has a busy daily schedule with patients at the office and hospital; perhaps he's been called to attend another emergency five minutes before you walked through the door. Bona fide and sudden emergencies should never have to wait for attention. These are given top priority and hospitals have triage systems to ensure that such emergencies are seen promptly.

When selecting a family doctor, it's important to know the scheduling patterns he or she prefers, especially if you are intolerant of long waits. Arrange your health care needs to suit your expectancy; but keep in mind that no one can control the uncontrollable. Also, don't assume that the lack of a wait reflects an efficient physician; it could simply mean a lack of patients—and that could worry you, too.

And if all else fails, try to take comfort from the wise words of your friendly physician-author: Patience and understanding—the key to survival!

CHAPTER SIXTY-FOUR

"I Have Nothing To Wear For My Visit To The Doctor"

I have been around for a long time and often think that I've seen it all. But, just about that time, something usually happens to remind me that every day is full of mystery and surprises.

The other day, a woman brought her 4-year-old son into my office. I thought nothing of the fact that he was dressed in a bathrobe until I asked his mother to undress him so I could begin my examination. To my surprise, that was all that he was wearing. As it turned out, he had experienced a painful run-in with a zipper and street clothes were out of the question. Live and learn.

This episode brings up the question of what to wear to the doctor's office. It's amazing what some patients will don. There are two extremes. One group, realizing that they will probably be asked to disrobe for an examination, wears clothing that is easy to remove. Others, probably for the same reason, wear clothing that is difficult to remove or maneuver around, thus making physical examinations more difficult than necessary. I believe the latter group is sending a definite message to their physician.

Unfortunately, physical examinations are often necessary, so you may as well make the best of the situation. On your next visit to the doctor's office, wear clothing that is appropriate and can be removed easily. But, while shorts and a halter top are fine for the beach, they may not be the best attire for the doctor's office.

Examinations should be performed with your modesty and dignity in mind. If your doctor requires you to wear a hospital gown that is slit up the back, ask for two and wear one facing each direction. Always insist on some type of gown before disrobing. I have heard horror stories from patients who were asked to undress and remain in the "altogether" until the physician arrived. I wouldn't sit there like that and you shouldn't be asked to, either.

Some doctors want to examine you with no one else in the room. If you are comfortable with this arrangement, fine. But, if you have reservations, ask the physician to have an attendant of your same sex present during the exam.

If you are unhappy with any of the arrangements set by your doctor to ensure privacy, speak up loud and clear. Do not allow timidity to interfere with your modesty. Walking down the hallway, or other public places, wearing only a gown; allowing excess traffic in the examination room; or any other practices you don't appreciate should not be part of your visit to the doctor. It's up to you to make your feelings known.

CHAPTER SIXTY-FIVE

Preparing For A Visit To The Doctor's Office

You've scheduled an appointment with your doctor, maybe you're sick or maybe it's just a check up. Or maybe, you were sick when you called for the appointment and it's taken so long to get in to see the doctor that you're well now. Any visit to the doctor, no matter the reason, can be more productive with a little preparation.

If this is the first time to visit this physician, certain information will be required. Even if you're going to see your regular doctor, he or she will likely need to review previously obtained information to ensure that situations haven't changed. In either case, doing your homework will pay off for both you and your physician.

Before you go, make a list of all the medications you are currently taking. Include the name and dosage of the drug, the name of the physician who prescribed the medication and why you are taking it. Also include the name and telephone number of your pharmacy so your doctor can call in prescriptions if necessary. Next, list your allergies—the substance you're allergic to and your reaction. Don't limit this list to medications, include foods, dust, pollen, etc.

A personal medical history, listing past illnesses and medical problems will come in handy. Your medical past may play a role in your current problem. Don't forget to include all past surgical procedures, when they were performed and the outcome.

Obtain the results of any tests or x-rays performed somewhere else and not immediately available to your doctor. You may have to return to the test location and sign a release to receive the results. But, this trip is well worth the effort, not only providing valuable information to your doctor, but also saving you the expense of repeating the examination. By the way, hospitals and laboratories are used to this practice, so your request for the result should not pose any problem.

Finally, list the symptoms of your current problem. Include the date the problem first occurred, what you did in terms of self-treatment and anything else you want the doctor to know about your illness. Your doctor may need to perform blood or urine tests when you are in the office. Plan ahead so that you aren't caught off guard by the doctor's request to provide the specimen.

I would be remiss if I did not remind you to bring appropriate financial information with you to the doctor's office. Supply the staff with the name of your insurance carrier, but also bring some form of payment since most physicians prefer to be paid for their services at the time of the visit.

In summary, if you take the time to prepare for your visit to the doctor things should go more quickly and efficiently. Compiling important information before visiting the doctor's office will provide the physician with the additional knowledge he or she needs to make a proper diagnosis and prescribe the correct treatment for what ails you. Refer to the back of this book, complete the forms and don't forget to bring the book with you.

CHAPTER SIXTY-SIX

Patients Sometimes Must Just Have Patience

Things have changed a lot since Norman Rockwell painted the ideal physician for the cover of the *Saturday Evening Post*.

After an hour in the waiting room, 10 minutes with the doctor and 15 minutes with the billing clerk, you may yearn for the past.

But don't be deceived. The past "ain't all it's cracked up to be." Sometimes a long wait in the doctor's office means much more than reading last year's magazine.

In the "good old days," everything was not rosy, although it might appear that way today if you are looking through the right pair of eyeglasses.

Sure, a visit to the doctor might have been faster and the time actually spent with him (almost no female doctors back then!) was longer, but the visit was neither as productive nor efficient as today.

For example, not too long ago, most lab tests that are commonly performed in the doctor's office today were sent to a local hospital or even to a larger hospital in another city. Worse, you sometimes had to go elsewhere to have the test done before it was sent off for analysis. Several visits could be required to get results from the first examination. Today, thanks to the "miniaturization" of sophisticated equipment, many tests can be done in the doctor's office. Although you might have to wait a little longer to get the test results, it's certainly faster than returning for another visit. Adding to your wait in the doctor's office is one unpredictable element—you, the patient. While the physician begins the day with a well-planned schedule, with every intention of sticking to it, the very nature of illness can throw the whole day out of whack.

It's a little like being stuck on a freeway that's been slowed to a crawl. You can't help but get irritable and impatient. Hopefully, your compassion will put things into perspective once you've passed the site of the accident that was the cause of the backup.

The doctor's office is no different. While you sit fuming in the waiting area and looking at your watch, the doctor is possibly taking extra time with a patient who needs special attention. A patient who walks in complaining of fatigue (and then shows signs of chest pains) should not be rescheduled for the sake of "being on time."

Similarly, if the doctor gets called to the hospital for an emergency, your 1:00 p.m. appointment can even be canceled. Patience is certainly required when visiting the Ob/Gyn physician. Babies don't keep schedules.

Once you do get in to see the doctor, don't be dismayed if you are examined for only 10 minutes. Rather, count your blessings. Some medical problems are more easily diagnosed and treated than others. Skin rashes for example, while annoying, do not require nearly as much of the physician's time as do gall bladder complications.

That is not to say that you cannot spend time talking with your doctor. You should never leave with unanswered questions about your health. It is your right to ask and the physician's duty to provide the answers, if possible.

However, a certain amount of understanding about how a doctor schedules patients can help you maintain your cool. Knowing and trusting your doctor helps, so find one that you are comfortable with and that you feel is treating you fairly and with confidence.

Next, pretend that you are leaving for an airplane trip when visiting the physician. Call ahead and confirm that everything is on schedule. If you have a 2:00 p.m. appointment and the secretary knows that the doctor is running two hours behind, then you can save yourself a lot of frustration by rescheduling, or rearranging your day.

Also, take along a book, magazine or something to keep you occupied (the doctor's office is a great place to catch up on some of that office work for which you never seem to find the time). If you must wait, at least you can be productive.

Finally, if you find that you are consistently waiting too long, that your time with the doctor is too short, and that in general, you're not satisfied with the services of your physician, then find another. It's your right.

CHAPTER SIXTY-SEVEN

What Should You Do When You Can't Find Your Doctor?

You're sick, it's Sunday afternoon, and you need your doctor. You'll have to wait hours at your local emergency room, and besides, all you really need is to have the doctor OK a refill for your prescription.

What do you do? Like millions of Americans each year, you dial your doctor's number and hear those words that strike fear into the hearts of all patients: "Answering service."

From a patient's point of view, it often seems that answering services were invented simply to prevent them from talking with their doctor. Not true! Regardless of their dedication to their chosen profession, doctors are people, too! And just like you, they need to be able to "get away." However, doctors recognize the need to be reached at all times; thus, answering services, pagers and now cellular telephones are making it easier for patients to locate their physicians, and for physicians to stay in touch with their patients.

Actually, while you are feeling victimized by the answering service, some physicians are beginning to feel that another diabolical device was developed solely to ruin their lives—the beeper!

But beepers are better than the alternative, the telephone. Before, doctors had to let people know where they would be every minute and were often paged in restaurants, at ballparks, in theaters and at various other public places, where they had to locate a telephone. (Have you ever tried to find a phone in the zoo?) Today, there are beepers that don't even make a noise. They vibrate silently and some are able to send and receive messages, so that the need for telephone contact is reduced.

It's a good bet that the next phase will be the miniaturization of the cellular telephone, so they can be carried easily in a shirt pocket or a purse. It's been done with calculators—why not telephones? And if that happens, the doctor will never be out of range.

Doctors know they must be accessible, and that their commitment to their patients takes precedence over the second act of a play or a tempting dessert. For them, beepers and telephones have become a way of life; for you, it's the answering service.

While doctors are more accessible than ever, they are also smarter about looking after their marriages, family life and their health—those things that keep them in a healthy physical and mental state so that they can be effective doctors. And this means "time off" for vacations and trips. Group practices allow doctors to "spell" each other and to have some relief from the pressure of 24-hour medicine.

So what can you, the patient, do on the weekend if the answering service refers you to your doctor's partner? The first rule is to be prepared for such a possibility and to investigate your doctor's medical practice before choosing his or her services. Make sure that the other physicians meet your expectation, both in qualifications and personality. Also, make your preference known ahead of time, so that "Plan B" can be implemented if your doctor is out of town.

There are other alternatives. You can go to the emergency room, but remember that the sickest are seen first, and there could be a wait. Immediate care clinics can treat minor injuries and illnesses, but should not be relied upon for major long-term health problems. Or, you could wait until Monday morning, by which time you might be feeling better, anyway.

Regardless, at least take the time to know your doctor's partners. They might treat you in an emergency. Also, know your doctor's schedule and availability; and of course, you could plan things a bit better and try to get sick between 8:00 a.m. and 4:00 p.m., Monday through Fridays.

CHAPTER SIXTY-EIGHT

What Does My Doctor Do All Day?

You're sick, and all you care about is feeling better. The answering service says your doctor will "call back" at some vague time in the future, and according to the doctor's receptionist, the next available appointment is three weeks from next Tuesday.

And you just know the doctor's out there playing golf, or shopping, or lounging in the pool. Glory be! Doctor's are supposed to be dedicated; to sacrifice everything for the patient's suffering. Well, Ben Casey, Kildare and old Marcus Welby were always available, weren't they?

But Kildare, Casey and Welby belong to a fantasy world; and now it's time to "get real." Doctors are people too—they have families, personal needs, and interests that have nothing to do with medicine. And while the doctor's inaccessibility at your time of immediate need can be frustrating, there's something to be said about "all work and no play," even for a doctor.

Everyone should have time to enjoy quality relaxation, and for patients to expect and receive the best possible care, the physicians must have time to nourish there own mental and physical well-being. An exhausted doctor is far more likely to make mistakes than is one who is refreshed and alert.

Certainly, you do not want to be attended by a physician who is so tired that he or she cannot think clearly about your problems. Be understanding of your doctor's needs as a human being. Acknowledge that your doctor has personal needs, but that this does not make him or her less dedicated. You will be the beneficiary of your own tolerance.

Of course, there are times that your doctor's absence means he or she is taking care of other pressing, professional needs. For instance, doctors are expected to update their knowledge through study and continuing medical education seminars. That's to your benefit also; who needs a physician who hasn't learned anything new in the past 10 or 15 years?

Then, there's the paperwork! Insurance forms must be completed (or you might have to pay your entire bill); and physicians do not escape the watchful eye of state and federal government agencies. Don't forget, medicine is a business these days, and being a doctor doesn't "let you off the hook."

So the next time you can't find you doctor, try not to get too impatient. Indeed, he or she might be playing golf, shopping or lounging in a pool. Perhaps a haircut was needed or a child is having problems at school. But dedicated doctors do still care primarily about their patients, and you can expect your needs to be met before very long.

And if they're not? Then respond as you would to any other poor service and considering transferring your "business" elsewhere. Call Kildare or Casey. Call another doctor.

CHAPTER SIXTY-NINE

My Doctor's A Jet Setter

You called your doctor this morning, and he's out of town. It's cold and raining, and your 5-year-old has an earache that's kept her and you awake all night. And your doctor is at a professional meeting—in Hawaii.

"Who's he kidding?" you yell, as you slam down the phone in frustration.

But it's true: Bona fide professional medical meetings are held all over the world at all times of the year. Your doctor is really attending scientific meetings and discussions most of the time, and one day, you or your child might benefit from the information and knowledge shared at those meetings. No, I won't try to kid you: There are social events too, but there's no law that says a hard-working doctor shouldn't have a good time too, is there?

Medical education does not stop when the student graduates or the young doctor completes a residency. In the past 50 years, there's been an enormous explosion of knowledge, and doctors must keep pace with this information. Although there are excellent medical journals and video tapes available to help doctors keep up-to-date, the truth is that more can be learned at two or three conferences a year than from articles and tapes.

You see, when a doctor attends a medical conference, his or her attention is focused one hundred percent on the subject matter under discussion. If that same doctor depends on reading even the best articles or listening to the best tapes, this must be done after a long day at work. And doctors are just like you: There never seems to be enough time. It's actually easier and more efficient to schedule a few days away from the office than try to "keep up" on a daily basis.

The value—indeed, the necessity—of continuing medical education is recognized nationally and internationally. In this country, some states require doctors to attend continuing education activities in order to maintain licensure. And this makes sense. (Would you really want to be treated by a doctor who hadn't learned anything new since 1960? I wouldn't!)

Well, yes, I understand all that, you say. But why Hawaii? Wouldn't Chicago be cheaper? After all, my doctor is using the money I pay to make the trip. Am I supposed to condone this waste of my money?

My answer to this is two-fold. It's true that these traveling expenses are paid by the fees you've been charged for treatment. But when you go on vacation, don't you pay for it from money saved from your salary? And isn't the doctor's salary nothing more than an accumulation of all the fees received throughout the year? Second, the potential value of continuing education shouldn't be measured in money. If a doctor learns something that later allows a faster diagnosis or a sophisticated technique that will save a life, the trip has been more than worth its weight in gold.

Does *your* doctor attend continuing medical education seminars? Is *your* doctor up-to-date with the latest medications or recommended courses of treatment? Why not ask your doctor about his or her continuing education activities? Let's face it: No one knows everything there is to know about anything; but if your doctor doesn't take the time to remain current, you should be more than just a bit concerned.

And please—don't begrudge that trip to Hawaii. Given the choice between Chicago and Hawaii, which would you choose?

CHAPTER SEVENTY

When The Doctor Becomes Ill

Doctors get sick. When we do we have extra troubles that the non-physician does not. We face all the usual trials and tribulations that you do. We have to fill out the same forms to get into the hospital. We have to deal with our insurance companies; face all the old and new rules to save money. And we have to put up with the same "insensitive and impersonal" health care workers.

On top of that, consider the problems we have because of our knowledge about diseases and illnesses. Sometimes knowing too much is not too good. Especially if you only know a little too much and not enough too much to really be an expert.

I suppose it would be OK if the doctor made sure the illness was in the same specialty area as his or her expertise. But even doctors have not mastered the ability to predetermine how we will get sick and what our disease will be.

In fact, many books and movies have been produced about doctors attitudes before and after they develop an illness. It not only makes good reading but also often does educate the physician about the real world of medicine—the world of medicine from the patient's point of view.

There is the old story about walking in the Indian's moccasins. Nowhere, that I know of, in the medical school curriculum is a course about what it's like to be a patient. Wouldn't it be a good idea to put every medical student (and all doctors already out of school) into the hospital for a while and do to the "patient" some of the same things that happen to real patients.

What are some of the things we could do? First of all we could dress the doctors in those specially tailored hospital gowns and let them walk out in the hallway with "you know what" exposed.

Then we could feed them hospital food. Give them all some of the special treatments like enemas and put tubes everywhere. We could wait until they just fall asleep and wake them up to ask them if they want a sleeping pill. We could wake them up again to take their temperature and blood pressure.

It's interesting just being wheeled about on a stretcher, so that all you can see is the moving ceiling. We could leave them outside the x-ray room for several hours and on the hard x-ray table for a few more.

How about a good bed bath? A few shots would also be nice, and we could finish the whole thing off by putting them in a room full of health care workers who wouldn't talk to them.

After that, the doctors would probably think marine boot camp a gentle experience. It would give them a new outlook on health care from the patient's point of view.

Oh, I almost forgot, when they are finished we will send them a bill and make them pay good money for the experience. Now that's realism. I know you could add many more such experiences to the list, but I do have some compassion for my fellow doctors.

This is all to point out that those of us in the health care business often do forget about the patient. We get so fascinated with all the new medical technology that we lose site of what we are supposed to be about. We are supposed to be caring human beings who have been entrusted by you to care for the well being of all. We are well paid for this trust. Although we have spent considerable time learning how to be successful, we must always remember that it was you who allowed us to do it.

If you did not desire to spend billions of dollars each year to teach new doctors, to build "state-of-the-art" hospitals and fill them with the latest equipment, and do all the other things necessary to develop one of the best health care delivery systems in the world, then we would not be able to do anything but make a few simple drugs out of plants and do a little blood-letting like our ancestors did before us.

Caring is still the key to successful medical care. Caring is cheap, it doesn't require major technology or equipment. It doesn't even require a great deal of training. It does require some effort and time, but it's worth it.

Are you getting the caring you desire? If not, fix it. You are the patient, and as the old expression goes, "the patient is always right."

CHAPTER SEVENTY-ONE

Do Doctors Deserve To Be Rich?

Here comes the doctor, driving down the street in his Mercedes. Oh, and look, there's his wife in her brand new Cadillac. They live in that mansion over there with the full-time maid and babysitter for the kids. That must be the life.

But, what about the other side of the story? The doctor awoke at 5:00 a.m., had a quick breakfast and got to the hospital by 6:30 a.m. He made rounds seeing patients and is off to a second hospital to make sure his patients there are doing well also. He then reports to the operating room (OR) by 7:30 a.m. for three operations that are completed by 1:00 p.m. Leaving the OR, he rushes to his office where he sees patients until 7:00 p.m. Then, it's back to the hospital to visit more patients before returning home by 9:00 p.m. (This is usually where he falls asleep and misses dinner, but it really doesn't matter since it's cold now anyway.)

At some time during the day, your physician has signed the medical records of several patients, answered countless calls from patients, met with his business manager on how the Medicare cutbacks are going to affect operations, and completed at least a dozen other chores necessary to keep his practice running smoothly.

And, life is not a picnic for a doctor's wife (or husband, for that matter. Even though this chapter is written in the masculine gender, it could just as easily have been the doctor and *her* husband). The household must be run as smoothly as the office and many times, the non-physician spouse can begin to feel like a single parent—having to raise the children essentially on his or her own while the doctor works long hours away from home.

I'm not about to tell you that doctors are not well paid. They are. And they do work hard, but their image certainly has changed over the years from the family physician making house calls to the sophisticated specialist with little time to spend hand holding or sitting at your bedside.

I don't believe any physician becomes "super rich" from income alone. But, the bottom line is that doctors are well-paid for their work and more work means more money. As in every profession, some physicians overdo and end up spending their income on ulcers and heart attacks rather than mansions and Mercedes. Other doctors have decided it's better to settle for less income and a more normal and longer life.

I believe the level of income and the life style of most physicians is appropriate. But, you'll have to judge for yourself (I'm obviously biased). Regardless of how you feel, as a consumer you must make sure you're getting your money's worth out of your physician. Insist on receiving adequate attention for the fees you are paying and make sure you and your doctor communicate clearly.

CHAPTER SEVENTY-TWO

Physician's Assistants Ease the Burden On Doctors

Some common complaints from patients are "my doctor hardly knows me," or "my physician sees me briefly." Unfortunately, the overbooked doctor is an all too familiar product of modern times. Increased demand for health care, new technological advances and added responsibilities mandated by insuring agencies have resulted in less time to spend with the patient.

But there is a solution that is rapidly becoming an accepted part of health care delivery—the physician's assistant. While relatively uncommon, this new profession is easing the physicians' work load, while maintaining the high quality of care that you, the public, require.

What is a physician's assistant? The "PA" is a professional who has completed a minimum of two years of college and a prescribed curriculum at a school specializing in training physician's assistants—usually a school of allied health sciences with close ties to a medical school.

The course of study is designed to encompass a great scope of the classes experienced by medical students (though it's a shorter and less intense program), and following graduation, PAs become affiliated with a physician.

Physician's assistants cannot work independently; they do not replace the doctor; and they must be associated on a one-to-one basis with a physician-sponsor. But the PA's contribution is invaluable; they take medical histories, conduct physical examinations, order diagnostic tests and see patients in follow-up examinations or during and following treatment. However, they are not allowed to develop treatment or therapeutic programs for patients without approval of their sponsor physician, and they are not allowed to write a prescription.

Physician's assistants should always introduce themselves as such to patients and should inform you of their role in your health care. It is important to understand that the physician's assistant is not your doctor, even though expected to be knowledgeable, intelligent, academic, compassionate and motivated.

While the presence of the physician's assistant might not mean that you spend more time with your doctor, it does allow your doctor to give you better care indirectly. During your initial visit, you should always see your doctor as well as the physician's assistant. Follow-up visits can include both the PA and the doctor but can sometimes include only the PA, depending upon the nature of the problem.

Physician's assistants, like doctors, specialize in certain areas of medicine, such as neurosurgery, family medicine, or hematology, and they are a valuable additions to the health care team. You should not feel offended or insecure about being seen by a PA. Everything you discuss with the PA will be brought to your doctor's attention.

Although PAs have only been part of the medical scene since the early 1970s, physician's assistants can now be found in doctors' offices, hospitals, operating rooms, outpatient clinics and just about anywhere else that a physician is practicing.

The advantage of such innovations is that the patient benefits from anything that improves the quality of health care. Without the physician's assistant, you would probably spend have less time with a qualified health care professional—and more time getting mad about it. Take my word— trust the PAs and be grateful for their presence.

CHAPTER SEVENTY-THREE

Today's Nurses Are A Far Cry From Florence Nightingale

Although there were nurses before her time, Florence Nightingale is generally credited with bringing pride and respectability to the nursing profession. And while the "Lady of the Lamp" might relate to the compassion and dedication that continues to be the core of the nurses' code, she would hardly recognize today's nurses, nor would she understand one fraction of their duties and responsibilities.

No longer relegated to emptying bedpans and changing the bedding, the modern nurse works in a variety of settings including hospitals, doctors' offices, schools, industry, governmental offices, businesses, at people's homes, and as administrators or faculty members in nursing schools. Nurses must be knowledgeable about sophisticated electronic wizardry, complicated therapeutic instructions, and the effects and dangers of new drug treatments as prescribed by a physician. They are often assigned an incredible patient load and encouraged to work extended hours, while being expected clean up after accidents, be courteous to visiting family and accommodate sensitive patients graciously.

And of course, nurses look far different from when Florence pursued her dream. For decades, nursing was considered, stereotypically, a woman's domain; not so today, as men are now claiming their share of this rewarding profession. And also for decades, nurses wore distinctive uniforms that identified the institution at which they were trained (when hospital training was the vogue) or educated, once degree programs in nursing were established. Today, they wear scrub suits, lab coats or business suits. For identification, nurses now wear badges that should display their name and their level of expertise.

A Licensed Vocational Nurse (LVN) has completed one year of undergraduate study and has passed the LVN licensure examination. The LVN does not have the responsibilities or knowledge of the Registered Nurse (RN) who has a two or four year degree in nursing from an accredited institution and who has passed the requisite state examination for RN status.

A more recent entry into the profession, however, is the Nurse Practitioner. This is a great opportunity for RNs who want to pursue advanced education, while continuing to apply their skills in direct patient care. The nurse practitioner enjoys a great deal of independence and can serve in the doctor's place for certain functions such as medical histories, physical examinations and follow-up examinations. But the nurse practitioner works closely with a physician.

A primary advantage for nurse practitioners is that they are registered nurses, simply attempting to add to their expertise through additional training. Many have worked with doctors in a clinical setting throughout their professional lives, and this proves to be invaluable experience for those who choose to seek nurse practitioner status. It's worth noting that some of the best and most compassionate doctors were nurses who decided to enter medical school.

As a physician, I welcome the help and expertise of nurse practitioners. Their presence helps to make health care even more accessible to those who are finding it more and more difficult to see the doctor. As a patient, it's to your advantage. Enjoy!

CHAPTER SEVENTY-FOUR

Who Really Runs The Place

We have talked about many contributors to the health care team and how each impacts your well-being. How about medical secretaries? Let us recognize the valuable roles of these individuals, and consider the potentially disastrous results if all the secretaries were to suddenly disappear from the health care scene.

You do not feel well, so you call your doctor. Who answers the phone? Rarely your doctor, right? Your initial contact is almost always with a secretary who treats you with respect and courtesy, fully mindful of the old saying: "First impressions are lasting impressions."

When you arrive at your doctor's office to keep your appointment, it is probably the secretary who greets you as you walk through the door; and before you leave, it is the secretary who arranges for additional appointments, discusses payment plans, calls a cab if you need one, and sends you on your way with a cheerful smile.

You are not the secretary's only concern. There are meetings to arrange, travel plans to confirm, and mail and correspondence to handle. There are patient appointments, phone calls, supplies to order, and a myriad of other details that take up hours of the secretary's time.

What if the secretary is sick or delayed and cannot come to work? The efficient office can turn into chaos, and the doctor is in deep trouble! Few people realize just how much a doctor's office depends on the expertise of the secretary. Let's face it, the physician's knowledge rarely extends to an in-depth comprehension of word processing software.

Yet, sad to say, secretaries rarely receive the kind of compensation that reflects the value of their contribution. Often, paychecks are barely adequate to meet basic needs: food, shelter, and clothing. Vacation time is usually minimal. Office hours are long and arduous.

You can help! Sometimes, a good secretary is taken for granted. My advice is to be nice, and for the doctor to do the same. When you find a secretary who will put up with all the problems of the office, the patients, and the doctor, you better do everything possible to keep him or her satisfied, and as happy as possible in their work. Show you recognize his or her worth by being pleasant and friendly when dealing with them. Indicate that you are aware of how much you benefit from their help.

Try to understand that the secretary is not always free to act in the way you would prefer, but is usually offering you the best available service. Send a letter or note to the boss (i.e. the doctor) that emphasizes the secretary's value. Such a gesture from a grateful patient would surely be appreciated.

Often, you are sick or worried when you walk into your doctor's office, so try to imagine what it would be like without the secretary's friendly smile, professional approach, and helpful attitude.

You have heard the expression: "It's a tough job, but somebody's got to do it?" Well, being a doctor's secretary is truly a tough job. Be thankful that someone is willing to do it!

Checklist
Chapters 56-74

Dealing With Your Doctor

✓ Have you met your doctor when you are well?

✓ Have you discussed your medical problems with your doctor?

✓ Can you really "talk" to your doctor?

✓ Have you learned your doctor's appointment systems?

✓ Have you evaluated your doctor's associates?

✓ Have you learned your doctor's financial policies?

✓ Are you happy with the care your doctor provides?

✓ Are you comfortable asking for a second opinion?

✓ Do you trust your doctor?

✓ Are you comfortable with the possibility that your doctor utilizes the services of a Physician's Assistant or nurse practitioner and that you may be seen by these individuals?

✓ Are you prepared to tell you doctor that you do not understand medical language and you would like to talk in simple, non-medical terms?

CHAPTER SEVENTY-FIVE

Painless Parker—Your Friendly Dentist

Let's talk about fear? Or pain? Or both? OK—let's talk about dentists!

Two of my uncles are dentists, and all my life, I've listened with some disbelief to tales about my uncle's dentist friend—Painless Parker. Even as a kid, I knew that "painless" and "dentist" were two words that simply didn't belong together. After all, just like you, I've seen and had first-hand experience of those weird-looking diabolical instruments, and I *know* there can be nothing painless about something called "root canal" or "trench mouth."

But the truth is that a visit to the dentist is usually something like having your ears pierced or being a blood donor: The thought is much worse than the actual doing! And isn't it strange that so many people go happily to have their ears pierced but those same people are so afraid of the dentist, they're prepared to face the consequences of not taking care of their teeth?

Think about this: Deer and many other wild animals will often die of starvation, assuming they escape the persevering hunter, because their teeth wear out and no one has yet invented deer dentures. But humans do not have to fall prey to the deer's fate: We have a choice. We have the dentist!

Visits to the dentist should begin during childhood. Just like you take your car for its annual lube job or your pet to the veterinarian for its shots every spring, you should practice "preventive maintenance" on your teeth. There is much to be said for the old expression "An ounce of prevention is worth a pound of cure."

And once you've taken the plunge, be sure to provide the dentist as much information as possible that could be helpful. What are your current symptoms? Are you under a physicians's care for any other medical problem? Are you allergic to any medication? Is there something in your past medical history that could affect a recommended treatment? Are you currently taking prescribed or over-the-counter medicine? There can never be too much information when your well-being is at stake.

Be prepared to accept your dentist's advice. Ask questions if you don't understand the recommended course of treatment, and if you're not satisfied, seek a second opinion—just as you would if you were uncertain about advice you'd been given by your family doctor. Seeking a second opinion is not unusual—and is even recommended when the suggested treatment might be complicated, lengthy and expensive.

Remember—dentists are trained in much the same way as are physicians; and they are usually sensitive to their patients' fears and anxiety. Most of them will be only too happy to take the time to explain the reasons for the recommended treatment and to answer your questions. Remember, too, that understanding the facts goes a long way to eliminating the fears—but if you don't ask questions, the dentist won't know that anything is bothering you.

So you've summoned up your courage and kept your appointment; you've even found that the dentist is friendly and helpful, carefully explaining the recommended course of treatment. And now it's up to you to decide whether or not to take the advice and act upon the recommendations.

The chances are that if you've come this far, you will take the next step. By now, you've realized that this is your opportunity to preserve your own teeth and perhaps avoid having to wear dentures some time in the future.

At least, if you make the right move, you'll avoid ending up like the deer—but if you go hunting, just make sure another hunter doesn't mistake you for a buck. Even a visit to the dentist is less painful than that!

CHAPTER SEVENTY-SIX

Prevention Takes the Bite Out Of the Dentist

Most people don't like to visit the doctor, dreading the thought of shots or maybe even some bad news. But even worse is the thought of a trip the dentist's office. (I've never yet met anyone who says, "Had a good time, today. Went to the dentist!!")

Don't misunderstand me. I have several friends and relatives who are dentists. They're all very nice people too, and I feel sorry for the way they've had to live with the never ending stream of abuse heaped upon their chosen profession.

Well, if my dentist is right, his job might be in danger, because medication could soon be available that would prevent tooth decay, especially if used from childhood. If this happens, the obligatory annual trek to the dentist's office will become a thing of the past, at least for the next generation.

But don't be discouraged. There are still ways for us, the older folks, to minimize the need for visits to the dentist's office. Dentists use the fancy name "prophylaxis," which simply means the prevention of dental problems before they occur. In other words, don't wait for the toothache to happen before you make your appointment!

Let's face it, it's not the actual visit to the dentist that's scary; it's the thought of what might happen when you get there.

Do visit your dentist regularly, but between visits, practice good dental hygiene. The chances are that after the first time around, your next check up might well be exactly that: A check up; no painful prodding or poking; no extractions or expensive root canal work. Could anything be better than that?

But be prepared for that first visit. Your dental hygienist will want to check for all signs of weakness or problems with your teeth and gums. Cavities might be discovered and repair recommended. Your mouth will be carefully scrutinized for tartar—that hard material that clings to your teeth and causes tooth decay if left to its own devices. Let your dental hygienist scrape away with those awful looking metal instruments. It will be to your advantage later. In other words, go for it at that first visit.

After that, follow your dental hygienist's advice. Brushing and flossing regularly will probably be recommended. Take control of your own dental destiny and do everything you can to prevent tooth decay or gum disease. The need for periodic check ups will not be eliminated altogether; but the chances are the fear and dread will diminish, when you discover how painless each visit becomes.

Of course, following this route is no guarantee that nothing will go wrong even if you follow your dentist's recommendations to perfection. But you will lessen the possibility of problems—and nobody will be able to say you've only got yourself to blame. (Don't you just hate it when people say that to you?)

It's really strange, though. Between discovering medication that could eliminate tooth decay and strongly recommending prophylaxis, dentists are setting themselves up to become an endangered species.

But then, I told you earlier that all the dentists I know are really nice people. Is it possible that I might be right?

Checklist
Chapters 75-76

Dental Issues

✓ Do you have a dentist?
✓ Have you consulted appropriate referral sources?
✓ Have you learned the personality of your dentist?
✓ Have you learned the financial system of your dentist?
✓ Have you resolved to practice preventive dentistry and follow the advice of your dental hygienist?

CHAPTER SEVENTY-SEVEN

FDA Plays Important Role In Your Health Care

The 1970s witnessed a sad chapter in the history of health care when thousands of Americans invested money and time traveling to other countries to obtain Laetrile, a new "cure" for cancer. Hopes were dashed, as it became obvious that this drug, derived from apricot pits, had no clinical or healing value as a treatment for cancer.

Like many drugs, laetrile was never tested or made available in the United States, because it failed to receive the approval of the Food and Drug Administration (FDA). And even though detractors might feel the FDA is too conservative, this federal agency provides a much needed service that ultimately results in better health for the American people.

History is replete with "home remedies" that can be effective. But an even greater number are ineffective and could be deadly. You can travel to other countries and find medications derived from goat glands or human urine, and both have been lauded as the solution to major illnesses. However, many of these countries do not have the stringent monitoring system provided by the FDA.

The FDA is a large organization that employs a lengthy and very complicated system for drug approval, leading to the criticism that the FDA prevents patients from benefitting from drugs that are still in the testing stage. And while it might be true in some cases, the overall benefit of keeping dangerous drugs out of general use outweighs the exasperation of lengthy testing procedures.

Regardless of its somewhat maligned reputation, the FDA plays an important role in your health, serving as a watch-dog over the nation's multi-billion dollar pharmaceutical industry.

Manufacturers invest millions of dollars in research and development (R&D), and many drugs are extremely expensive—an investment you help to support when you purchase costly medications. Drug companies face the same marketing challenges as does any manufacturer of any commodity, and to be profitable they try to ensure that their product is available before that of their competition.

While most drugs are carefully tested during the R&D stage of development, corporate shareholders demand a return on their investment; marketing becomes a primary motivator. But the FDA looks only at product effectiveness and safety, demanding a lot of tests and satisfactory results before it will release a product for general sale to the public.

As a potential purchaser of drugs, either through a prescription or directly from your drug store's shelf, it is important that you understand (and support) the FDA's involvement. For instance, if you buy a product that cures your headache but causes your kidneys to malfunction, your health is endangered.

Though drug companies test their products carefully, the FDA's vigilance forces an even broader examination of each product. Usually, you will not be able to purchase that magic cure for your headache, until the FDA is convinced that it will have no adverse side effects.

There are ways to benefit from drugs that have not yet received FDA approval, however. If you live near a major medical center, you may qualify to participate in drug studies. Your physician can usually advise you whether or not you are a suitable candidate for such a study.

The FDA is an official branch of the U.S. Department of Health and Human Services and was established to protect you. That should give you some peace of mind the next time your doctor tells you to "take two and call me in the morning."

CHAPTER SEVENTY-EIGHT

To Work Drugs Must Be Taken Correctly

It's called the *Physician's Desk Reference* (PDR); it weighs about 20 lbs., and it lists most of the currently available drugs that a patient might require during medical treatment.

But heavy books are useless, if the patient refuses either to take the prescribed medicine or to follow instructions correctly.

Oh, for those simple times, when the doctor showed up at your house with bottles of medicine and boxes of pills in his little black bag and gave you nice clear instructions.

Today, we have prescriptions, drug stores, check out lines, generic brands and a lot of other complications. It's really not true that a doctor is required have terrible handwriting; and neither is it necessary for you to be able to read a prescription; that's the pharmacist's domain. The prescription tells the pharmacist which medicine to give you, in what strength and how it should be taken. The notations are usually abbreviations of medical terminology and often in Latin—which is why a prescription is visually confusing.

Even though you might not understand the prescription, the pharmacist should always explain the directions for use. Never walk away from the counter not fully understanding how you are to take the medicine.

Your medicine should be labeled with your name and expiration date. *Never* take another person's medication, and never take your own after the expiration date. The chemical properties of drugs can change as they age; you wouldn't eat a rotten apple; don't take outdated medicine! The label should also tell you when and how often to take the medicine: Three times a day? Before food? In the morning? Also, refill instructions and even warnings (e.g., "can make you drowsy") should appear when appropriate.

Many containers are equipped with "childproof" caps. Although these do protect your young children, they can be frustrating or even dangerous for older adults or others who have difficulty removing these caps quickly. Perhaps you have arthritis in your hands; or perhaps you have a broken wrist. To be sure you can get to your medicine quickly (and as long as there are no children around), ask your pharmacist to provide containers with "old-fashioned" caps that can be unscrewed.

Some people might also need help in remembering to take their medicine. Pillboxes with separate plastic pockets for each medicine can help. Also, some pharmacists can package the medicine in blister packs on a large card—labeled with the appropriate instructions.

If your prescription allows for refills and is intended to treat a long-term illness that requires regular medication, then plan ahead. Allow for weekends, holidays and vacations when renewing your prescription. Don't take chances; running out of medicine can be dangerous—even deadly. Diabetics who take insulin, for example, should always have a supply on hand. And know the location of your nearest 24-hour pharmacy. It could be a life saver.

If yours is a short-term problem, and you have only a two-week supply of medicine, this should be sufficient to eliminate your problem. But you can call your physician if symptoms persist; it might be possible to get a second prescription called to your local drug store—but don't argue if your doctor prefers that you come to his or her office for a check up first.

Medicines are a bit like television programs. They can be good or bad, depending on your need. Take them cautiously; apply a dose of common sense; and use the off switch when your doctor advises you to do so.

CHAPTER SEVENTY-NINE

Generic Drugs Offer Good News and Bad

Let's talk about big money, billions of dollars. Let's talk about the pharmaceutical industry.

But, first: Raise your hand if you've ever complained about the high cost of medication, any medication—whether it was something your doctor prescribed or a box of headache pills you picked up at the local drug store.

Some people think that there's something immoral about the high cost of drugs. But pharmaceutical companies are no different than any other publicly-owned business: They have boards of directors, stockholders and annual reports. And their continued existence depends upon their ability to make a profit for their investors.

Millions of dollars are spent on research and development, as each drug manufacturer attempts to gain a head start on its competition. And as medical research continues to find more ways to treat or cure life-threatening diseases, so the drug industry has expanded to accommodate the demand for ever expanding drug needs. And of course, the consumer must pay for associated escalating costs.

Enter generic drugs! While generic drugs have been available for decades, only comparatively recently has a cost-conscious public started to abandon its love affair with brand names and opt for the same cure at half the price! In general, generic drugs are as effective and as safe as their brand name counterparts. But how do you know which choice to make?

Depend on your doctor's expertise when a prescription drug is involved. He or she can specify whether or not a generic drug can be substituted and will instruct the pharmacist accordingly. If your doctor does not indicate an option, ask for an explanation. The doctor probably knows that, on this occasion, the generic drug is not appropriate for you. There will be a good reason for your being asked to purchase the more expensive name brand.

Your pharmacist can be a source of information, especially if you're considering a non-prescription generic drug. The knowledgeable pharmacist will choose only high quality products and should be able to provide the name of the manufacturer; information on comparative prices; and even the difference between the generic and the brand name, in terms of their content. Also, some insurance companies and health care programs offer an incentive for using generic drugs, by providing low-cost generic drug plans.

Be sure that the generic drug you buy has a "Made in America" label. Other countries might not have the stringent inspection requirements mandated by U.S. state and federal laws. The drug could be less effective or even dangerous. Since some American firms subcontract with foreign companies to manufacture generic drugs, it's important to know that your medication is All-American.

Generic drugs will probably not look the same as the name brand equivalent. They are often a different color and shape and carry their own identification symbols. Manufacturers of generic drugs try to create their own identity; they are not ashamed of their product and strive to build their own base of loyal customers.

Generic drugs are not new. It just took a long time for the consumer to "find" them, and they are gaining in popularity. Usually it will be to your financial advantage to choose the generic brand; but be a smart shopper. Ask the right questions, and take the advice of experts, rather than the promises of television ads or screaming billboards.

CHAPTER EIGHTY

Do Some Homework Before Trying Quick Fix

Pick up any newspaper or magazine and you're likely to find at least one advertisement describing ways to combat baldness, impotence, obesity, or menstrual cramps. The radio, T.V. and roadside billboards carry similar message of hope. Are they accurate? Do the products work? Should you pay attention?

For centuries, unscrupulous individuals (some even calling themselves doctors) have been fooling a vulnerable public with potions and nostrums to cure every imaginable disease.

By wagon or pushcart or even on foot, they hawked elixirs with ease and enthusiasm. Most of the salesmen left town the next day, not wanting to be confronted when their customer realized that the medicine was made of roots and extracts with enough alcohol added to make the sickest customer feel better about life.

Such "snake-oil" salesmen still exist today. But because anything made of all natural ingredients does not require approval by the Food and Drug Administration (FDA), many "medications" or other "cures" are largely unregulated.

Today's salesmen are far more sophisticated, using glitzy ads and carefully circumventing truth-in-advertising laws by promising but not guaranteeing success.

How does the concerned citizen determine what is or is not legitimate? Do your homework! Ask questions! Be careful. Read labels carefully to determine the products' ingredients. If you have any doubts, don't use it. Seek advice from a pharmacist or doctor. Ingredients should always be listed.

Determine whether the manufacturer is reputable. Are you familiar with the company name? Ask your pharmacist or doctor. Contact the Better Business Bureau. If the product is sold in the drugstore, and you still have doubts—you guessed it—talk to your pharmacist.

Ask your family, friends or coworkers whether they are familiar with the product—and did it live up to either their expectation or the manufacturer's claims. And if you are influenced by the experiences of someone you know, be sure it's someone you trust, too.

Is the product warranted with a money back guarantee? This does not always assure legitimacy, but at least you should be able to get your money back. If the company is willing to stand behind its product (and its guarantee), there appears to be a sincere commitment.

Is the cost reasonably competitive with the marketplace value for similar products? Beware of the overpriced "quick fix."

Can you reach the company only through the mail? And is there a two-three month delivery time. Reputable companies offer easy access, usually through a customer service department, as well as prompt delivery.

Above all, never depend on unknown medications or treatments for serious illnesses. Mail order houses do not stock cures for cancer, heart disease or diabetes. Consult your physician who might even suggest a medication you have seen advertised, as one component of an overall treatment plan.

Some highly advertised health products do work. Vitamins can make you feel better, some diet products can help you lose weight if used in a sensible manner, and even some baldness remedies appear to be effective. But always remember to check with your physician.

Don't risk your health to save money or to chase the impossible dream. And if it sounds too good to be true, it probably is too good to be true!

CHAPTER EIGHTY-ONE

Poison, Poison Everywhere—It's Your Responsibility

Now that my youngest child is nineteen, I wonder how my wife and I ever survived the past two decades. In fact, when my older daughter asked for my opinion about something the other day, I realized that as my kids got older, I must have somehow gotten smarter.

As with everyone who's "married with children," our kids were hardly immune from having accidents, and we had our share of problems: Visits to the emergency room; broken bones; and even pills eaten by a toddler who thought he'd found a new kind of candy.

The need to "childproof" your home against poisonous materials is extremely important. Infants cannot read, and a pretty red pill is very enticing—whether it's a jelly bean or medication for a stomach ulcer. Be sure that all medications are out of reach of tiny fingers; that cleansing materials are stored on top shelves; that the fancy, wild plant you found in your back yard won't poison your adventurous two year old; and the cute little furry creature on the back porch isn't some kind of poisonous mini-monster.

But regardless of how much care you take, it seems that small children can always find a way to stay one step ahead of mom and dad. And that could mean the need for help from the Poison Control Center.

Although the Center's phone number should be in the local telephone book, you should make sure it's even more readily available.

An emergency situation requires immediate action; there is no time for you to hunt around for the appropriate telephone number. So be prepared! Find the number *now* and spend a few minutes that could prove invaluable at some future time.

Fix the number of the Poison Control Center to every telephone in your house; find a prominent place on you refrigerator door; tape it to your medicine cabinet; write it in you address book; keep it in your glove compartment.

The Poison Control Center can also provide you with a supply of "Mr. Yuk" stickers which you can put on all the dangerous and poisonous articles in your home. Teach your children *not* to touch anything with Mr. Yuk on it. Believe me, even toddlers can learn.

Should a possible emergency arise, call the Center for advice or information—and don't ever allow a friend or family member to convince you that such a call is not necessary. Even if you think the stuff that junior just ate might not be harmful, make the call to the Center, anyway; particularly in this type of situation, there is much to be said for the old expression: "It's better to be safe than sorry."

Checklist
Chapters 77-81

Drugs and Medications

✓ Have you resolved to follow your doctor's and pharmacist's advice about taking your medications?

✓ Have you developed a system to remember to take your medications?

✓ Do you understand the reason the medication was prescribed?

✓ Do you understand the side effects of the medications?

✓ Have you considered requesting generic medications?

✓ Have you realized that medications that are prescribed for you should be taken by you and only you, and that you should not share your medications with others?

✓ Are you prepared to follow the advice of your doctor and pharmacist and not listen to any slick salesman selling unknown medicine?

✓ Have you "childproofed" your home and removed or secured all poisons?

CHAPTER EIGHTY-TWO

Why Are Hospitals So Expensive

A few weeks ago, a friend of mine raised the rates at the hotel he manages. He told me he couldn't keep up with the disappearing towels and washcloths. He said you'd be amazed at the things people take with them when they leave hotel rooms. And eventually, someone has to pay the bill for these and many other hidden costs. Hence, an increase in room rates this summer.

Hospitals are the same way. People don't usually take stuff; but hospitals have a lot of hidden costs (sometimes called "overheads"), just like my friend's hotel.

Consider the hospital building itself: by its very nature, the building must incorporate dozens of special needs that allow it to fulfill its intended purpose—caring for the sick. It must be built to adhere to the strictest building codes to ensure your safety; emergency generators are standard, in case of a power cut; and you might not even notice the outlets on the wall behind your bed unless you need oxygen or suction in your treatment. So you won't realize that walls contain special pipes to accommodate these outlets.

Diagnostic and treatment equipment is extraordinarily expensive. x-ray machines, magnets, radiation counters and hundreds of other testing devices have surely enhanced medical care; unfortunately, they've enhanced your bill, also.

The major cost of hospital operations, however, is devoted to its people. In addition to the doctors, nurses, technicians, therapists and all those others people who are directly involved with your health care, a hospital would cease to function without housekeepers, administrators, dietitians, electricians, transportation personnel, billing and accounting experts, air conditioning gurus and so many more, it's virtually impossible to list them all.

Then consider the specialized areas of the hospital. An emergency room has its own specific needs, as do the operating and recovery rooms, the kitchens, and the security department.

And then there are more hidden costs—those that usually surprise even the most prepared administrator! A storm damages the roof; the bandage company raises its prices; a nursing shortage forces higher salaries to retain qualified and experienced personnel.

I know it's hard for you to believe, especially if you've received a hospital bill recently, but cost containment and efforts to control expenses are primary concerns of all hospital administrations. Attempting to reconcile these spiraling costs with a commitment to providing the finest possible health care is an ongoing conflict. Hospital costs consistently defy the old maxim of "What goes up, must come down." The theory of gravity just doesn't apply in this case.

All we can ask is that patients understand our predicament and do whatever they can to reduce their personal health care costs, without compromising their health: Keep your hospital stay as brief as you can; use generic drugs, if possible. And please, never, never take the towels or the washcloths.

CHAPTER EIGHTY-THREE

Here's How You Can Control the Costs of Health Care

In the old days, doctors made house calls. They had few overhead expenses, a bag of simple instruments and payment was often a chicken or two for the doctor and some hay for his horse. But the patient's recovery was frequently as much as matter of good luck as the result of medical knowledge.

Today, health care is far more sophisticated, and people are living longer, healthier lives. But everything has its price, and the cost of health care is far greater than the value of two chickens and a stack of hay.

As costs continue to escalate, the patient is faced with the basic problem of trying to keep those costs at an affordable level, when even routine treatment involves countless lab tests and the interaction of health care specialists—nurses, technicians, radiologists, and so forth.

While the money to pay the doctor (or hospital) comes from your income either in the form of cash or through your insurance premium, it is the doctor who tells you which test you need or sends you off for several, expensive x-rays.

Think about this: Is buying health care really any different from buying anything else? You purchase and you pay. So just as you shop around for the best in cars, shoes or groceries, so you should play a role in the cost of your health care.

Ask the physician to have your tests processed at a lab that will provide the best quality at the best cost; and feel free to seek a second opinion. While this might be somewhat time consuming, once you've determined which lab offers the best deal, then you can insist that all your future testing be done at the same place.

The same principle applies for prescription drugs. If a quality drug that will meet your needs is available in generic form, then insist on this when your physician writes a prescription.

Still another way to save begins with you. Be sure you are confident of the support of your insurance company; it's extremely important that the insurance company be there for you when health care costs are incurred. By cutting corners and obtaining second-rate insurance (or worse, no insurance), you could easily pay much more in the long run.

At the grocery store, you receive a receipt that itemizes all your purchases. Request a similar accounting of costs from your physician or hospital. Scrutinize it carefully to ensure that you were not charged for a service or product you did not receive. Mistakes are made.

Regardless of the complexity or size of your bill, you have every right to go to the billing office and ask someone to review the bill, line-by-line, to make sure that the charges are correct. A busy hospital might be reluctant to comply, but it is your right.

Even after your insurance has paid for the agreed upon percentage of health care, the remainder can still be a major blow to any budget. Rather than ignoring the request for payment and risk harming your credit rating, talk to the billing personnel and see if there is a payment plan that can be established. Most will be happy to work with you.

However, if you ever feel that you have been charged for something you didn't receive; or if you feel a mistake has been made ("the computer did it"); or if you simply do not understand the itemized bill that lands with a sickening thud in your mail box—be a responsible consumer. Ask questions and insist upon clear answers.

Of course, since prevention is the best cure, the best cost cutting technique is to research the cost of tests and procedures ahead of time. But this gets us into a whole new discussion (How to talk to your physician); and that's the subject of another chapter.

CHAPTER EIGHTY-FOUR

How Do You Know If You Really Need That Medical Test?

Last week, I took my car for its annual check up. The mechanic glanced under the hood and then turned his attention to the vast array of plugs, electrical contraptions and computers, as he began his diagnostic evaluation of my car. That's when I began to think about the changes that have taken place in health care in the second half of the 20th century,

In the past 50 years, there has been a huge explosion in high-tech lab procedures, and today, a complex battery of tests are now an accepted routine part of any proper medical examination. This can place the patient at a distinct disadvantage. It used to be easy to ask the doctor to explain the visible and simple procedures of a stethoscope or a finger on your pulse. But faced with intimidating technology, how do you say, "Thanks, but no thanks," simply because you don't understand the test that's been recommended?

Actually, it's easier than you think. You ask for an explanation; you demand to know if there are alternatives; you require to know whether there are any drawbacks to the test—and the extent of its reliability. You are the patient; you have a right to know what is being done to your body. And you have a right to know that when you receive the bill, the tests were well worth the money.

The costs of tests can become exorbitant and often exceed your doctor's fees. They are more sophisticated, more complicated, could be dangerous, and sometimes are sufficiently routine that you might think they're unnecessary. And you are faced with difficult decisions!

As a consumer, you want to reduce the amount of money you spend for health care, but you want the best health care you can buy, which includes any tests that might help your physician to arrive at a proper diagnosis for treatment.

Well, there is no hard and fast rule. But if you understand the test and what it can do for you, you can make an informed choice with some peace of mind. First, you should realize that choosing a test is an "art" based on hunches and education. Your physician decides which tests might shed some light on your medical problem by evaluating your medical history, your physical condition, and your symptoms, and by drawing upon his or her own medical expertise and, at times, that "sixth sense."

The tests are usually ordered to confirm suspicions, to screen for other possible problems, to clarify unclear results, and to follow the progress of the patient. But if you have any doubts about the necessity of a specific test, ask all the appropriate questions. Physicians who react negatively when patients ask questions about any aspect of their health care are out of touch with modern medicine—so ask your questions, and don't be intimidated by your doctor's knowledge or position.

It's never wrong to learn more about your medical problem and about the tests that might help unravel the solution to treatment. Nor is it wrong to want to save money. More and more patients are insisting on the explanations that allow them to reject a prescribed test. And it's your doctor's job to help you understand the consequences of such a decision.

CHAPTER EIGHTY-FIVE

Patient Is Ultimately Responsible For the Bill

No matter how much you enjoy dining in a fine restaurant, it always ends the same way—the bill arrives. It's no different with health care. You "hire" a service temporarily, and then you pay for it.

But the similarity between restaurant checks and medical bills ends there. Complex? Often. Confusing? Yes, if you don't understand how the billing system works. Impossible? No. But to cope with the "billing blues," you need to understand billing.

If you don't have medical insurance, you have to pay the bill personally. Write a check, bring money to the hospital in a wheelbarrow, melt down your credit card. But pay. Or work out a plan with the hospital that will allow you to liquidate your debt gradually and less painfully.

For those of you with insurance, your bill takes on a whole new meaning—someone else is paying. But since you are ultimately responsible for the bill should the insurer reject or question payment, and since mistakes can be made, you should review the bill. And remember, even if the insurance company pays the bill, you have provided the money through months or years of paying insurance premiums.

In most cases, the bill is merely a statement of which services you incurred while at the hospital or under the doctor's care. Generally, you will receive two or more bills; there should be one bill from the hospital and one bill from the doctor. Depending on where you are hospitalized, you could receive separate bills also for a lot of related services: X-rays, pathology, emergency room, and so forth.

The hospital bill should be an exact picture of the services you received during your stay, including medications, use of surgery facilities, your room, and lab tests. However, some hospitals contract with outside organizations for some services (radiology, for example), and that's why you could receive additional bills. In this instance, you are expected to pay the outside service directly and separately from the hospital.

Take the time to go over the bills to ensure that you were not charged for items unnecessarily. Of course, it's hard for the average layman to remember if they received a "liter of D5W" or a "dose of cephalosporin." But you do have the right to request explanations: Don't hesitate; and don't pay the bill until you're satisfied.

Often, the first statement you receive is not a demand for payment but an indication that your insurance company has been billed for the listed items. When the insurance company has settled its debt, you will receive a statement and bill for the balance of payment; this is the amount for which you are responsible.

If you are uninsured (and therefore responsible for the entire amount) or if your portion of the bill is unmanageable, contact your hospital and doctor. Work out a payment plan that is satisfactory to all those involved—most hospitals and doctors do not find this to be an unusual or unacceptable request.

One way to avoid incurring a bill that you cannot pay is to find out whether your insurance company will pay for the procedure, prior to going into the hospital. Most insurers publish and provide booklets that specify those items for which they will and will not pay. Check with your benefits department if you are covered through a work-related plan, or call your agent if you are privately insured.

If you are depending on Medicare or other governmental programs, then stay tuned for another chapter. That's very different.

Flexibility, planning and communication are perhaps the key words when billing is the subject. Plan for medical needs by having insurance, or by having the cash to pay for such services. And be patient with the billing process. Allow it to function as it does—don't flip out if you receive 32 bills before your insurance company pays, but make sure your insurance company has been billed. And remember, the hospital and physicians can be flexible if you demonstrate sincerity. Communicate if there are problems with your bill. Question those items you are unsure of and insist on satisfaction if wrongly charged.

CHAPTER EIGHTY-SIX

Medicare and DRGs: Be Sure You Know What's Covered

Back to school! Quiz time: Which of the following involves your health care?

A) GNP   **B) MPG**   **C) DRG**   **D) ABC**

If you chose "DRG," and know exactly what it means, you're ahead of the class and might not need to read this chapter. For the rest of you—read on.

If you are one of millions of Americans who rely on the federal government to help you pay the high cost of medical care, then you are probably aware of changes in the way that Medicare operates.

First, a little history. In the old days, people depended on their life savings to see them through medical treatment during their "golden years." Then along came private insurance and the words "premium" and "deductible" became common terms, hated by everyone except the insurance industry. Still, this was not enough. A large percentage of our elderly population could not afford private insurance, and their life savings were unable to meet the demands of ever-increasing cost of health care.

Enter Medicare, the Social Security-funded program that began in the 1960s, promising cost-free care for the nation's retirees and reimbursement to America's doctors and hospitals. But the reimbursement became too costly and there were too many retirees, and in the 1980s, Medicare realized that there were three possible answers to the exploding health care costs. One, stop Medicare altogether; two, charge Medicare recipients increasingly larger fees; and three, reduce overall costs of health care.

Since it was not feasible (or appropriate) to disband Medicare, and since most Medicare recipients were on fixed incomes, the solution of choice had to be to reduce health care costs. Consequently, Diagnostic Related Groups (DRGs) were invented.

As a conscientious health care consumer, it is imperative that you understand these strictly regulated "illness categories" and how the new

Medicare operates. It could mean the difference between contained costs and a high bill which you cannot afford to pay. DRGs—approximately 470 categories of medical conditions—have changed the way in which hospitals are reimbursed. It has made them more accountable for true costs and therefore, directly impacts you, the consumer, since Medicare will not pay for treatment unrelated to the "category" for which you were admitted, and will not pay more than a predetermined "price" for that category.

It works like this. If you need to have a hernia operation, then Medicare will only reimburse the hospital a set amount of money, based on a average cost for hernia operations. If the hospital and physician perform the service for a smaller amount than Medicare has determined, then the hospital pockets the difference. If the cost exceeds the estimate, the hospital must absorb the overage. This has resulted in a dramatic drop in the number of days a patient is likely to stay in the hospital and has also led to a boom in outpatient visits, day surgery and other forms of health care that advocate short (and cost-cutting) visits.

On the surface, this system appears to be the answer to saving the taxpayer's money and to promoting efficient health care; but there is a negative side to the picture. The DRG system requires extensive documentation, and has complicated health care for patients as well as for physicians and hospitals, since they are carefully regulated through utilization review committees to ensure that the system is not abused.

The biggest threat however is that changes in Medicare means that patients can accidentally incur large medical bills which they cannot pay. How? Read on, my friends.

Medicare does not cover *every* medical condition within its DRGs. If you undergo some types of cosmetic surgery, for example, without first talking to a Medicare representative, your physician or the hospital finance officer, you could find a huge bill in your mailbox. Familiarize yourself with the types of health care that are open to coverage under Medicare.

Another "negative" involves deductibles and co-payments. In addition to DRGs, Medicare has implemented a system much like private insurers where the patient is responsible for a portion of the initial costs. If you are unaware of this, you could be in for a shock. It's highly advisable to consider supplemental private insurance coverage to offset these unexpected expenses.

There is no question that Medicare has made a tremendous impact on the availability of quality health care to a large segment of the U.S. population. But as with any service or product that appears problem-free: buyer beware!

CHAPTER EIGHTY-SEVEN

Get Your Free Health Care Here

THERE IS NO SUBSTITUTE FOR A VISIT TO THE DOCTOR WHEN YOU ARE ILL!!!

Now that I have made that disclaimer, I want to share some tips with you on receiving health care free, or at a greatly reduced rate.

That's right, you can reduce your health care costs and still receive quality information, but to do so you must be attentive to what's going on in your community. Pay attention to local advertising outlets, like the newspaper, for information on health fairs planned for your area. Health fairs are sponsored by a variety of organizations and may be aimed at a single medical issue or a broad range of health care needs.

One of the most important benefits of health fairs is education. Fairs provide a wonderful place to learn more about health issues and problems. You will not only find a variety of written materials, but also many knowledgeable professionals who can explain things to you. Talk to these people, ask them questions. If they don't know the answers, they can direct you to someone who does.

Not only is there a great deal of information and education conducted at health fairs, but also there is usually some type of testing offered free of charge. Often free blood sugar screening is offered at the diabetes information booth, or participating agencies might provide blood cholesterol screening, vision and glaucoma testing, hearing testing and so forth. Depending on the sponsoring organization, the free tests can be quite comprehensive.

More and more health related businesses, such as pharmacies, offer free blood pressure screening. All you do is slide in your arm, push a button and the machine takes over to give you a blood pressure reading. A word of caution though, automated blood pressure readings are not a substitute for blood pressure checks by a trained professional. Things can go wrong with a machine, but usually it can provide you with a general blood pressure range and advise you to seek medical attention when necessary. Don't panic if the machine gives you a high reading, instead have the report verified by your physician.

Periodically other types of tests, for example mammograms, are offered to the general public. Often these tests will require a doctor's order, but this should not be difficult to obtain if you have a family physician. If no doctor's order is required, make sure the results of your test are provided to your physician.

Free prostate screenings are also conducted by doctors and hospitals across the nation. These tests are usually offered in the fall and consist of a short questionnaire, a blood test and a prostate examination. The tests are offered free of charge and the results are reported to the physician of your choice.

These are only examples of reduced price health care opportunities. Keep an eye out for additional opportunities in your community, they can provide you with valuable medical information. You must make the first step toward taking advantage of these programs by identifying the activities and getting yourself to the right place at the right time.

Checklist
Chapters 82-87

Financial Considerations

✓ Are you prepared to pay your medical bill?

✓ Are you prepared to understand the bill?

✓ Are you prepared to question the bill if you do not think it is accurate?

✓ Do you know where to go to question the bill?

✓ Are you prepared to have the utmost patience with the billing agencies, recognizing that they all need time to complete the billing process?

✓ Are you prepared to discuss medical costs with your doctor and to question the cost and necessity of tests and procedures?

CHAPTER EIGHTY-EIGHT

Malpractice and You

If you've received a bill from your doctor recently, I bet you've spent a few minutes complaining bitterly about the high cost of health care. I couldn't blame you, if you've muttered a few bitter words about "rich doctors" or something similar.

All I ask, though, is that you believe that your doctor is just as concerned about the skyrocketing costs of medical care as you are. Most doctors try to minimize these costs as much as possible; they know that health care costs can be tough on your budget.

Even if you have insurance, you will usually have to satisfy a deductible before your insurance company pays anything; and health insurance is big business. Insurance companies have stockholders who expect them to make a profit; so if the company's expenses increase, they are passed along to you and your premium goes up.

Your doctor has expenses too. Just as you must pay electric, gas and phone bills at home, the doctor's office must meet these monthly obligations. Equipment and supplies are expensive. Staff salaries, employer social security contributions and similar items are as much a reality to your doctor as they are to your own employer.

But in recent decades, health care costs have been affected by another major but essential expense to the doctor: Malpractice insurance.

In the "old days," doctors were expected to do the very best they could when treating a sick patient, and most people accepted that their physician lived up to this obligation. If the patient did not survive, it was generally accepted as a reality of life. People got sick, and a total cure was not always possible.

Of course, those were less sophisticated days, before the arrival of microsurgery, fertility drugs and so many other complicated treatments, aimed at prolonging life or improving its quality. Those were less complicated days with few opportunities for "things to go wrong."

My, how times have changed. Today, physicians are frequently blamed for anything less than a complete recovery or a fairy tale ending to a patient's illness. There is often an unreasonable level of expectancy, and when less happens, the doctor might be sued for malpractice, with huge amounts of money at stake.

Indeed, malpractice suits have become so threatening, that many young doctors are turning their backs on some areas of medicine, rather than take the risk of being ruined by a malpractice lawsuit. Even legislators have recognized this major problem, and some states are attempting to introduce limits to the amount for which a doctor can be sued for malpractice.

Don't get me wrong. I'm not trying to tell you that doctors never make mistakes. And considering that they deal with human life and enjoy the trust of their "customers," a doctor's mistake should be open to question.

I'll even take this a step further. If a doctor makes a mistake with disastrous results, then the patient and family should certainly seek compensation. But less than acceptable results does not always add up to malpractice.

No one wants to think about the possible death or permanent disability of a loved one. But we have to face the fact that these things happen; regardless of whether we feel that "more could have been done," we have to face the fact also that medical science has its flaws and limits.

Malpractice law suits have forced doctors to pay high premiums for malpractice insurance and these costs are passed back to you on your bill. The only way to remove this burden from you, the innocent victim, is to rethink the whole issue of malpractice. When something goes wrong, fault (if it exists) should be determined with a resulting fair compensation. But if a physician does everything possible, this should be recognized also with no resulting accusations of malpractice.

Let's get our act together on this—all of us.

CHAPTER EIGHTY-NINE

With Computers, Doctor Visits Will Never Be the Same

Being a doctor used to be so uncomplicated. Appointments were noted in a schedule book; bills were recorded in a ledger; and patient examinations involved using simple, hand-held instruments.

Today, without a mainframe, a modem, a laser printer, a fax machine, computer programs and at least one mouse, the modern physician could barely cope! In other words, the health care professions have not escaped the 20th century's technological revolution.

Beginning with a call to schedule your next doctor's visit and ending with the last payment on your medical bill, computers play a role in your total health care experience.

For instance, in the old days, lab technicians worked with solutions, glass tubes and dishes to study bodily functions. Such tests have increased, both in number and complexity, and today, virtually every minute chemical in your body can be tested by computers. The lab technicians have had to master the appropriate computer technology, although they retain the expertise to handle the tests manually, if required. And upon completion, the computer-analyzed test results are sent (by computer, of course) to your doctor or hospital.

X-rays are now computer-linked, also. Earlier machines used film that had to be developed in chemical solutions much like the film from your home camera. Today's x-rays send a picture directly to a computer that analyzes the data and provides a much more sophisticated result. Other new and extremely sophisticated diagnostic machinery that are computer-assisted include the CT scan and magnetic resonance imaging (MRI).

Intravenous fluids (IVs) used to be monitored and adjusted manually every few hours. The nurse counted the drops of medication as they entered the IV tube to ensure that the patient was receiving the proper dosage. Today, IV tubing runs through a computer that regulates the medication automatically. Not only has this eliminated the chance for human error, but it allows more time for the nurse to respond to other patient care needs.

Modern technological devices are emerging that can automate almost every aspect of health care. Automatic thermometers and blood pressure cuffs are commonplace. Patients are monitored on banks of screens at a centrally-located station. In the operating room, lasers are used to remove tumors, while anesthesiologists depend on computers, as they administer the appropriate amounts of drugs and gases. Even the lowly weight scale is computerized!

Let's face it—we all know that fast food restaurants can place our order at the touch of a button. So we're probably safe in assuming that it won't be long before our doctor will be able to order diet plans, tests and medications through a computer. It will be just like McDonalds. No, you won't get a hamburger and fries, but you will get to skip the long wait at the pharmacy check-out.

A word of caution. As with anything else, computers are not infallible. Mistakes can be made, and your right to quality health care is beyond question. "The computer did it," is never an acceptable excuse, especially when your health is concerned. So stay in touch with your physician, and if you suspect a computer confused your appendectomy with another person's heart surgery, press a button or ring a bell—very loudly!

CHAPTER NINETY

Chin Up: Your Attitude Makes A Difference

Wouldn't the world be a wonderful place if medicine was an exact science and all the bugs had been worked out? But you can't compare medicine to the new car you just drove out of the showroom. Billions of dollars are spent annually on medical research, and much remains a mystery.

You read about it in the newspaper. A relatively simple surgery goes perfectly, but the patient died. Or the patient who'd been given no hope for recovery and is pronounced disease-free weeks later.

And there never seems to be a simple explanation. But one thing on which most doctors agree is that your attitude can make a significant difference to the success or failure of your health care. Realistically, if a patient abandons hope and refuses to fight, there is little that medical science can do to help.

Don't misunderstand! I'm not telling you that all you have to do is "think recover," and all will be well. But a positive attitude and self-determination can help you to accept the treatment that might restore or improve your health. Easier said than done. You're right—but what have you got to lose—other than maybe your good health or even your life?

Participate in your health care. Don't let someone push you around in a wheelchair, if your legs are in good working order and the doctor says it's OK for you walk. Bathe yourself—don't wait for the nurse to scrub your back. Be as independent as your medical condition and your physician will allow you to be.

Learn about your medical problem. Ask questions. Read material. Talk to your doctor and nurses. As a doctor, I'm disheartened when people show no interest in their own health problems. It usually indicates that they could be passive (perhaps dangerously so) about their recovery.

Smile frequently. Did you know it takes fewer muscles to smile than it does to frown? And smiling makes you feel a whole lot better, too. There's something to be said for the old cliche that laughter is the best medicine. Watch comedy shows or movies; talk to friends who make you laugh.

Set short and long-term goals; try to fulfill them. For example, walk across your room, today; walk down the hallway, tomorrow; and walk around the nurses' station on Friday. Achieving such goals will make you feel wonderful, and you'll want to try for more. Plan next year's budget or an exciting vacation. A philosopher once said that you should always be striving to reach something slightly beyond your grasp. Well, keep striving—good health is waiting for your reach.

Pray or meditate; take note of the birds or trees outside your window; consider the grass, the flowers or simply the beauty of nature in general. Make peace with yourself; you'll be surprised how relaxed you can be, if you come to terms with your own shortcomings and conscience.

Follow instructions with diligence. Listen, understand and make every attempt to do what must be done to improve your health. No pain, no gain! Many a cancer patient has added years to his or her life after accepting the unpleasant experiences of chemotherapy.

Be realistic and consider the total health problem. Medicine, therapy, good food, exercise, and the expertise of your health care team are essential to your recovery. But they cannot succeed without your help—without your positive attitude.

I had a patient once who refused insulin to control diabetes and died from a very treatable disease; another patient contributed every ounce of energy and desire to accepting unpleasant but effective treatment for cancer—and went on to live a productive and happy life.

In the world of war and athletics, it's often said that the best defense is a good offense; join the team, and you'll have a whole lot better chance of winning the game.

In Changing Society, Support Groups Abound

Families used to be larger; towns were smaller; and everybody knew their neighbors. When I was a kid, I couldn't get away with anything; someone who knew my family was sure to see me, and that spelled big trouble for little Mikey! But in those days, if one family suffered a setback or tragedy, help and emotional support was never far away.

It's so different today; this is a mobile society in which success is often measured by the number of times you've paid the moving van to haul your belongings from one large city to an even bigger city. When you experience a crisis, there's a chance you might not have known your neighbors for more than a few months—and your parents live hundreds or even thousands of miles away.

Yet, except for expert medical treatment, nothing can help someone to recover from a variety of medical and social problems like emotional and moral support. In recent decades, many support groups have been founded, often acting as substitutes for family members or close friends. The results can be amazing. I've witnessed many patients who joined such groups as Reach for Recovery (breast cancer patients) and the Stroke Club who made remarkable recoveries. Buoyed by the support they received, they were able to move ahead with their lives and deal with their misfortune.

Most people are familiar with the reputation of Alcoholics Anonymous (AA); but did you know there are similar groups to help people with drug and gambling addictions? There's also support groups for people with weight problems and for those struggling to accept their fate, perhaps as a result of a stroke or a crippling accident. Probably the largest and most powerful support group is the American Association of Retired Persons (AARP) whose concern is for the senior citizens of America. Indeed, there are support groups for virtually every problem—but the onus is on you to find the one you need.

Usually, support groups do not seek out "clients," believing that an individual's desire to belong must motivate him or her to search for and find the appropriate group. Some groups advertise in the phone book (and some even have toll-free numbers); your local hospital should be able to give you some helpful information; local health agencies, coworkers, and ministers are also excellent sources for referrals.

Support groups ask you to make a commitment to attend meetings and to develop a positive relationship with the other group members. Sometimes, family members are asked to participate also—but the fact that you have made the initial move to seek help is the primary consideration.

Most people hesitate to join support groups and resist the group process, hating to share their troubles with "strangers." With the realization that everyone in the group has a similar problem—and can, therefore, offer help, sympathy and advice, most participants take a massive step toward resolving their personal conflict.

Of course, the problem that you must face is usually shared by your family; if you drink too much, it impacts the lives of everyone around, and they must cope also. Several support groups have been founded with such families in mind; for instance, Alateen is for the teenage children of alcoholics. And there are support groups for families of patients with Alzheimer's disease, and the hospice movement offers comfort and aid when there is no hope for recovery.

I'm a good example of the positive influence of group support. After joining a support group, I was able to lose 40 pounds; I looked better and felt healthier; but then I made the classic error. Instead of continuing to attend my group meeting, I decided I didn't need the group any more. What a mistake! Within a few months, I had gained back all the weight I'd struggled to lose.

Take some friendly advice, will you? If you suspect that a support group could help you through a crisis—look for one; find one; join one.

Let's face it, folks! Everybody needs somebody. Why should you be so different?

CHAPTER NINETY-TWO

Patients Have A Responsibility to Learn About Health

I remember as a child visiting the Amish area of Pennsylvania and learning about their customs. They have so many wise sayings, and at an Amish restaurant, I saw a sign that read: "We get too soon old and too late smart." It must have made an impression, because I never forgot its wisdom, and recently, I saw another sign that gave me more food for thought: "If you think education is expensive, try ignorance."

I know you don't have the time to listen to all my views on education, but let's take just a few minutes to think about one aspect: Education and health—your health. No, I'm not suggesting that everyone goes to medical school and becomes a doctor; but I am suggesting that when it's your health at stake, making the effort to get explanations and to understand what is happening is to your advantage.

It is important for a patient to be knowledgeable about his or her body and health problems; and you don't need a college education or a medical degree. The one necessary prerequisite is a determined desire to know and to be informed.

Before you arrive at your doctor's office, make a list of questions you want to ask. Don't allow the physician to overpower you with long, complicated words; insist on explanations being given in language you understand. As I tell my students: There is no such thing as a dumb question. Make a note of each answer—don't trust to memory. Later, if you think of more questions, write them down and ask them next time. If you feel an immediate answer is truly necessary, call your doctor's office.

There are many other ways you can help yourself to understand. For instance, visit your local library; most libraries have ample information about virtually every medical problem known to science.

Maybe you could attend patient education classes. Check within your community to see if there are any provided by hospitals, medical societies, civic organizations or other concerned groups. It is not unusual to find that organizations such as the American Diabetes Association or the American Heart Association provide opportunities for the public to become educated in these specific subjects.

Videotapes are available (often from libraries, bookstores, hospitals or concerned organizations), and even television can be helpful. Some channels (for example, Discovery, Lifetime and Public Television) are very cognizant of the public's desire "to know," and offer a lot of medicine-oriented programs.

But be careful. Medical information that is designed to help you understand your health needs or health problems is not intended to be a substitute for "the real thing." Just as you can't expect to win the US Open after watching one or two Arnold Palmer tapes, neither can you expect to be a medical expert without the necessary years of formal training. Work with your doctor; talk to your doctor; but please, don't try to play doctor!

**Checklist
Chapters 90-92**

Self Help

✓ Are you prepared to participate in your health care?
✓ Are you willing to be educated about your medical problems?
   Medical Library
   Local library
   Newspaper and Magazines
   Television
   Reading material supplied by your physician
✓ Are you willing to seek help from family, friends and support groups when such help is needed?
✓ Are you prepared to work to regain your health, follow instructions by the medical team and suffer some pain for the gain?

CHAPTER NINETY-THREE

Imagine Yourself Handicapped—Act To Help Others

One of the best ways to take care of your own health is to be concerned about the health of others! In health care, as well as in most other areas of life, there's something to be said for treating others the way you would want to be treated.

For instance, you don't have the flu, but someone arrives at work complaining of aches and a fever. Everyone knows "its" going around! Well, if you suspect your co-worker has "it," you should insist that your friend goes home and takes care of him or herself. You will sound extremely caring and compassionate; however, you are acting in your own best interests, too. You don't want to catch "it" as well, do you?

Let me ask a question or two: Do you ever try to understand the other guy's point of view? Have you ever really set aside some time to consider what you would do or how you would handle your life if you were blind or hearing impaired or physically handicapped?

Consider this: Suddenly, you are struck down in a major accident and find that you will never be able to walk again; you will have to use a wheelchair for the rest of your life. You recognize that you are fortunate: you can see and hear; touch and think; and you set out to continue your life. But your world has changed. You can't cross the street, because there's no ramp for your wheelchair, and your favorite restaurant is lost forever, for the same reason. It's difficult to get in and out of your office building, because the doors are not automatic; and the handicapped parking spots always seem to be taken by others whose only problem appears to be laziness.

You are outraged! The world does not consider the needs of the handicapped. And then you feel a sense of shame, because you know that before your accident, you never took even a minute to think about the problems of the physically challenged. Never once did you wonder whether there was something you could do—because you would appreciate some consideration under similar circumstances. And although the above scenario is fiction for you, it's a fact of life for thousands of

Americans—but you can help. If you notice areas in your community that do not accommodate the handicapped—speak up. Talk to store owners who have not yet installed access ramps; write letters to your congressman, city officials, and county representatives complaining about public facilities that continue to ignore the needs of the physically impaired.

There might be a support group or lobby organization for physically challenged individuals that would welcome your help; you can stuff envelopes or make phone calls. You can get involved.

The world can be a hazardous place even for the healthiest of people. But for the visually handicapped, those in wheelchairs or the hearing impaired, it can provide untold obstructions to their most valiant efforts to lead a normal life.

Show compassion and support (not pity) for those who face such obstacles. Care about the other guy—just as you'd want others to care about you. You just never know, do you?

CHAPTER NINETY-FOUR

Vacation Can Be A Health Care Nightmare

We're a jet-set society. In a matter of hours we can be anywhere—or nowhere.

The middle of the Atlantic Ocean at 30,000 feet can be "the middle of nowhere," if your health is threatened. We often forget about the hidden dangers of travelling, as we hop on a plane, blithely assuming that most of the comforts of home have somehow boarded the plane with us. After all, there's hot food, cocktails, well-cushioned seats and pleasant company. But the interior of an airplane, a ship, train or bus can become a very remote site if you have a heart attack or go into a diabetic shock.

Two of my cousins had vastly different experiences while travelling. While on a Caribbean resort island, one of them developed a painful condition that required minor surgery. Fortunately, he was in an English-speaking country with reasonably good health care, and he found a surgeon who treated him smoothly and efficiently.

The other cousin had a heart attack aboard a cruise ship. The ship had limited medical facilities and a doctor who could not provide the appropriate care. My cousin was evacuated by a small boat, across rough seas to a hospital. The trip took several hours and he was lucky to survive.

Nothing can be more relaxing than a vacation to an exotic, faraway place, and a fear of the medical consequences should not prevent the adventurer from exploring the world. If you are planning a trip outside the United States, be prepared.

Know your body and its limitations. Choose a place that suits your health. If you burn easily in the sun, avoid tropical climates. Vacations in high altitudes are not advisable for people with heart trouble. If you have problems with walking, don't visit somewhere that requires a lot of "getting around." Choose your destination wisely.

Investigate the need for immunizations and other preventive or protective measures. It might not be required, but it's safer to have the shot, if in doubt.

If you are taking medication, be sure to have an adequate supply and an extra supply packed separately. Not that I'm suggesting that some of your luggage could get lost! (I once asked an airline to check two bags—one to Chicago and the other to San Francisco. The agent said "I can't, you're going to Houston." I said, "Why not? You did it last week!")

You could need additional "preventive" medicine you wouldn't require at home, such as motion sickness pills, or medications for intestinal problems. It can't hurt to carry a supply in your purse or pocket, can it?

Plan ahead and assume the worst. Most people plan for the best, knowing the names of the best restaurants and the whitest beaches. But they've no idea what to do if they get ill, or even what kind of health care is provided. Do your homework. It could save your life.

If you should get ill or seriously hurt while travelling, there are several sources of help. If you are in a major hotel, then there might be a doctor on the premises, but if not, the hotel manager can get medical services for you. You could call the police or contact the American Consulate for advice or support. If you are with a tour group, the group leader should be able to assist in finding medical help. And before you leave home, ask the travel agency about existing arrangements to take care of medical emergencies.

If you do visit a hospital or doctor's office in a foreign country, follow established customs and rules. Try to make sure that your physician has the appropriate credentials—maybe there is a diploma or two on the office wall—and if you have to ask, be discrete! And most importantly, be sure you are understood and that you understand the doctor. Don't assume the doctor speaks English—you are the guest in his or her country!

Getting proper health care abroad can be difficult, but it is manageable if you plan ahead. So have a good trip—and send me a postcard: All is well, doc, glad you're not here?

Checklist
Chapter 94

Vacation Preparation

✓ Before leaving have you:
    Received appropriate immunizations?
    Packed a good supply of appropriate medications?
    Packed enough preventive medications?
    Determined what medical facilities are available at your
        destination?
✓ During travel have you reserved enough medications to carry
    with you should you become separated from your luggage?
✓ Have you evaluated the health care available and made contin-
    gency plans should you need help?
✓ Have you and your travel companions learned CPR?

CHAPTER NINETY-FIVE

Prevention Beats Treatment Every Time

Cancer! One word that strikes fear into the hearts of almost every person who hears it. We lower our voices, as if this will make a difference, much as young children think that if they cover their eyes and can't see you, then you cannot see them either. But cancer is a reality, and we must accept its existence and deal with its effects.

Cancer is one of the major causes of death each year. There are many kinds of cancer, ranging from the types that are easily treated (if caught early enough) such as some types of skin cancer to the devastating, harder-to-treat tumors, such as brain cancer.

It's time to rethink cancer, AIDS and other tragic diseases that conjure up abject fear and feelings of hopelessness; it's time to remember that there are other diseases that are life-threatening also. For instance, heart disease is the leading cause of death among Americans. Diabetes kills thousands each year. Addictions to alcohol and drugs can be fatal, as well as causing immeasurable emotional distress.

But even though cancer should not be feared, because it can be treated and managed aggressively through prompt care, isn't it even better to deal with it before the disease invades our body and forces us to fight back?

The key is preventive medicine. We must respect our bodies and conduct our lives such that we protect ourselves as much as possible. For instance, quit smoking and reduce the risk of lung cancer; adjust your diet (more fiber and less fat;) breast examinations, mammograms and PAP smears for women and testicular and prostate examinations for men should be mandatory; regular physical examinations should be automatic. No, we don't guarantee that following this advice will protect you from cancer; but early detection means a faster and better chance of survival.

If you are overweight and have a history of diabetes in your family, your chances for diabetes increase every day. Do what you know you must do. Join a weight-loss support group, adopt a sensible diet and exercise program—take care of yourself. Diabetes can be fatal.

If you believe that you may be at risk for AIDS, then get tested for the antibody to the AIDS virus. Knowing you are positive will not mean instant death. Rather it will allow you to manage your condition. Many people have been HIV-positive for years and have shown no signs of the disease. But the wise ones go in for periodic checks of their T-cell levels and monitoring of certain blood components. If signs of the disease begin, they can be given anti-viral drugs such as AZT.

Risk for heart disease can be lessened by quitting smoking, cutting down on drinking, adopting a regular exercise program, and reducing fat, cholesterol and salt in the diet. Remember that heart disease is an accumulative disease. Poor diet for long periods of time can lead to that sudden heart attack. (And keep this in mind as you fix dinner for the kids!)

Practice preventive medicine. Take charge. Look to the future.

CHAPTER NINETY-SIX

Help Yourself With Proper Self Examinations

The adage "What you don't know can't hurt you" doesn't ring true in the case of medicine, especially in the practice of preventive health care.

What you don't know about the changing conditions of your own body can lead to severe medical complications if left unattended. Whether male or female, I believe each of us must take an active role in our own health care. And, self-examination of our bodies is one of the most important steps we can take along the path of preventive health care.

Disease can pop up when we least expect it. Prevention and/or early detection of disease are keys to successful treatment. You can help in this regard. In fact, you are the most important factor in a successful preventive health care program. Self-examination before visiting your physician will help to ensure your good health.

Frequent breast examination is essential for all women. This fast, easy and pain-free process could save your life. Your doctor can demonstrate how to perform the examination and can provide educational materials on it, as well. If your physician does not bring up the subject, then you should ask him or her about it yourself.

Women are not alone in the area of self-examination. Self-examination of the testicles is as important for men as examination of the breast is for women. This also is a painless and easy to perform procedure that takes only a few minutes. Ask your doctor for details on how to perform this important examination.

Each of us has moles, marks and blemishes on our bodies. Regular self-examinations should include checking these blemishes to ensure they don't change in appearance and that new ones do not develop. Any unusual lump, bump or sore that does not heal can potentially cause trouble and should be examined by your doctor—the sooner, the better.

Physicians do not expect you to replace their examinations with your own. You will not be asked to make a diagnosis. All you are expected to do is recognize that the results of your latest self-examination are different from the previous one. You know something has changed and should now make an appointment to have the change further examined by a doctor.

There are other precautions you can take in addition to self-examinations. Periodic visits for such things as eye exams, mammograms and prostate gland checks are some of the necessary steps to help prevent the development of disease. Ask you doctor for details.

CHAPTER NINETY-SEVEN

Blood And What To Do About It

Blood is a life-giving fluid. It carries oxygen from the lungs throughout the body, supplying tissues with the nutrients necessary to function properly.

Blood is transported by way of the veins and arteries and it was only a few centuries ago that the function of the veins and arteries was fully understood. The arteries carry oxygenated blood to the tissues and veins return the blood to the lungs (via the heart) for more oxygen.

That's the way everything is supposed to work. But, things don't always function as they're supposed to. The same goes for blood. For a variety of reasons, blood often escapes from the veins and arteries (the vascular system) unexpectedly appearing elsewhere in the body. When this happens, trouble may not be far behind.

Many people are scared by the sight of blood. Actually, this is one of blood's most important functions—to alarm. The sight of blood can draw attention to a health problem that might have otherwise gone unnoticed.

Still, some people choose to ignore the warning sign of blood. They may not understand the seriousness of the situation, or perhaps their fear of the unknown keeps them from seeking professional help. I call this "the ostrich syndrome." Never ignore the presence of blood, it does no good to stick your head in the sand and hide from the truth.

Bleeding can result from a simple problem. Take a nose bleed, for instance. A sneeze can be enough to cause the fragile tissue lining of your nose to bleed. But, a nose bleed can also signal a more serious problem, especially if the bleeding does not stop quickly with the application of pressure.

The same is true for bleeding from the skin, mouth or ears. While the injury may be minor in nature, bleeding from these locations may also be the sign of a more serious condition and should not be neglected. Also, blood that appears in the eye that does not result from a trauma, should be promptly investigated.

You should always visit a physician if blood is found under these circumstances:

1. *Vomiting up blood*
2. *Blood in your urine*
3. *Blood in your stool (bowel movement)*

Even if the bleeding occurred only once or twice, still mention it to your physician, who will likely investigate further to determine the source of the bleeding.

Any unusual vaginal bleeding should always be investigated by your physician. Normal menstrual periods are one thing, but if you experience bleeding between or after periods, or heavy and unusual bleeding, then consult your doctor.

The bottom line is that blood is essential to life but its presence outside the vascular system is a warning that should never be ignored.

CHAPTER NINETY-EIGHT

Relaxation On A Budget

Sounds great, doesn't it? Who wouldn't want a visit a luxurious resort spa frequented by the rich and famous for expensive and exotic treatments like volcanic mud baths, boysenberry facials and Yugoslavian massages?

Probably neither of us could afford to visit places like these, but wouldn't it be wonderful? What this world really needs is a poor person's spa.

But, what does the spa really do for you? Once you weed through the gimmicks and special features each spa uses to distinguish itself from the crowd, what's left? The real answer, I think, is that visiting such a place allows you to take a break from your daily routine and relax without interruptions from the real world.

There is no question in my mind that the ability to get away from it all and not be forever tied down to your work or other daily activities, plays a major role in maintaining your sanity and rejuvenating your spirit so you can face the daily grind more easily. And, I believe you can do this at a relatively modest expense.

Don't get me wrong. I have absolutely nothing against fancy spas. If you can afford them—great! (In fact, if you can afford to treat yourself *and* your family physician, I'll gladly volunteer as your doctor!) If, on the other hand, you can't afford several thousand dollars for a week-long visit to a spa, then you need to find an alternative.

You don't have to take a full week away from the office, but perhaps you can find time for a long weekend. You may be amazed that your office or business will run smoothly even without your daily presence. However, that realization may produce some anxiety. Just remember that if arranged properly, you probably could take several days—even weeks off and not be missed. When this is the case, your's is a job well done in an atmosphere conducive to efficiency and cooperation.

Now, where to go and what to do? If the real secret is to just get away from the daily grind, you shouldn't have to go very far. In fact, you only have to go the next town or the closest hotel. That's right. Make a reservation at a local hotel, don't tell anyone where you're going and don't make or accept any telephone calls. You might also unplug the television and avoid the newspaper.

Don't worry, there will still be plenty to do. Many hotels offer a variety of activities for their guests. Visit the swimming pool, enjoy the jacuzzi or work out in the fitness center. Exercise is important to your general good health and if you haven't exercised in a while this would be a good time to begin again.

If you choose a resort type hotel, you have even more choices, perhaps tennis, golf, the beach or all three. You will be able to keep as busy or become as lazy as you desire. Just make sure to do whatever YOU want, not what your spouse or children or anyone else demands of you.

This is your treat to yourself.

There will certainly be a dining room or nearby restaurant at the hotel. Check out the menu. Does it include healthy choices? As it turns out, the healthiest choices are often the least expensive items on the menu. So, you win twice—once in the fat department and again in the pocketbook. If you took a survey of expensive spas, you would likely find the most expensive are the ones that include diet control during your stay. But at your less expensive hotel, you can enjoy leisurely meals of your choice.

I know you will be a different person upon your return to civilization and your daily routine. But should your symptoms reappear, this prescription can be refilled at any time.

CHAPTER NINETY-NINE

When the Mind Gets Ill, Treatment Is Available

For centuries, society refused to recognize mental illness as a medical condition. We've all seen old movies or read books whose mentally-ill characters exist in the deplorable conditions of an insane asylum or are victims of cruelty or derision.

Unfortunately, even in today's enlightened age, the perceptions have not changed greatly. Many people continue to view mental illness as something less than a bona fide medical problem; they reject its existence; it is often a matter for shame and rejection.

Isn't it time we put an end to the ignorance and dispel the myths of mental illness? To put this whole thing into perspective? To understand the problems?

Your mind is just as much part of you as your legs. If you break your leg, you seek treatment and do whatever is necessary to repair the damage. By the same token, if you are mentally ill, you should seek treatment; and you should do whatever is necessary to repair the damage. It's that simple.

Today, most hospitals that specialize in treating mental disorders are modern facilities, often located in pastoral settings designed to create a peaceful atmosphere; they are staffed with medical and mental health professionals dedicated to their work. Such hospitals employ psychologists, psychiatrists, social workers, nurses, therapists, counselors, clergymen and other qualified professionals.

Mental health professionals understand your problems, this is their specialty, and they understand the potentially horrendous consequences of an illness that is left untreated. The clinically depressed can become suicidal; the alcoholic might self destruct, ending a promising career; while a schizophrenic can live a devastating life, alienating family and even joining the ranks of the homeless.

Early diagnosis and treatment are essential. No major illness—diabetes, cancer, AIDS or mental disorder—will cure itself, and all will become progressively worse and life threatening if left untreated.

But there is a truly strange phenomenon. You suspect that you might be a diabetic, and you go to a doctor; you suspect that you might be depressed, and you make excuses: "All I need is a long weekend away from the office." "If Frank would just quit giving me a hard time, I'd be OK."

Additionally, many people fear that if they admit to mental illness, they might lose their job. Perhaps the doctor will not honor patient confidentiality. Maybe the insurance company won't pay for therapy. The family will be embarrassed.

Well, folks, it's time to get a few things straight. First, it's illegal to fire someone for seeking medical treatment for a legitimate illness; so you've got that one covered. Second, most insurance company's include treatment for mental illness. Check with your company or switch to one that offers the appropriate coverage. Third, patient confidentiality is mandatory; mental health professionals are committed to this philosophy just as much as any other professional in any area of medicine. And finally, if your family and friends have stuck with you during the dark days, they'll surely be delighted to support and help your endeavors to recover.

It takes courage to admit that you have any medical problem (ask a cancer or AIDS patient how they reacted upon hearing the news). It's no different for patients with mental health problems. But help is available.

Find a good treatment facility and mental health physician (your family doctor or clergyman can usually point you in the right direction). Make a commitment to the prescribed treatment and stay with it. It can take years to develop mental health problems, and it can takes years (even a lifetime) to recover; there is no miracle cure or wonder drug. But you can win. It's up to you.

You Can Help, If You Know First Aid

You're walking down the street. Suddenly, a teenager loses control of his bike, falls into a plate glass window and cuts his arm severely. Blood spurts in all directions, a crowd gathers, and someone dashes off to the nearest phone to call for help. But, the unfortunate reality of this scenario is that the young man could actually bleed to death before an ambulance arrives, because no one in the crowd was qualified to apply even the simplest first aid to stem the flow of blood from an injured artery.

You do not have to be a doctor or a nurse to understand how to apply pressure to a teenager's arm to stop the bleeding or how to help a child whose fallen into your backyard pool. Indeed, first aid classes are available in most towns and usually at a very reasonable cost. Such an investment is particularly worthwhile when you consider that the ability to render first aid in an emergency situation—and perhaps save a life—might be the most valuable thing you learn throughout your entire life.

If you've never considered taking a first aid class, perhaps now is the time to sign up! Contact the American Red Cross, your local "Y", or even your personal physician; first aid classes will be available somewhere in your area—and someone can point you in the right direction. It could even be a good idea to make first aid classes a "family affair." A certain amount of comfort can be gained from the knowledge that if you get sick or need immediate help, someone else in your home is qualified to assist you. In addition to actual first aid training, programs will often teach participants peripheral skills, such as how to remain calm in an emergency; how to incorporate the help of bystanders; how to summon professional help quickly; and how, in general, to assume the leadership role on a temporary basis.

Not many years ago, people (including doctors and nurses) were afraid to stop at the scene of an accident, because they could be held liable for any negative results of the first aid they might render. Today, however, there are "good samaritan" laws that protect medical professionals and others from such liability, if their intent was to provide help in such an emergency situation.

There are other possible advantages to taking a first aid class, too. Once exposed to the basic concepts, you might well be motivated to learn even more advanced techniques. It's not beyond the realm of possibility that you could be tempted to pursue a new career—to become an emergency medical technician or a paramedic.

I have to admit—I am a bit of a nag, as far as first aid training is concerned. Why? Well, as a doctor, I have witnessed so many incidents when a life might have been saved or an injured patient might have suffered less, if someone—just one person in that crowd of curious bystanders—had been able to help; had been able to apply the techniques that he or she had learned at first aid class.

CHAPTER ONE HUNDRED ONE

Don't Be A Helpless Bystander; Learn CPR

In my business, I do a lot of travelling, attending scientific meetings and visiting other doctors. However, in all my travels, only once have I been called upon to use my knowledge of emergency care to help a passenger in distress, fortunately with a happy ending.

I am a firm believer in the fact that cardiopulmonary resuscitation (CPR) should be required instruction in every American school. Seldom are there warning signals when someone is about to need help from this life-saving technique. And to find yourself in the role of helpless by-stander can leave you feeling angry and frustrated that there was nothing you could do to help.

Yes, CPR has saved thousands of lives. It is comparatively easy to learn; you don't need a medical degree; and classes are usually offered in most communities through such agencies as the American Red Cross, local hospitals, churches, first aid organizations, and the fire department or similar EMS group. Learning CPR is not limited to the physically strong or muscle-bound individual. Anyone can learn; even those with certain physical disabilities can use their expertise by guiding others through the process.

It takes but a few hours to complete a CPR course, but the skill you learn will be with you for the rest of your life. Just think, if you save one life, because you took a few hours to learn CPR, can you imagine a greater sense of accomplishment or reward? And if that life is your father's or your child's?

One of the greatest improvements to CPR education has been the introduction of "Resusci-Annie," one of the smartest dummies ever created. She will tell you if you are applying CPR correctly or incorrectly; she will help you to master the right way to breath and to do chest compressions. You will be delighted when you see the light that indicates that you have saved Annie's life!

We are all fortunate that there exists a CPR method that is both easy to learn and effective. CPR is for everyone. It can be performed easily on adults and on children; and you don't need special tools or medications—just some training, a little common sense, and the desire to save a life. (I've even heard of instances when people saved their pet's life by applying CPR. But don't try it on your goldfish—that would get a bit messy!)

Do yourself a favor! Enroll in a CPR class as soon as possible. Like the proverbial boy scout—be prepared.

CHAPTER ONE HUNDRED TWO

Most Accidents Happen In The Home

It's no accident that one of the most common causes of trips to the doctor's office or emergency room is—accidents. How do we avoid these unpredictable occurrences? The best advice is that "an ounce of prevention is worth a pound of cure."

Statistics show that most accidents occur in the home. A quick trip around the premises will reveal whether your home is "accident proof." Begin outside. Is the entry in good repair or is someone likely to trip on uneven pavement or broken steps? How quickly can you enter and leave the house?

Moving indoors, examine the halls and stairways. Could rugs that slip and slide cause someone to fall? If elderly Aunt Alice were to take a tumble, could she injure herself further on the sharp objects decorating the hallways and tabletops? And, what about the banisters? Are they secure enough to give aid in climbing the stairs?

Fire hazards in the home can be numerous. Examine the electrical wiring. Install plug protectors in unused outlets and make sure those outlets in use are not overloaded. Are space heaters located near flammable materials? And most importantly, make sure your smoke detectors are in proper working order.

Let's move on to the kitchen and bathrooms, two of the more dangerous rooms in the house. Sharp objects, boiling liquids on a hot stove, microwave ovens and numerous other obstacles make kitchens an accident waiting to happen. And, the combination of electrical appliances and running water can make accidents in the bathroom a "shocking experience."

Your home can be a dangerous place for your family and visitors. (And you thought physicians stopped making house calls for reasons involving time and money!) It's impossible to completely rid your home of all hazards, but many accidents could be prevented if homeowners would take these initial steps. Make a thorough examination of your house and property. Identify problem areas and correct any potential dangers. Then, review your home periodically for future problem development.

CHAPTER ONE HUNDRED THREE

You Can't Be Too Safe—Use All The Devices You Can

When I was a kid, I wanted a motorbike in the worst possible way! And I vividly remember the bitter arguments with my parents, when they refused to consider even the possibility. Years later, the scenario was replayed between my son and me—and I became the "bad guy."

It's not that I have anything against motorcycles—not really. Most of us realize that a two-wheel vehicle is less stable and potentially more dangerous than a four-wheel vehicle. And one visit to a hospital emergency room after a motorbike accident victim has been admitted is sufficient to confirm a parent's worst fears when a son or daughter makes an ardent plea for this form of transportation.

But any type of machinery or mechanized equipment can be dangerous, if the right precautions are not taken. It always amazes me that airplane passengers don't hesitate to fasten their seatbelts when requested to do so, but many of those same people struggle with rush hour traffic on the freeway without applying the same precaution. Even though most states have introduced laws enforcing the use of automobile seat belts, it's unbelievable how many people find excuses not to use them. Yet statistics show clearly that seatbelts save lives. Many law enforcement officers have been quoted as saying that they have never unbuckled a dead person!

And what about eyeglasses, especially the protective kind? Regular eyeglasses can shatter if struck by a piece of flying metal, and specially constructed safety glasses should always be worn when you're working around any type of material that can damage the eyes. No one wants to be blinded, because he or she was too stubborn to wear safety glasses either at work or while pursuing a favorite hobby. It can take but a split second for an unexpected or "freak" accident to change a person's life forever.

But let's get back to the motorbike for a minute! No, I can't make you wear a safety helmet; but I can tell you that most motorbike accident victims suffering from devastating or fatal head injuries were not wearing a helmet. And safety belts in your car? Maybe it's sufficient to say that after many years of tending to accident victims in the emergency room, I think there are very few tragedies that can top the sight of a badly injured child whose been hurled into the dashboard or through the windshield of a car because he or she was not wearing a safety belt.

Of course, nothing is 100 percent absolutely safe! But every safety device used brings you a whole lot closer to being protected than if you make no effort at all.

CHAPTER ONE HUNDRED FOUR

"No Pain, No Gain, No Beautiful Body"

I hope you don't mind, but I'm not writing this chapter for you; I'm writing it for me! We all have our faults, right? And I confess: I'm really good at giving advice but leave a lot to be desired when it comes to taking it. So I thought if I wrote a chapter about the benefits of exercise, with your help, maybe I could be persuaded to heed my own words.

We all know people who are into aerobics, jogging, health clubs or running marathons. Keeping fit is their obsession, and if they miss a day or two they suffer withdrawal symptoms and feelings of guilt. We choose to ignore their lean, muscular bodies, their thinly disguised smile as they survey our flab, and the knowledge that they'll probably enjoy longer, healthier lives than we will. We have good reasons to avoid exercise, right? Too busy. Overwhelmed with work. Too cold. Too hot. Don't want to sweat. (If it's any comfort, horses sweat; men perspire; and women glow!)

Let's face it! There really is no good excuse to avoid exercise, and as the old expression goes: If you can't beat 'em, join 'em. First, check with your doctor to make sure your planned program is right for you. This is especially important if you suspect you might have some genuine physical problem that should limit your amount of exercise. Then start slowly, gradually increasing the amount of time and the level of difficulty. Remember, you can't become an incredible hulk in two or three days!

There are many types of good exercise, depending on your personal preferences. Walking, jogging, cycling and swimming are all extremely healthy forms of exercise that require little or no expense and can be personally monitored. Aerobic classes, from beginners to advanced levels, can be found in most communities. And don't forget the video tapes aimed to please all age groups (and tastes in music!)

For the more ambitious, health clubs abound, ranging from the "Y," to the more expensive private clubs. I realize that to the uninformed, much of the equipment might look like shiny tools of torture; but with the correct plan and qualified supervision, most people can benefit from the conglomeration of bars, weights and pulleys. You won't become another Arnold Schwarzenegger overnight—but you could be fitter and healthier than you ever dreamed possible.

Over and above the generally-accepted notion that "exercise is healthy," there are many specific benefits. Usually, people who exercise have a better chance to avoid cardiovascular diseases and problems with their blood pressure. They are stronger and faster. If you're involved in a weight loss program, exercise is virtually mandatory. Not only will it help you to burn up the calories, but you'll want to tighten up the muscles and get rid of the loose skin when you shed all those pounds, won't you?

And exercise can save you money! In itself, it is a form of preventive medicine, creating a healthier you and reducing the number of times you have to visit your doctor's office.

I started my own aerobics and muscle building program some time ago, but to date, my devotion has not reached the proportion of a magnificent obsession. Unfortunately, I don't feel guilty if I miss a day—and have used all the available excuses. Of course, I don't have a beautiful body, either.

CHAPTER ONE HUNDRED FIVE

I Discovered Something New—Medical Research Is Essential

It's every scientist's dream! To discover something new! To become a Louis Pasteur, a Madame Curie or a Jonas Salk. To become an immortal in medical research history because of an invaluable contribution!

There is no question that medical research, particularly in the last 50 years, has made incredible progress. Some diseases have been rendered virtually extinct; transplant surgery prolongs life; and dozens of treatments and techniques now give hope to millions of people every year.

But scientific advancement is neither a new phenomenon nor an accidental occurrence. Just as today's discoveries often depend upon yesterday's efforts, progress in the 21st century will be a continuation of everything that preceded it. Scientists will continue to be challenged by the need to invent new surgical techniques or frustrated by the emergence of diseases for which there is no cure.

But the scientific community needs your help. Look at it this way: Maybe, your grandfather's generation was the first to benefit from the invention of anesthesia; perhaps your parents were the first to benefit from antibiotics; and you might well be the first to benefit from a kidney transplant. But what will your children and grandchildren need? How can we help to ensure that scientific research continues, so that future generations benefit, as we have done?

We must not forget that scientific research and the resulting progress require huge amounts of financial support—and we must find a way to provide that backing. Yet, the medical profession understands that a plea for support for expensive research efforts might appear somewhat outrageous—given the ever-increasing costs of patient care. But an investment today can decrease tomorrow's costs, as future patients experience faster cures, shorter hospital stays, fewer visits to the doctor's office, and longer, more productive lives.

Future support for medical research will require everyone's blessing as larger amounts of tax dollars are dedicated to research through state or federal funding. We ask that you understand this need, realizing and accepting that you and all future generations will benefit from that acceptance.

Truthfully (and with great regret), I don't think I'll ever personally invent anything that will make me a "legend in my own mind." I've tried to get a local restaurant to help out be naming something for me—Dover Sole Michael or Warren a la Mode, maybe—but that's not happened yet, either.

CHAPTER ONE HUNDRED SIX

Donations to Medical Research

You probably don't need me to tell you that health care costs are high and continue to rise at a phenomenal rate. I try to keep costs down for my patients but their bills still strain their budgets and upset their insurance companies.

One reason for the increase in health care costs, particularly in the past two or three decades, is the incredible expense of maintaining and updating equipment in our technological world.

There's no doubt that technology is allowing medicine to diagnose, treat and even cure more efficiently and more often that ever before. Computer enhanced x-rays, magnetic resonance imaging, and radioactive materials are used to view the body's interior; and new and more effective antibiotics and other drugs have been developed.

But new technology does not happen accidentally; there is no magic wand. It takes research; and research costs money—for people, materials, and testing and a lot of other elements that ultimately combine to give you better treatment and a longer life expectancy.

Funding for research comes from a variety of sources; but just as you find toward the end of the month when your check book is almost empty, there never seems to be enough.

One major source for research funding is the federal government. And there is little doubt that without the government's involvement, medical research would still be stumbling around in its infancy. Other public funds are made available from state and local agencies; and private foundations and corporations contribute heavily to research efforts.

The health care industry has also become an important funding source for research, especially pharmaceutical companies which recognize a potential benefit for their organizations. Physicians, too, have donated, either individually or through major foundations, some of their private income to medical research, recognizing the benefits of enhanced medical knowledge to mankind.

Finally, donations from private individuals can make a difference. Such donations can be given directly to research institutions or through contributions to charitable organizations that support research endeavors. Private donations of this nature also help to reduce health care costs by supplementing governmental and other sources of research funding.

Would you like to help? No amount is too little or too much; and every dime will be appreciated.

Perhaps you'd like to make a contribution to honor someone else: Your parents' golden wedding anniversary; your child's college graduation; the birth of a grandson; a memorial.

Hospitals and medical schools usually have a development department whose function is to take care of raising funds. Most development officers will be happy to send you some brochures or similar literature that describes the ways your contribution can help medical research. And sometimes, you can benefit directly—with such things as tax-deductible contributions.

Ultimately, medical research benefits everyone; perhaps not this generation; but your children or grandchildren, for sure. And what's wrong with that!

CHAPTER ONE HUNDRED SEVEN

New Technology In Health Care

I'm writing this today! But by the time you read it tomorrow, it will need updating, because new technology will already be available to bring additional expertise to the world of medicine.

In a way, the ultimate goal of medicine is to eliminate the need for all doctors! A pipe dream maybe—because can we ever cure all diseases? Will there ever be a time when we eradicate one scourge from the face of the earth without finding that another, unknown, mysterious sickness has emerged?

But the medical progress of the past few decades cannot be denied. Diagnostic procedures, surgery and treatment often include medicine and methodology that just twenty or thirty years ago might have sounded like something from science fiction. Computers, lasers, magnets and a host of other technological marvels allow physicians to scrutinize every part of your body, from the smallest cell to the largest organ.

Today, patients often benefit from faster and more diagnoses, less painful surgical procedures, briefer hospital stays and shorter recuperation time.

Unfortunately, however, progress cannot be made without paying a price; and when medical research is involved, that price can be astronomical. Sophisticated equipment, years of research, and more years of testing all combine to impact the final cost of progress. And the question remains: Is the cost worth the benefit?

The immediate answer is, of course, obvious: New technology prolongs and saves lives. The young grow to adulthood and the maimed can recover to enjoy productive years. Advances must be encouraged and supported—but are we, as a nation, prepared to pay the price?

Necessarily, insurance costs will increase and personal contributions to health care will escalate. And when government programs are involved, expenses are passed on to the public in the form of taxes.

Some might suggest alternatives. For instance, the concept of rationing expensive tests could be considered. But who will make the decision? Who will choose between one patient or another? Organ transplantation is particularly vulnerable to the possibility of debate and choice, since the need far outweighs the availability. But each life is precious, and who is to say which is more valuable or deserving to be saved?

Another alternative is to create a national policy to slow the development and application of new technology. But this raises yet another moral issue: It is simply contrary to the nature of a thinking humanity to turn its back on progress and refuse to apply new technology, once it's a *fait accompli*. Just imagine having penicillin and the polio vaccine and not using them! Unthinkable!

Of course, we must all be grateful for medical progress and thankful for recent and future developments. But we must be prepared to play a role in the ethical debates that will surely arise regarding their use; and we must be prepared to pay the price.

CHAPTER ONE HUNDRED EIGHT

New Parts For Old—Artificial Body Parts

Most of us have viewed at least one episode of the television programs *Six Million Dollar Man* or *Bionic Woman*. Though the plots may have seemed farfetched, the premise of these programs is more fact than fiction.

Artificial body parts are becoming more and more readily available. In fact, you may have a friend or relative with an artificial hip, knee, heart valve or eye lens. It's difficult to compile an accurate listing of all the available artificial body parts. As soon as it's complete, that list could be outdated by the invention of a new device. To date, almost every joint found in the body has been duplicated in plastics and/or metals.

Artificial hearts are constantly being improved upon. Although somewhat inconvenient, artificial kidneys have been available for years. And today, investigators are working to lessen the inconvenience of these lifesaving inventions. There are many devices that also have been developed to improve appearance. Breast implants, facial implants and penile implants are all currently available.

In the future, the sky (in combination with funding sources) is the limit. I'm not willing to estimate how far this science will go, nor its implications, but I will predict that many of us, or our children, will be faced with the decisions involving artificial organs and limbs.

Who's to judge the benefits of this science versus the complications? As with everything good, there is the possibility of bad. For example, there is no question that the discovery of penicillin and other antibiotics has saved countless lives, but serious complications from allergic reactions to these drugs have also occurred and some patients lose their lives to these reactions. Likewise, recent reports of problems with silicone breast implants have sparked the Food and Drug Administration (FDA) to recommend halting the use of these devices until their safety can be evaluated.

Any of us could be faced with the immediate decision of whether to allow our body parts to be replaced with artificial devices. Sometimes the decision will be an easy one. The replacement of a lens or a hip for the one that won't work are somewhat complicated procedures that work well and could eliminate pain while allowing us to function more normally. But, consider an artificial heart. This difficult operation is a "horse of a different color" and one that requires careful decision making.

What should you do? As always, ask questions and make sure that you understand the answers. Your doctor can supply you with the facts, but ultimately you must decide. All too often, these situations have no clear-cut answer, leaving the patient with a difficult decision. It's then that the answers to your questions and the guidance of your physician will help you determine what's best for you.

CHAPTER ONE HUNDRED NINE

The Future Of Health Care

I like to think I'm a reasonably intelligent person, but every once in a while, I'm tempted to do something stupid. Like losing my money at Las Vegas or trying to predict the future. Actually, I'd probably win a small fortune, if I bet all my nickels and dimes on the certain fact that health care costs will continue to rise in the years ahead.

Not only will the cost of health care rise very quickly, but it might well spiral to a point that it becomes unaffordable for many Americans. And unless efforts are made to control these costs, quality health care could become only a memory for thousands of people in this country.

In the past 50 years, we have experienced an explosion of discovery that has produced more sophisticated equipment, "miracle" drugs, and amazing treatments that allow us to live longer and healthier lives. But for us to enjoy those longer and healthier lives, we must provide the financial support for medical research to provide the equipment and the drugs, and for physicians to treat emerging, unknown illnesses or the various health problems that accompany our later years.

Provisions must be made so that treatment is available for those who simply cannot afford to pay for health care; and we cannot ignore the fact that, historically, the cost of living our daily lives has always increased over time for everybody—including health care providers.

Obviously, some help should be expected from local, state and federal authorities. But while governments can provide some funding to ensure availability of health care, this is a form of "band-aid" treatment: It is a short-term remedy and not a long-term solution.

And what will the government do to "correct" the problem? If their past actions are any prediction for the future, they will concentrate on reducing their cost of health care. They will do so from two angles. They will pay less and less to the providers of health care, so that doctor and hospital fees for everything from office visits to cardiac surgery will be reduced. And they will require the beneficiaries of health care (that's you) to pay more and more of their "share" of the costs.

Managed Health Care is a new term that will become more familiar to you as time passes. It means just what it says. The government or your insurance company or your employer will develop prepackaged plans in association with hospitals and doctors to manage all your health care needs, in one place, by one group of providers. Of course, the place and group will be determined by the owners of the plan—not you. An HMO is an example of a managed health care plan. If you choose not to participate in the plan, your medical costs will be reimbursed at a reduced rate. If you choose to participate in the plan, you will have to play the game by their rules. Either way, you will be squeezed. Nevertheless, everyone agrees that something must be done.

Controlling the costs of health care can begin with the patient-doctor relationship. Often, a doctor might recommend tests or a course of action simply as a precaution: To make sure he or she has done everything possible, when the symptoms are baffling or obscure. Sometimes, a physician might think he or she might be accused of malpractice, if the most modern technology is *not* used at all times—whether it's needed or not.

The patient should question the validity of prescribed tests before agreeing to taking them; perhaps generic drugs can be substituted, at a lesser cost, for brand names; day surgery could be more appropriate than hospitalization; or maybe, diet, medication, therapy or other treatments might eliminate the need for surgery altogether.

Currently, insurance companies are carefully monitoring health care expenses, fully aware that their industry has been greatly affected by spiraling health care costs. Second opinions, pre-certification, and preferred provider organizations have become commonplace terminology; gone are the days when a patient visited the physician and sent the bill to the insurance company, without a second thought.

Some physicians resent this input from the paying agency, since it affects the traditional physician-patient relationship; they feel the physician must be allowed to prescribe the best route for the patient, without the cost (to the insurance company or government agency) becoming an intrusion. But if health care costs continue to increase at their current rate, it will be impossible to eliminate the cost factor as a major matter for consideration; and physicians will just have to get used to this fact of life.

We cannot turn back the clock; we cannot ignore state-of-the-art technology or miraculous (but expensive) medications or surgical techniques. And it would be immoral to discontinue our research to provide even greater opportunities for better health for future generations. What is the solution? Is there a way to get back to "the good old days"? What do you think?

CHAPTER ONE HUNDRED TEN

New Year Is A Good Time To Make Health Resolutions

My primary New Year's resolution is usually to try and stick to the other resolutions. Some are easy, some difficult, some important, others insignificant. Regardless, the new year is the perfect time to commit to new plans and to begin afresh. Especially when it concerns your health.

While adding daily jogs, oat bran and sufficient sleep to your "must do" list is important, there are other far more critical health resolutions you might decide to pursue. And keeping these resolutions could be difficult, if not impossible, without careful research, proper medical supervision and the support of your loved ones.

A commitment to better health is a wonderful New Year's resolution. Begin a dietary program, start an exercise regime, get an annual physical. But if you're an alcoholic or a drug user, or if you are seriously overweight or a smoker, you have a life-threatening habit. Find a program that appeals to you and has a documented record of success. Give yourself a chance. Do yourself a favor.

People who suffer from these addictions offer many excuses for not seeking help: "It's too expensive." "I have a problem with confidentiality." "It's inconvenient."

We all know that it's absolute nonsense to blame anyone but yourselves for personal shortcomings—and the health care industry is far from responsible for your failure to seek treatment.

Increasingly more reputable programs are covered by health insurance policies; so expense should not be an issue. Confidentiality should not be a problem either, since there are many safeguards designed specifically to protect patients' right to confidentiality. And programs abound that recognize the need for many to combine treatment with as little disruption as possible to their daily lives.

The social stigma once associated with addicts and alcoholics has changed in recent years. Politicians, movie stars and professional athletes have helped to raise the public's level of awareness, by acknowledging their personal struggles with alcohol or drugs. Consequently, friends, employers and family members are more understanding, and an alcoholic is not just a drunk who should know better but someone with an illness who needs treatment.

Once you've admitted that you have a disease (and an addiction to anything, be it drugs or food, is a disease) and that there is a program that is right for you, take the necessary time to find it! Search among the many outpatient and inpatient programs that are designed to help you make the transition and provide emotional support throughout the rest of your life, if necessary.

Many substance abusers misunderstand such fine programs as Alcoholics Anonymous, Cocaine Anonymous, Narcotics Anonymous and other support groups that depend on the 12 Steps, believing they are religion oriented, since they rely heavily upon the concept of a "higher power." Be aware that the higher power is anything you wish it to be from God to the group leader; and the happy fact is that these groups work. When attended regularly during and following qualified medical treatment, they have amazing track records for restoring happy lives to alcoholics and addicts.

The program you need depends largely upon the severity of your problem. For outpatients, there are home-based or residential (hotel/motel or some other type of "group" arrangement) daily programs. Sometimes, the schedule can allow you to work normal hours and receive treatment and counseling during the evenings and/or weekends. But the most intensive program is inpatient treatment. Most hospitals that have a substance abuse program offer a separate unit or even a building where a home-like environment is maintained. Private treatment facilities can range from traditional hospital settings to near country club surroundings. Some depend on psychiatric evaluation with the physician playing a key role. Others use group therapy with assistance from psychologists. Many combine the two.

Treatment programs can be sponsored by private business, religious organizations, state or non-profit groups. But all have the same goal: to help you with your addiction.

How can you be sure the program you choose is reputable? Ask. Talk with a respected physician, state or federal agencies, your clergyman, the county medical society. Look for credentials such as licensure and accreditation. Conduct your research carefully and with some skepticism. Your mental health should not be taken lightly. And neither should your wallet. These programs are costly (either to you or your insurance company), and you don't want to spend three weeks in treatment only to discover you made the wrong choice.

Substance abuse is a family problem. Most substance abuse health professionals know that the family unit needs just as much help as does the abuser. Reputable programs include family counseling, since treatment and counseling of the patient's "co-dependents" is crucial to overall recovery. If you put a fresh coat of paint on a rusty bicycle and stick it back out in the rain, it will soon rust again. Place an abuser back into a home where the family does not understand the "new rules" and the abuse can begin again.

These same principles are equally applicable to those who need to stop smoking or have an obesity problem. If either excessive weight or smoking is your main concern, the path to successful treatment is no different. Evaluate your personal needs, query your sources, check credentials, and elicit support from family and friends.

But keep in mind that most facilities and physicians would advise that you deal with a drug or alcohol problem first, before attempting to lose weight or stop smoking. While all are major threats to your health, sometimes you are faced with handling one problem at a time. Don't try to "make it up all at once" (as the sportscasters are fond of saying). Each touchdown counts, and combined, they can provide a winning result.

And if only one person decides to rid themselves of a destructive addiction or habit because of this chapter, then the ink is worth it.

Happy New Year!

CHAPTER ONE HUNDRED ELEVEN

Getting On The Right Side of The Needle

So you want to get into the health care business, you say? That's good! We need your help—and your desire to help is probably your best qualification, regardless of prior training and educational background.

Of course, the specific areas that are available to you depends on a variety of factors. Obviously, the younger you are when you decide upon your career path, the greater the opportunity to reach your goal. And if, right now, you are a grade school or a high school student, you have a huge range of choices.

How about becoming a doctor? And yes—it does take a long time. First, you must go to college, usually four years. Then, medical school takes up another four years of your life; and after that, several more years are devoted to a residency or specialty training.

Becoming a doctor requires a great deal of hard work, and commitment—the same hard work and commitment that is needed to become a nurse, a physical therapist, a radiologic technician or any other professional health care provider.

If you are past high-school age (or even, maybe, past middle age), there are still many career opportunities—as long as you have that much-needed desire and determination.

For instance, some schools offer programs for students who must seek a part-time education; completing the program takes longer and might be more challenging for students trying to juggle jobs, families, studies and various other demands on their time. But the end result is worth the effort: a rewarding career as a health care professional.

You might think you're too old or too busy or too something else to begin a new career—but would still like to contribute *something* to the health care field.

Contact your local hospital and offer your services to its volunteer program. There probably isn't a hospital in the country that couldn't use more volunteers who are, of course, an essential part of the health care team. And if you have teaching qualifications, hospitalized children can certainly benefit from your expertise.

Art and music are now recognized as extremely valuable aids to the recuperation of some patients. Do you have either of those talents? Can they be utilized by your local hospital?

But regardless of whether you are a health care professional or a volunteer, your efforts will be worthwhile. You will experience a kind of personal satisfaction that cannot be gained from alternative professions or pastimes. Your efforts will be appreciated by some people who take the time to thank you—or by others you might never even meet. Either way, you will contribute to the well being of the world around you. And you'll never regret wanting to get into the health care business.

CHAPTER ONE HUNDRED TWELVE

Managed Health Care

As this book goes to press the country is about to address significant changes in our health care system. President Clinton (either Bill or Hillary) intends to completely revamp and hopefully improve the way we receive medical care. There are two major issues. One is the continually escalating cost of health care, with no plateau for the steep annual increases in sight. The other is the unfortunate fact that not all of our citizens can afford this care, and therefore, go without.

Clearly, changes need to be made. Both problems need to be addressed. Unfortunately, the tendency is to rush into unclear solutions that lead to inefficient systems requiring greater expenditures of public funds. Please remember that the term "public funds" translates into taxes.

My crystal ball tells me that we will end up with some form of managed care program for all citizens (perhaps even non-citizens). Managed care means that our health care will be "managed" by "professionals." Patients may have little to say about such matters as who their doctors are; where, when and how they receive medical care; and possibly even if they are entitled to any care at all.

Should a 75-year-old gentlemen who has lost his kidney function be allowed the use of an artificial kidney? If we are truly trying to contain health care costs, serious consideration must be given to denying this treatment. How old are you? Do you know anyone who is 75?

Specific managed care programs can vary greatly, assuming many forms; for example, health maintenance organizations (HMOs) or preferred provider organizations (PPOs). Each insurance company has one or more varieties they offer to firms who finance health care for their employees and families. It is important to become educated about these new managed care plans, since we are likely to become involved with one or another of them in the near future. Some of the more common managed health care formats are described below:

MCO—Managed Care Organization. This is a general term that refers to organizations designed to provide health care benefits to patients in other than the traditional insurance company style.

HMO—Health Maintenance Organization. An organization that provides health care to enrolled members in return for a preset amount of money. Members must choose their physician from a limited panel of doctors, who are employed by the HMO. Member patients must first visit their primary care physician and obtain approval for any specialized care. Obtaining care from unauthorized health care providers voids the organizations responsibility to pay for the care.

PPO—Preferred Provider Organization. Another organization that provides health care to enrolled members in return for a preset amount of money. The PPO enters into agreements with health care providers for their services, usually at a negotiated discount price. Patient members can choose care from any physician, regardless of specialty, as long as the physician is a member of the PPO.

IPA—Independent Practice Association. An organization that has a contract with a managed care plan insurance company to deliver services in return for a single payment rate, called a capitation rate (a fixed amount of money per patient, per month). The IPA then turns in contracts with health care providers to deliver the necessary medical services.

EPO—Exclusive Provider Organization. Similar to HMOs requiring patient members to stay within a defined network of health care providers to receive benefits.

EAP—Employee Assistance Program. An employer-sponsored program designed to coordinate the delivery of mental health and substance abuse services to employees.

PHO—Physician Hospital Organization. Legal or informal organizations that bond hospitals with attending physicians. Frequently developed for the purpose of contracting with managed care plans.

POS—Point of Service. A plan where members do not have to choose how to receive services until they need them. These plans incorporate elements of both HMOs and PPOs. They are also known as "swing-out HMOs," or "primary care PPOs."

TPA—Third Party Administrator. A firm that performs administrative functions such as claims processing, membership verification and the like for self-funded employers or small managed care plans.

OWA—Other Weird Arrangement. A general term that applies to any new and bizarre managed care plan that has thought up a new twist.

Managed Competition. There are no currently available initials for this program. It will probably be the first attempt to resolve health care cost and availability issues. It will force competition between the various insurance companies and all of the managed care plans in order to reduce the costs of plans.

What will our health care program look like in the year 2010? It might not be represented by any of these examples. There may be a totally new set of initials to consider. But the next few years will see discussion, debate, pilot projects and political maneuvering in an effort to identify and implement a new health care strategy. We have to be ready.

Actually, we have to be more than ready. We need to participate, as much as possible, in the development of these new health care programs. Since these programs will be developed and implemented by politicians, we do have an opportunity to influence the outcome of health care reform. But we need to be proactive, paying constant attention to developments and communicating our feelings about them to our elected officials.

The crisis in health care costs will continue unless we do something about it. We must be certain that what we do will produce the desired effect. And that end result or desired effect, in my opinion, should be the highest level of medical care for all citizens at an affordable cost.

Remember, it's *our* health!

CHAPTER ONE HUNDRED THIRTEEN

Conclusion

Well, my friends, good health is indeed a complicated business! And I address you as my friends, because if you've read this much of my book, we're far more than mere casual acquaintances. Thus, I feel pretty comfortable offering you one final piece of advice.

Keep this book as a handy reference; and if a question arises, check the index to see if that particular topic is covered. Unlike the information in most medical books, the advice on these pages should not become outdated; it is as equally applicable to you as it is to your parents or grandparents; to your children or grandchildren.

Regardless of how many times you read or refer to this book, I hope, sincerely, that some of its advice will be remembered. Please do take charge of your health care; become educated about your health needs; and don't be intimidated by the increasing complexity of the medical profession.

You have enough to worry about, when you're faced with sickness or serious injury. Perhaps this book can help you to recuperate quickly and successfully from the complicated and confusing worlds of medical science and health care bureaucracy.

REMEMBER, IT'S *YOUR* HEALTH!

Medical Record

PRESENT ILLNESS OR SYMPTOMS

The following list includes many possible symptoms that could indicate a medical problem. Although this list does not cover every potential medical problem, it is quite extensive and spans a broad spectrum. Read the list carefully and answer either "yes" or "no" to each question. If any of the boxes are marked "yes," consider an appointment with your physician. It is possible to have more than one box checked "yes" and it is also possible that even if you have checked several boxes in the "yes" column, it does not indicate a severe problem. But it is clearly best to let your physician decide.

In addition to the presence of any of these symptoms, your doctor will also want to know: When did the symptoms start? Do they come and go? Are they associated with pain? These (and many more questions) will be asked when you visit your doctor, so be ready for them.

Even if you answered "no" to all of the questions, it is wise to repeat the process yearly. Therefore, I have provided sufficient space for several years.

DATE

	YES	NO
1. Have you lost weight without trying?	☐	☐
2. Have you lost your appetite?	☐	☐
3. Do you feel tired all the time?	☐	☐
4. Do you tire easily, even after mild exercise?	☐	☐
5. Do you ever feel hot or feverish?	☐	☐
6. Do you crave a lot of water or liquids?	☐	☐
7. Have you developed recent headaches?	☐	☐
8. Do you have nosebleeds?	☐	☐
9. Is your hair very dry?	☐	☐
10. Do you have unexplained lumps or bumps?	☐	☐
11. Do you have sores that will not heal?	☐	☐
12. Are you losing hair rapidly?	☐	☐
13. Do you have light patches of skin?	☐	☐
14. Is your skin yellow? (Look in sunlight)	☐	☐
15. Is your skin very dry?	☐	☐
16. Do you eat a lot and not gain weight?	☐	☐
17. Are you excessively overweight?	☐	☐
18. Can you see as well as you used to?	☐	☐

	DATE			DATE			DATE	
YES		**NO**	**YES**		**NO**	**YES**		**NO**
☐		☐	☐		☐	☐		☐
☐		☐	☐		☐	☐		☐
☐		☐	☐		☐	☐		☐
☐		☐	☐		☐	☐		☐
☐		☐	☐		☐	☐		☐
☐		☐	☐		☐	☐		☐
☐		☐	☐		☐	☐		☐
☐		☐	☐		☐	☐		☐
☐		☐	☐		☐	☐		☐
☐		☐	☐		☐	☐		☐
☐		☐	☐		☐	☐		☐
☐		☐	☐		☐	☐		☐
☐		☐	☐		☐	☐		☐
☐		☐	☐		☐	☐		☐
☐		☐	☐		☐	☐		☐
☐		☐	☐		☐	☐		☐
☐		☐	☐		☐	☐		☐

DATE

	YES	NO
19. Are the words on this page blurred?	❐	❐
20. Can you see distant objects clearly?	❐	❐
21. Have you difficulty moving your eyes up/down?	❐	❐
22. Have you difficulty moving them right/left?	❐	❐
23. Are there yellow patches on the white parts of your eyes?	❐	❐
24. Are your eyes yellow? (Look in sunlight)	❐	❐
25. Do the black inner portions of your eyes stay the same size if light is shined into them?	❐	❐
26. Do you see double or spots?	❐	❐
27. Do your eyes burn?	❐	❐
28. Do your eyes drip?	❐	❐
29. Can you see at night as well as you do in the daytime?	❐	❐
30. Can you see colors?	❐	❐
31. Do you hear as well as you used to?	❐	❐
32. Do you hear buzzing in your ears?	❐	❐
33. Do your ears drip?	❐	❐
34. Do your ears hurt?	❐	❐

DATE		DATE		DATE	
YES	**NO**	**YES**	**NO**	**YES**	**NO**
☐	☐	☐	☐	☐	☐
☐	☐	☐	☐	☐	☐
☐	☐	☐	☐	☐	☐
☐	☐	☐	☐	☐	☐
☐	☐	☐	☐	☐	☐
☐	☐	☐	☐	☐	☐
☐	☐	☐	☐	☐	☐
☐	☐	☐	☐	☐	☐
☐	☐	☐	☐	☐	☐
☐	☐	☐	☐	☐	☐
☐	☐	☐	☐	☐	☐
☐	☐	☐	☐	☐	☐
☐	☐	☐	☐	☐	☐
☐	☐	☐	☐	☐	☐
☐	☐	☐	☐	☐	☐
☐	☐	☐	☐	☐	☐

DATE

		YES	NO
35.	Are you able to smell as well as you used to?	❑	❑
36.	Is your nose stuffed all the time?	❑	❑
37.	Can you breathe through your nose with your mouth closed?	❑	❑
38.	Does your nose drip?	❑	❑
39.	Do your lips droop?	❑	❑
40.	Do your eyelids droop?	❑	❑
41.	Do you have an uneven smile?	❑	❑
42.	Do you have slurred speech?	❑	❑
43.	Can you see unusual bumps, lumps, sores in your mouth, lips or tongue?	❑	❑
44.	Do you have difficulty moving your tongue up or down?	❑	❑
45.	Do you have difficulty moving your tongue right or left?	❑	❑
46.	Does your breath smell bad?	❑	❑
47.	Are your gums swollen?	❑	❑
48.	Do you have holes in your teeth?	❑	❑
49.	Do you have a sore throat?	❑	❑
50.	Do you feel lumps behind your jaw?	❑	❑

DATE		DATE		DATE	
YES	**NO**	**YES**	**NO**	**YES**	**NO**
☐	☐	☐	☐	☐	☐
☐	☐	☐	☐	☐	☐
☐	☐	☐	☐	☐	☐
☐	☐	☐	☐	☐	☐
☐	☐	☐	☐	☐	☐
☐	☐	☐	☐	☐	☐
☐	☐	☐	☐	☐	☐
☐	☐	☐	☐	☐	☐
☐	☐	☐	☐	☐	☐
☐	☐	☐	☐	☐	☐
☐	☐	☐	☐	☐	☐
☐	☐	☐	☐	☐	☐
☐	☐	☐	☐	☐	☐
☐	☐	☐	☐	☐	☐
☐	☐	☐	☐	☐	☐
☐	☐	☐	☐	☐	☐

DATE

		YES	NO
51.	Do you feel lumps in the middle of your neck?	☐	☐
52.	Does it hurt to move your neck?	☐	☐
53.	Is your neck stiff?	☐	☐
54.	Does it hurt when you swallow?	☐	☐
55.	Do you have any swellings in your neck or head?	☐	☐
56.	Do you wheeze?	☐	☐
57.	Has it been longer than a year since a doctor listened to your lungs?	☐	☐
58.	Is your mouth dry?	☐	☐
59.	Do you have trouble breathing?	☐	☐
60.	Do you cough a lot?	☐	☐
61.	When you cough to you bring up mucus?	☐	☐
62.	Do you cough up blood?	☐	☐
63.	Are you short of breath?	☐	☐
64.	Do you get short of breath when walking?	☐	☐
65.	Can you lie flat in bed without pillows?	☐	☐
66.	Do you wake up short of breath?	☐	☐
67.	Do you get pains in your chest?	☐	☐

	DATE			DATE			DATE	
YES		**NO**	**YES**		**NO**	**YES**		**NO**
☐		☐	☐		☐	☐		☐
☐		☐	☐		☐	☐		☐
☐		☐	☐		☐	☐		☐
☐		☐	☐		☐	☐		☐
☐		☐	☐		☐	☐		☐
☐		☐	☐		☐	☐		☐
☐		☐	☐		☐	☐		☐
☐		☐	☐		☐	☐		☐
☐		☐	☐		☐	☐		☐
☐		☐	☐		☐	☐		☐
☐		☐	☐		☐	☐		☐
☐		☐	☐		☐	☐		☐
☐		☐	☐		☐	☐		☐
☐		☐	☐		☐	☐		☐
☐		☐	☐		☐	☐		☐
☐		☐	☐		☐	☐		☐
☐		☐	☐		☐	☐		☐

DATE

	YES	NO
68. Do you feel lumps in your breasts? (Men also)	☐	☐
69. Do you feel lumps in your armpits?	☐	☐
70. Are there red spots on your breasts?	☐	☐
71. Are your breasts dimpled?	☐	☐
72. Are your breasts sore?	☐	☐
73. Do your breasts have any discharge?	☐	☐
74. Is one breast much larger than the other?	☐	☐
75. Does one breast hang much lower than the other?	☐	☐
76. Do you get pains in your chest with exercise?	☐	☐
77. Do you wake up with pains in your chest?	☐	☐
78. Do you have pains in your stomach?	☐	☐
79. Do you feel as if you need to vomit?	☐	☐
80. Do you vomit?	☐	☐
81. Do you have cramps in your stomach?	☐	☐
82. Is your stomach swollen?	☐	☐
83. Do you have lumps around your belly button?	☐	☐

DATE		DATE		DATE	
YES	**NO**	**YES**	**NO**	**YES**	**NO**
☐	☐	☐	☐	☐	☐
☐	☐	☐	☐	☐	☐
☐	☐	☐	☐	☐	☐
☐	☐	☐	☐	☐	☐
☐	☐	☐	☐	☐	☐
☐	☐	☐	☐	☐	☐
☐	☐	☐	☐	☐	☐
☐	☐	☐	☐	☐	☐
☐	☐	☐	☐	☐	☐
☐	☐	☐	☐	☐	☐
☐	☐	☐	☐	☐	☐
☐	☐	☐	☐	☐	☐
☐	☐	☐	☐	☐	☐
☐	☐	☐	☐	☐	☐
☐	☐	☐	☐	☐	☐
☐	☐	☐	☐	☐	☐

DATE

	YES	NO
84. Do you have bulges around your belly button when you cough or strain?	☐	☐
85. Do you have dilated veins on your skin?	☐	☐
86. Do you have pains anywhere when you press on your belly?	☐	☐
87. Are there any lumps in your stomach?	☐	☐
88. Are there any lumps in your groin?	☐	☐
89. Do you have any pains in your back or sides?	☐	☐
90. Are you constipated?	☐	☐
91. Do you have diarrhea?	☐	☐
92. Do you pass any blood in your bowel movements?	☐	☐
93. Are your bowel movements an unusual color?	☐	☐
94. Are your bowel movements black?	☐	☐
95. Are your bowel movements white or gray?	☐	☐
96. Have your bowel movements changed in size?	☐	☐
97. Do you have to strain to pass your urine?	☐	☐
98. Do you have a very weak stream of urine?	☐	☐

	DATE			DATE			DATE	
YES	NO		YES	NO		YES	NO	
☐	☐		☐	☐		☐	☐	
☐	☐		☐	☐		☐	☐	
☐	☐		☐	☐		☐	☐	
☐	☐		☐	☐		☐	☐	
☐	☐		☐	☐		☐	☐	
☐	☐		☐	☐		☐	☐	
☐	☐		☐	☐		☐	☐	
☐	☐		☐	☐		☐	☐	
☐	☐		☐	☐		☐	☐	
☐	☐		☐	☐		☐	☐	
☐	☐		☐	☐		☐	☐	
☐	☐		☐	☐		☐	☐	
☐	☐		☐	☐		☐	☐	
☐	☐		☐	☐		☐	☐	
☐	☐		☐	☐		☐	☐	

DATE

	YES	NO
99. Do you have trouble starting to urinate?	☐	☐
100. Do you have to get up at night to urinate?	☐	☐
101. Does your urine leak when you don't want it to?	☐	☐
102. Does your urine stop completely?	☐	☐
103. Do you pass blood in your urine?	☐	☐
104. Does your urine smell bad?	☐	☐
105. Do you urinate too frequently?	☐	☐
106. Do you have sores on your arms or legs?	☐	☐
107. Are your toes or finger tips bluish?	☐	☐
108. Have you lost sensation or coordination of your hands, feet, toes or fingers?	☐	☐
109. Do you have dilated veins?	☐	☐
110. Do you have swelling of your arms or legs?	☐	☐
111. Do you have trouble holding a cup or pencil?	☐	☐
112. Do you have trouble raising you arms above your head?	☐	☐
113. Do you have trouble touching your toes with your fingers?	☐	☐
114. Do your knees give way?	☐	☐

DATE		DATE		DATE	
YES	NO	YES	NO	YES	NO
☐	☐	☐	☐	☐	☐
☐	☐	☐	☐	☐	☐
☐	☐	☐	☐	☐	☐
☐	☐	☐	☐	☐	☐
☐	☐	☐	☐	☐	☐
☐	☐	☐	☐	☐	☐
☐	☐	☐	☐	☐	☐
☐	☐	☐	☐	☐	☐
☐	☐	☐	☐	☐	☐
☐	☐	☐	☐	☐	☐
☐	☐	☐	☐	☐	☐
☐	☐	☐	☐	☐	☐
☐	☐	☐	☐	☐	☐
☐	☐	☐	☐	☐	☐
☐	☐	☐	☐	☐	☐
☐	☐	☐	☐	☐	☐

DATE

	YES	NO
115. Does you spine appear crooked?	☐	☐
116. Do you have difficulty standing straight?	☐	☐
117. Do you have difficulty standing on one leg with your eyes closed?	☐	☐
118. Do you have difficulty walking a straight line?	☐	☐
119. Do you have a weak handgrip?	☐	☐
120. Do you have difficulty clapping your hands with your eyes closed?	☐	☐
121. Do you have numb areas on your skin?	☐	☐
122. Do you have difficulty swallowing?	☐	☐
123. Do you have difficulty feeling the difference between hot and cold water?	☐	☐
124. Do you have difficulty touching your fingertips with your thumb?	☐	☐
125. Has it been more than one year since you have had your blood pressure checked?	☐	☐
126. Do your feet swell?	☐	☐
127. Do your legs hurt when you walk?	☐	☐
128. Do you have pain in your joints?	☐	☐
129. Do you have lumps on your arms or legs?	☐	☐

	DATE			DATE			DATE	
YES		**NO**	**YES**		**NO**	**YES**		**NO**
☐		☐	☐		☐	☐		☐
☐		☐	☐		☐	☐		☐
☐		☐	☐		☐	☐		☐
☐		☐	☐		☐	☐		☐
☐		☐	☐		☐	☐		☐
☐		☐	☐		☐	☐		☐
☐		☐	☐		☐	☐		☐
☐		☐	☐		☐	☐		☐
☐		☐	☐		☐	☐		☐
☐		☐	☐		☐	☐		☐
☐		☐	☐		☐	☐		☐
☐		☐	☐		☐	☐		☐
☐		☐	☐		☐	☐		☐
☐		☐	☐		☐	☐		☐
☐		☐	☐		☐	☐		☐

DATE

	YES	NO
130. Do you have any ulcers on your skin?	☐	☐
131. Has your skin changed color?	☐	☐
132. Do you bleed easily even with small cuts?	☐	☐
133. Do you bruise easily?	☐	☐
134. Are you nervous all the time?	☐	☐
135. Are you under a lot of stress?	☐	☐
136. Do you feel everyone is against you?	☐	☐
137. Do you anger very easily?	☐	☐
138. Do you let your temper get the best of you?	☐	☐
139. Are you a violent person when angry?	☐	☐
140. Do you feel "blue" all the time?	☐	☐
141. Do you see visions or have strange dreams?	☐	☐
142. Do you have difficulty walking?	☐	☐
143. Do you get dizzy or light headed?	☐	☐
144. Do you faint or have convulsions?	☐	☐

****

For Women

145. Are your periods very heavy?	☐	☐

DATE		DATE		DATE	
YES	**NO**	**YES**	**NO**	**YES**	**NO**
☐	☐	☐	☐	☐	☐
☐	☐	☐	☐	☐	☐
☐	☐	☐	☐	☐	☐
☐	☐	☐	☐	☐	☐
☐	☐	☐	☐	☐	☐
☐	☐	☐	☐	☐	☐
☐	☐	☐	☐	☐	☐
☐	☐	☐	☐	☐	☐
☐	☐	☐	☐	☐	☐
☐	☐	☐	☐	☐	☐
☐	☐	☐	☐	☐	☐
☐	☐	☐	☐	☐	☐
☐	☐	☐	☐	☐	☐
☐	☐	☐	☐	☐	☐
☐	☐	☐	☐	☐	☐

| ☐ | ☐ | ☐ | ☐ | ☐ | ☐ |

DATE

	YES	NO
146. Do you have a vaginal discharge?	❏	❏
147. Do you have sores, lumps or pain on your vaginal lips or in your groin?	❏	❏
148. Do you have pain during sexual intercourse?	❏	❏
149. Have your periods stopped suddenly?	❏	❏
150. Do you have sores or lumps in your private area?	❏	❏
151. Has it been longer than a year since you have seen your gynecologist?	❏	❏
152. Have you missed your yearly PAP smear?	❏	❏
153. Are you having trouble with your sex life?	❏	❏

****

For Men

	YES	NO
154. Do you have a drip from your penis?	❏	❏
155. Do you have sores or lumps in your private area?	❏	❏
156. Do you have bulges in your groin?	❏	❏
157. Do you have swollen veins in your sac?	❏	❏
158. Are your testicles hard or painful?	❏	❏

DATE		DATE		DATE	
YES	**NO**	**YES**	**NO**	**YES**	**NO**
☐	☐	☐	☐	☐	☐
☐	☐	☐	☐	☐	☐
☐	☐	☐	☐	☐	☐
☐	☐	☐	☐	☐	☐
☐	☐	☐	☐	☐	☐
☐	☐	☐	☐	☐	☐
☐	☐	☐	☐	☐	☐
☐	☐	☐	☐	☐	☐
☐	☐	☐	☐	☐	☐
☐	☐	☐	☐	☐	☐
☐	☐	☐	☐	☐	☐
☐	☐	☐	☐	☐	☐
☐	☐	☐	☐	☐	☐

DATE

	YES	NO

159. Is one testicle much larger, harder or more painful than the other? □ □

160. Do you have a testicle that you cannot feel? □ □

161. Do you have a testicle that has not come down? □ □

162. Does your penis curve when erect? □ □

163. If you are uncircumcised do you have difficulty pulling the skin back over the head? □ □

****

164. Do you have problems that you wanted care for but have been putting off? □ □

165. Do you just want to talk to your doctor? □ □

DATE		DATE		DATE	
YES	**NO**	**YES**	**NO**	**YES**	**NO**
☐	☐	☐	☐	☐	☐
☐	☐	☐	☐	☐	☐
☐	☐	☐	☐	☐	☐
☐	☐	☐	☐	☐	☐
☐	☐	☐	☐	☐	☐
☐	☐	☐	☐	☐	☐
☐	☐	☐	☐	☐	☐

ALLERGIES

Allergies can be much more than just a nuisance. Anyone can develop allergies to various foods or pollens or just about anything in our environment. Drug allergies can be very serious and can even result in death.

If you are aware of any allergies you have to medications or drugs, it is essential that you avoid these materials. It is serious enough that your physician needs to be aware of these allergies and even reminded of them often. Each time you are prescribed a medication either for treatment or investigation purposes, you should remind your health care worker of your allergies; and you should ask whether your allergies will interfere with the material you are being given. If your allergies are severe, consider acquiring a warning device, usually available in the form of jewelry that can be worn constantly and will warn the health care team of your allergies. These are available in a variety of formats and are relatively inexpensive. Also a card in you wallet or purse describing the allergies, along with your doctor's phone number, should be kept in an obvious place.

List your allergies below.

Allergy   **Type of Reaction**

_____

_____

_____

_____

_____

_____

_____

_____

_____

MEDICATIONS

Most important is the list of current medications that you take on a regular basis. List these medications below. It is a good idea to keep a "running list" adding new medications to the bottom of the list but not removing discontinued medications, just noting when you finished them.

Medication	Dosage	Frequency	Date Begun	Completed

CHILDHOOD ILLNESSES

Strange as it may seem, you childhood illnesses, even though they occurred many years ago, could still play a role in your current medical problems. Such illnesses as measles, mumps, chicken pox etc. should be noted.

Illness	Age or Date	Any Remaining Problems

IMMUNIZATIONS

Your immunizations, which were begun as a child and should have been continued during your adult life, should be listed so that any further immunizations can be tracked and given when needed. Your doctor will know when to give you which immunizations, but only if he or she knows what you have already received. A continuous record is very helpful.

Immunization	Suggested Age	Done
Diphtheria, tetanus, pertussis, polio____(DTP/P)_____	2months	_____
(DTP/P)_____	4months	_____
(DTP)_____	6months	_____
(DTP/P) and Measles, mumps, Rubella_____	15 months	_____
Influenza type b_____	18-24 months	_____
(DPT/P)_____	4 to 6 years	_____
Tetanus_____	14 to 16 years	_____
Tetanus_____	every 10 years	_____
Other _____		

PAST MEDICAL ILLNESSES

Just as with your childhood illnesses, the adult illnesses and injuries you have experienced in the past can play a role in your current health problems. It is important to keep a list of these, adding to the list as new illnesses and injuries occur.

Illness or Injury	Date	Outcome

PREVIOUS SURGICAL PROCEDURES

Your previous surgical procedures also need to be listed so that your doctor can easily review them and decide if any of them are related to your current health problems. List them below and add to the list as additional procedures are performed.

Operation	Date	Result

FOR WOMEN

You menstrual (periods) history is important and could play a role in your current problems. Please record:

Date (or age) of first period: _____

Frequency of periods (# days apart): _____

Estimate of amount of flow: _____

Bleeding or spotting between periods: Yes_____   No_____

Your pregnancy history is also important. Please record the appropriate information below.

Date of Pregnancy	Full Term	Abortion	Complication
_____	_____	_____	_____
_____	_____	_____	_____
_____	_____	_____	_____
_____	_____	_____	_____
_____	_____	_____	_____
_____	_____	_____	_____
_____	_____	_____	_____
_____	_____	_____	_____

FAMILY HISTORY

Illness that your blood relatives have experienced can impact upon your own health. Many diseases are inherited and are known to run in families. It is important, therefore, to identify illnesses in your immediate family and list them below.

	Age	Illnesses	Cause of Death
GRANDFATHER			
GRANDMOTHER			
GRANDFATHER			
GRANDMOTHER			
FATHER			
MOTHER			
CHILD 1			
CHILD 2			
CHILD 3			
CHILD 4			
CHILD 5			

SOCIAL HISTORY

Your social history is also important and can seriously affect your health. Please list the pertinent facts below.

Smoking

Number of packs/day: _____
Number of years smoked: _____   ❑ Filters   ❑ Non filters
Have you ever quit? _____   For how long? _____

Alcoholic Beverages

Type of Alcohol: ❑ Beer   ❑   Wine   ❑   Liquor   ❑   Other
Amount consumed each week: _____
Number of years of drinking: _____
Are you *addicted*? _____

Drugs

Names of Drugs: _____

Amounts taken: _____

Number of years: _____

Are you *addicted*?

Drug _____

Drug _____

Drug _____

Sexual History

Your sexual history can also impact your medical care. It is important to complete the following questions.

1. Are you sexually active?

2. How often do you have sexual intercourse?

3. When did you become sexually active?

4. Do you have any pain with sexual intercourse?

5. Have you ever had any sexually transmitted diseases?

6. Have you ever been tested for HIV?

7. What is the result of that test?

Post-Test

1. Health care costs have levelled off in recent years thanks to intervention by the federal government.

    ❑ **True**   ❑ **False**

2. Depending on your medical problem, a small community hospital can be just as effective as a major teaching hospital in providing for your health needs.

    ❑ **True**   ❑ **False**

3. If a hospital has been approved by the Joint Commission on Accreditation of Health Organizations (JCAHO) it is equal to all other approved hospitals.

    ❑ **True**   ❑ **False**

4. If available hospitals are of equal quality in the care they provide, then it is appropriate to choose one based on amenities.

    ❑ **True**   ❑ **False**

5. Either your physician or the hospital administrator can grant your admission to the hospital.

    ❑ **True**   ❑ **False**

6. It is not necessary to notify your insurance company of your elective admission to the hospital, since they trust your doctor.

    ❑ **True**   ❑ **False**

7. Making a will before your hospitalization is a waste of time and money.

    ❑ **True**   ❑ **False**

8. It is important to bring large amounts of cash with you to the hospital so that you can buy extra food and clothing.

    ❑ **True**   ❑ **False**

9. Hospital security personnel perform the same sort of functions as other law enforcement individuals as well as many additional services for the patients.

    ❑ **True**   ❑ **False**

10. Consent forms you will be asked to sign in the hospital are standard forms and don't require your careful attention.
    ❏ **True** ❏ **False**

11. You have every right to expect all health care workers and hospital employees to respect your right to keep your health care confidential.
    ❏ **True** ❏ **False**

12. Your insurance company has access to your medical information automatically, without your consent.
    ❏ **True** ❏ **False**

13. A private room is always preferable to a semi-private room, if you can afford the cost.
    ❏ **True** ❏ **False**

14. Hospital food should be appetizing as well as nutritious. You should expect your meals to provide both.
    ❏ **True** ❏ **False**

15. Since a hospital room is a bedroom, living room, dining room, bathroom and family room, it is natural to find a few insects and bugs now and then. Don't worry about them.
    ❏ **True** ❏ **False**

16. Hospitals take special precautions to ensure the operating rooms are insect free.
    ❏ **True** ❏ **False**

17. Some noise in a hospital is acceptable, but noise without good reason is not.
    ❏ **True** ❏ **False**

18. When you visit an emergency room you should be seen first by a health care worker before you are asked about your medical insurance.
    ❏ **True** ❏ **False**

19. Hospital employees wear name tags so you can tell who they are and what they do.
    ❏ **True** ❏ **False**

20. Hospital volunteers provide many services to patients that would not be available without them.
❑ **True**   ❑ **False**

21. Private nurses are generally hospital employees and therefore they must be satisfactory or you can complain to the hospital administrator.
❑ **True**   ❑ **False**

22. Although private nurses are expensive, they are essential to good nursing care, particularly in the intensive care units.
❑ **True**   ❑ **False**

23. Hospital housekeepers' tasks are quite simple since they have all the most modern cleaning equipment available and since hospital construction is designed to maintain a clean environment.
❑ **True**   ❑ **False**

24. Hospital administrators are responsible for a smooth running, efficient business in the face of ever increasing costs.
❑ **True**   ❑ **False**

25. Hospital administrators are lucky to have many employees providing patient care and do not have to worry about day-to-day problems. They can sit in their offices and develop long-range plans.
❑ **True**   ❑ **False**

26. When choosing a gift to bring to a hospitalized friend or loved one, flowers, books and candy are always appropriate.
❑ **True**   ❑ **False**

27. Ambulance services are licensed by the state and are therefore equal in quality and service.
❑ **True**   ❑ **False**

28. You have the right to demand ambulance service to the hospital.
❑ **True**   ❑ **False**

29. Helicopter ambulances' main advantage is the speed with which you can be taken to the hospital.
❑ **True**   ❑ **False**

30. Because they are small and light, helicopter ambulances cannot be as well equipped as ground ambulances.
    ❑ True ❑ False

31. Emergency rooms must provide you emergency care regardless of your ability to pay.
    ❑ True ❑ False

32. If the hospital emergency room cannot provide the level of care you need, they have to find you a place that does.
    ❑ True ❑ False

33. Emergency room care is provided on a first-come, first-served basis.
    ❑ True ❑ False

34. Depending on the nature of your problem, waiting in an emergency room even after you have been examined may be necessary, even though it is not busy.
    ❑ True ❑ False

35. The feasibility of day surgery for surgical operations is due to advances in medical science and cost containment needs.
    ❑ True ❑ False

36. There are a variety of anesthetics available for your surgical procedure. Trust your anesthesiologist to pick the best one for you.
    ❑ True ❑ False

37. Operating rooms are places of life and death decision making. They are usually full of tension.
    ❑ True ❑ False

38. There are many types of pain medication available, but your doctor may not want to give you any—for your own good.
    ❑ True ❑ False

39. You may be asked to do several things after your operation that may be uncomfortable. Understand why and do them anyway.
    ❑ True ❑ False

40. Donating blood is painful and dangerous even though it is important.
    ❑ True ❑ False

41. If you are worried about receiving someone else's blood, there are still ways to use your own blood during surgery.
   ❑ True   ❑ False

42. X-rays are completely safe and can be used without fear of complications.
   ❑ True   ❑ False

43. Inserting needles into your body can be uncomfortable but information they provide about you is so important that it is worth the pain.
   ❑ True   ❑ False

44. Using needles can save you surgery, at times.
   ❑ True   ❑ False

45. Having your body invaded by tubes is uncomfortable and embarrassing. Know the reason why your doctor suggests it.
   ❑ True   ❑ False

46. The AIDS virus is an extremely fragile organism which is easily killed with common household bleach.
   ❑ True   ❑ False

47. Even if your hospital stay involves an unpleasant experience, don't bother complaining, it will do no good.
   ❑ True   ❑ False

48. You, the patient, have a right to refuse medical treatment.
   ❑ True   ❑ False

49. You have both the right to know the hospital rules and the responsibility to follow them.
   ❑ True   ❑ False

50. Prayer and faith can make a positive contribution to a patient's recovery.
   ❑ True   ❑ False

51. It is important for family members to participate in their loved one's care.
   ❑ True   ❑ False

52. Extra time spent visiting patients in the hospital during holiday periods helps to diminish the depression often associated with illness during these times.
    ❏ True ❏ False

53. It is possible to be given the wrong medication in the hospital although great care is taken to avoid this.
    ❏ True ❏ False

54. Since hospitals are so clean and sterile, it is not possible to develop an infection while hospitalized.
    ❏ True ❏ False

55. Planning for your discharge from the hospital should begin even before you are admitted.
    ❏ True ❏ False

56. Medical care has become so sophisticated and complicated that it can only be done in a doctor's office or hospital. Care at home is impossible.
    ❏ True ❏ False

57. The best time to choose a physician is when you are well.
    ❏ True ❏ False

58. All doctors, who are licensed by the state, are pretty much the same so you might as well select any of them.
    ❏ True ❏ False

59. Your doctor needs an accurate description of your symptoms so he or she can make an accurate diagnosis.
    ❏ True ❏ False

60. You need to be careful about asking doctors for a "second opinion" so that they don't feel you don't trust them.
    ❏ True ❏ False

61. It's a physician's responsibility to stay up to date on all aspects of health care, regardless of his or her specialty. You should expect to pay for the latest and best care.
    ❏ True ❏ False

62. While it may be OK for a doctor to say "I don't know," it is essential that he or she help you find out or find someone who does know about your medical problem.

❏ **True**   ❏ **False**

63. Medical students learn how to become physicians by participating in actual health care programs.

❏ **True**   ❏ **False**

64. If you don't have an appointment, but you need to see your doctor, calling ahead will help minimize your wait.

❏ **True**   ❏ **False**

65. You have every right to expect as much time as necessary with your physician but so do other patients, which may delay your care.

❏ **True**   ❏ **False**

66. You can be sure that if you like your doctor you will also be satisfied with his or her associates who substitute when your doctor is away.

❏ **True**   ❏ **False**

67. Medical conferences in exotic places allow the doctor to "refuel" both mind and body.

❏ **True**   ❏ **False**

68. Physician's assistants allow the doctor to extend his or her health care activities.

❏ **True**   ❏ **False**

69. All women in white uniforms are not nurses and all nurses are not alike in training and expertise.

❏ **True**   ❏ **False**

70. Dental problems are limited to your mouth, so the dentist doesn't have to worry about the rest of your medical problems.

❏ **True**   ❏ **False**

71. Appropriate tooth and gum care at home will help to decrease your chances of developing dental problems.

❏ **True**   ❏ **False**

72. Medication bottles should be labeled with the name of the drug inside. This is helpful so that you can identify other peoples prescriptions to use for your medical problems.
    ❏ True ❏ False

73. The medications you take are expensive. One reason is that you are helping to pay for the development of new drugs by the drug manufacturers.
    ❏ True ❏ False

74. Generic drugs can be as safe and effective as non-generic drugs.
    ❏ True ❏ False

75. The main purpose of the Food and Drug Administration (FDA) is to delay drugs from being sold so that non-legitimate drugs will be kept off the market.
    ❏ True ❏ False

76. The new technology in diagnosis and treatment is very expensive and is the single biggest expense in a hospital.
    ❏ True ❏ False

77. Hospitals try to curtail costs but not at the expense of providing the best health care.
    ❏ True ❏ False

78. Health care is expensive and unfortunately beyond the ability of the patient to control.
    ❏ True ❏ False

79. Virtually all known illnesses can be diagnosed using laboratory or other tests. These tests are expensive but specific alternatives are generally not available.
    ❏ True ❏ False

80. The main value of health insurance is that the insurance company will pay for your medical bills.
    ❏ True ❏ False

81. Hospital bills are done by a computer and are extremely accurate.
    ❏ True ❏ False

82. Most hospital billing departments will be happy to work out a payment plan with you if you have difficulty paying your bill.
   ❏ **True**   ❏ **False**

83. "DRG" is a system the Medicare program uses to pay hospitals for medical care.
   ❏ **True**   ❏ **False**

84. Malpractice law suits are increasing in number and resulting in greater costs to patients as malpractice insurance premiums increase.
   ❏ **True**   ❏ **False**

85. Don't even try to understand what doctors tell you. They speak the way they write—in shorthand and abbreviations.
   ❏ **True**   ❏ **False**

86. Medications available from mail order companies may be effective but can't cure what your doctor cannot.
   ❏ **True**   ❏ **False**

87. Modern medical care uses computers in many areas. They are sophisticated and foolproof.
   ❏ **True**   ❏ **False**

88. Participating personally in your recovery may be painful but will help.
   ❏ **True**   ❏ **False**

89. Smiling and maintaining a positive attitude makes the medical staff feel good but really can't influence your recovery.
   ❏ **True**   ❏ **False**

90. Support groups are nice but your medical recovery really depends on you alone.
   ❏ **True**   ❏ **False**

91. Fortunately, all city, state and federal buildings are equipped for the handicapped.
   ❏ **True**   ❏ **False**

92. Planning ahead for health problems on your vacation is important, since you may find yourself in a part of the world without much medical support.
    ❑ True ❑ False

93. While traveling, make sure all your medications are in a single, safe place in your luggage to be certain you can find them easily.
    ❑ True ❑ False

94. Prevention of illness is good in theory, but humans can't really do much to control the development of illness or injury.
    ❑ True ❑ False

95. Mental illness should be treated just as seriously as any other disease.
    ❑ True ❑ False

96. Your doctor will ask you a multitude of questions during your visit, so you don't need to worry what to tell him or her.
    ❑ True ❑ False

97. Your doctor spent eight or more years getting an education. Don't try to learn about your illness. He or she will tell you what you need to know.
    ❑ True ❑ False

98. Learning CPR is difficult and requires extensive exertion. You will probably never need to use it, so knowing how to do it is not essential.
    ❑ True ❑ False

99. A well planned exercise program is essential to maintaining good health.
    ❑ True ❑ False

100. This is a superb book and certainly worth the price.
    ❑ True ❑ False

Test Answers

Question	Answer	Question	Answer	Question	Answer
1	False	34	True	67	True
2	True	35	True	68	True
3	False	36	False	69	True
4	True	37	False	70	False
5	False	38	True	71	True
6	False	39	True	72	False
7	False	40	False	73	True
8	False	41	True	74	True
9	True	42	False	75	True
10	False	43	True	76	False
11	True	44	True	77	True
12	False	45	True	78	False
13	False	46	True	79	False
14	True	47	False	80	True
15	False	48	True	81	False
16	True	49	True	82	True
17	True	50	True	83	True
18	True	51	True	84	True
19	True	52	True	85	False
20	True	53	True	86	True
21	False	54	False	87	False
22	False	55	True	88	True
23	False	56	False	89	False
24	True	57	True	90	False
25	False	58	False	91	False
26	False	59	True	92	True
27	False	60	False	93	False
28	False	61	False	94	False
29	True	62	True	95	True
30	False	63	True	96	False
31	True	64	True	97	False
32	True	65	True	98	False
33	False	66	False	99	True
				100	True

Glossary

The following list of words and their associated definitions is designed to provide a brief compilation of some of the more common medical terms you are likely to encounter. It does not represent all known disease processes. A complete list would fill a book much larger than this one. The definitions I have provided are not the "sophisticated" definitions; rather they are designed for the lay reader, the so-called "average person."

More extensive information can be obtained from a medical dictionary. Several are generally available in book stores. They contain complete information *but* in medical terminology. Remember, if you don't understand the meanings of words your doctor uses—Ask! Ask! Ask!

A

AA—abbreviation for "Alcoholics Anonymous." A self help group for those people who recognize their illness. Other groups for other drug and chemical dependencies exist.

AARP—abbreviation for the "American Association of Retired Persons." A support group for senior citizens (over the age 50) that provides many benefits for its members.

ABDOMEN—anatomical location. Below the chest. Sometimes referred to as the belly or stomach (an inappropriate term since the stomach is only a part of the abdomen.)

ABORTION—loss of pregnancy. May be voluntary or involuntary due to some medical problem.

ABRASION—a scrape or roughening of the skin, usually due to some type of injury.

ABSCESS—a localized collection of pus. May grow to large size, and require drainage or other treatment.

ACETABULUM—the hip joint socket.

AIDS–abbreviation for "Acquired Immune Deficiency Syndrome." Caused by a virus and incurable at the present time.

ACUTE–short and severe. Of sudden onset. Many illnesses start suddenly and last only a brief period of time.

ADDICTION–a severe craving for a substance, ie. alcohol or drugs.

ADENOCARCINOMA–a malignant tumor containing or arising from glandular tissue, for example pancreas, kidney or thyroid gland.

ADENOPATHY–a disease of a gland, usually a lymph node. Characterized by a swelling of the gland.

ADIPOSE–fatty tissue.

ADRENAL GLAND–a gland lying above each kidney that secretes chemicals to maintain bodily function.

AFEBRILE–without fever. The normal body temperature is 98.6 F. but actually can vary from that number and still be normal.

ALS–abbreviation for "Advanced Life Support," usually describing a vehicle and its capability. ALS vehicles carry sophisticated, life-saving equipment and specially trained paramedics that can begin treatment even before the ambulance reaches the hospital.

ALLERGY–a susceptibility to foreign agents or substances, especially foods, medications and pollens.

ALOPECIA–baldness. Baldness may be a normal type of process or may represent significant illness.

ALZHEIMER'S DISEASE–a specific brain disease characterized by memory loss.

AMNIOCENTESIS–removing amniotic fluid from a pregnant woman (with a needle) for diagnostic purposes.

ANALGESIA–loss of pain without loss of tactile sense. The patient can feel but not feel pain.

ANASTOMOSIS–interconnection, usually referring to surgical procedures like attaching two pieces of bowel together.

ANATOMY—the science dealing with structure of the body. Usually one of the first courses taught to medical students.

ANEMIA—a deficiency of blood. This may be due to a variety of reasons that will require medical evaluation.

ANESTHESIA—loss of sensation. May be general, regional or local.

ANEURYSM—dilation of a blood vessel due to a fault in the wall of the vessel. It may explode if it is not corrected.

ANGINA—sense of suffocation or constriction. Usually referring to heart symptoms. It is a valuable warning system of potential serious heart disease and should not be ignored.

ANGIOPLASTY—plastic surgery of blood vessels. Often can be accomplished internally, without the need for open surgery.

ANOREXIA—loss of appetite. It may occur to a severe degree causing abnormal weight loss and severe illness or even death.

ANTERIOR—front. A medical term of anatomical description.

ANTIBIOTIC—antibacterial substances derived from fungi and bacteria. Penicillin was one of the first to be discovered but now there are many available for treatment of many types of infections.

ANTICOAGULANT—chemical that prevents or retards clotting of blood. This is a very useful medication but must be closely watched by the physician because too much is quite dangerous.

ANTISEPTIC—a chemical which destroys or inhibits the growth of microorganisms. Usually used to clean instruments and hospitals.

APPENDICITIS—inflammation of appendix. Usually requires surgery to remove the appendix.

ARTERIOSCLEROSIS—degenerative arterial change with age. Severe degrees of this problem in important arteries (in the heart, for example) may produce blockage of the artery and a heart attack.

ARTERY—blood vessels that carry oxygen rich blood from the heart to the organs of the body.

ASTHMA—wheezing and difficulty in exhaling. This condition can start suddenly and may require emergency treatment.

AUSCULTATION—listening to body sounds. Part of a general physical examination. A stethoscope is used to amplify the sounds so they can be more easily heard.

B

BACTERIA—a group of microorganisms. The same bacteria that may be normally present in your body (in your bowel, for example) may cause illness when they move to a different part of your body (your bladder, for example).

BARIUM ENEMA—barium placed into the large bowel for purposes of x-ray diagnosis. The barium will show up as white on the x-ray film.

BENIGN—non-invasive, non cancerous. Usually referring to tumors, they rarely cause serious illness or death.

BICU—abbreviation for "Burn Intensive Care Unit." A specialized area equipped for the care and treatment of patients with severe burns.

BILE—a chemical substance produced by the liver and stored in the gall bladder eventually used in the digestive process of food.

BIOPSY—removal of tissue from a living body for examination. The tissue may be removed with a surgical procedure or with a needle but only a small portion of the organ is removed.

BLADDER—a sac made of tissue, containing air or fluid. Most commonly used in reference to the gall bladder or urinary bladder.

BLISTER—separation of epidermis skin layer from dermis by fluid. The fluid may be clear or bloody depending on the cause.

BLS—abbreviation for "Basic Life Support." Usually used in referring to emergency vehicles. BLS represents the simplest form of emergency transportation with only first aid provided en route to the hospital.

BLOOD—a fluid circulating throughout the body that carries red blood cells with oxygen to nourish tissues. It also carries many other chemical products to maintain life, and waste products to the kidneys and other organs for removal.

BLOOD PRESSURE—pressure exerted by blood on blood vessel walls. If the pressure gets too high it can damage the blood vessels and other internal organs.

BONE—part of the skeletal system. The way we literally hang all our muscles and organs together.

BOWEL—the term generally used to describe the intestinal tract, usually referring to the large and small intestine.

BRAIN—located in the skull, the brain regulates all our bodily functions and controls our life.

C

CALORIES—actually a unit of energy but in general used as a measure of dietary indiscretion, since the number of calories eaten is related to weight gain or loss.

CANCER—a malignant growth in any part of the body.

CAPILLARY—the smallest blood vessels that connect arteries and veins and through which the oxygen, nutrients and waste products enter and leave the organs of the body.

CARCINOMA—a cancerous growth of epithelial tissue. All tissue types can develop cancer (such as blood, lymph nodes) but the most common type is carcinoma.

CARDIAC—pertaining to the heart. This is a general term that usually modifies additional words (for example, cardiac patient, cardiac vessels.)

CATARACT—an opacity of the crystalline lens in the eye. Cataracts interfere with clear vision. They can be corrected surgically.

CATHETER—a hollow tube. Catheters can be inserted into bodily orifices and used to drain internal secretions.

CCU—abbreviation for "Cardiac Care Unit." A hospital unit for the intensive care of patients with severe heart disease.

CERUMEN—the waxy substance secreted by the ear. If produced in excess it can make hearing difficult.

CESAREAN SECTION—delivery of fetus (baby) through an abdominal incision. This may be necessary if there is difficulty in the normal delivery process.

CHEMOTHERAPY—use of specific chemical agents to stop or remove a disease in the body. Usually referring to treatment of those patients with malignant diseases.

CHOLECYSTECTOMY—surgical removal of the gallbladder.

CHOLESTEROL—a chemical substance normally produced by the body but also extracted from certain foods. Some cholesterol is essential for life but too much can lead to damage of blood vessels and other organs.

CHRONIC—lingering, lasting—as opposed to acute. Many diseases can be classified as chronic if they persist for a long time and are difficult to cure.

CIRCUMCISION—removal of the foreskin from the male penis. This is often done to newborn children and aids in maintaining cleanliness of the penis and avoiding malignancy of the penis in later life.

CIRRHOSIS—a chronic condition of the liver that can result in liver failure due to extensive scarring of that organ. Often due to prolonged alcoholism.

CLAP—a common term for gonorrhea, a sexually transmitted infection.

COLIC—severe pain from periodic spasm of an abdominal organ. Often associated with kidney stones.

COLON—large bowel from the cecum to rectum.

COLONOSCOPY—visual inspection of the walls of the large bowel, using an instrument with lenses and lights.

COMA—state of unarousable unconsciousness. It may be prolonged and last for days, months and even years.

CONDYLOMA—warts. May be found anywhere on the skin but usually in moist dark areas and often in the genital area.

CONGENITAL—abnormal conditions present at birth. They may vary from insignificant to major medical problems.

CONSENT—agreement. In the medical sense it is the written permission the patient gives to the hospital or doctor specifically allowing for medical care.

CORONARY ARTERIES—arteries supplying blood to the heart. Narrowing or spasm results in angina, or pain and even may result in heart damage.

CPR—abbreviation of "cardio-pulmonary resuscitation." An emergency procedure used to revive patients who have stopped breathing or have no heart activity. Everyone should learn how to do this procedure.

C-T SCAN—abbreviation for "Computerized Tomography Scan." An x-ray examination that utilizes computer enhancement or improvement of x-rays to allow better pictures.

CYSTITIS—inflammation of the urinary bladder, usually caused by bacterial infection.

D

D & C—an abbreviation for "Dilatation and Curettage." A form of examination and treatment for women having problems with the lining of the uterus.

DIABETES—a disease of metabolism in which the body is unable to control the level of blood sugar. Insulin, made in the pancreas is the chemical control mechanism. If too little insulin is produced by the pancreas then diabetes is the result. It is a chronic disease that produces many symptoms and may even lead to eventual death if not well controlled.

D.O.—abbreviation for "Doctor of Osteopathy," the degree obtained after graduation of a school of osteopathy which is a specialized graduate school that includes a medical curriculum in its program.

DOA—abbreviation for "Dead On Arrival." A term used in emergency medicine to describe a patient who died before care could be given.

DRG—abbreviation for "Diagnostic Related Group," a term used by insurance companies such as Medicare, to categorize medical diagnoses for payment purposes.

DSA—abbreviation for "Day of Surgery Admission." The patient who will have elective surgery is admitted the same morning as the surgical procedure instead of the night before.

DSU—abbreviation for "Day Surgery Unit." The hospital unit that cares for surgical patients before and after the surgical procedure, but who are not admitted to the hospital overnight.

E

EDEMA—excess fluid in the tissues. When it occurs in the skin, swollen legs, eyelids, etc. are the result.

ER—abbreviation for "Emergency Room."

EMS—abbreviation for "Emergency Medical Service," the ambulance service in your community.

EMT—abbreviation for "Emergency Medical Technician," an individual specially trained to provide ambulance service on a transfer or emergency basis.

ENDOTRACHEAL TUBES—tubes that are placed into the lungs, through the mouth or nose, thereby allowing the patient to breath without any blockage to the flow of air or oxygen.

ENURESIS—involuntary urination, usually at night. Also known as bed wetting, this problem plagues many children and their parents.

EPIDERMIS—outer layer of skin.

EPILEPSY—convulsive seizures.

ESOPHAGUS—muscular tube connecting the mouth to the stomach.

ETHER—a chemical that has anesthetic properties. It was the first chemical widely used to put patients to sleep for surgery.

F

FATIGUE—tiredness, weariness. Often a symptom of illness.

FDA—abbreviation for "Food and Drug Administration." The federal agency charged with protecting the public from dangerous medications or medical equipment.

FEBRILE—having a fever.

FLUOROSCOPE—an x-ray machine that allows the doctor to look inside the patient and see the organs as they move and function.

FOOD AND DRUG ADMINISTRATION—the federal agency charged with protecting the public from dangerous medications or medical equipment.

G

GALL BLADDER—the muscular sac, found just beneath the liver in which bile is stored for later use in the digestive tract to aid in the digestive process.

GANGRENE—death of tissue. It may occur in the extremities and may result in loss of the limb.

GASTRITIS—inflammation of the stomach.

GENERIC DRUGS—copies of drugs made by pharmaceutical companies after the patent granted the original drug has expired. They are usually less expensive than the original drug.

GP—abbreviation for "General Practitioner." Often a family doctor who sees the patient first and seeks consultation with other physicians if necessary.

GLUCOSE—sugar. An essential chemical required to provide energy for bodily function.

H

HEADACHE—a pain in the head. Although it may be due to many different reasons, some may be minor but others serious.

HEART ATTACK—the common term for myocardial infarction. Major destruction of the heart muscle and even death may occur.

HEMORRHAGE—discharge of blood in large amounts. May be from any part of the body.

HEPATITIS—inflammation of the liver. This contagious disease may be quite serious.

HERNIA—protrusion of an organ into a cavity. These most often occur in the groin area and should be evaluated by a doctor because they can become serious.

HMO—abbreviation for "Health Maintenance Organization." Such health care organizations are become increasingly popular forms of medical care since they supposedly reduce costs. They do limit the types and sources of medical care available to the patient.

HORMONE—chemical messengers produced by many of the glands of the body. Hormones are essential to good health maintenance.

HOSPICE—an organization dedicated to care for the dying patient and the family of such a patient. This group provides superb support.

HYPERTENSION—an elevation of the blood pressure. Increased blood pressure may damage the organs in the body, even in the short term. Periodic blood pressure checks are essential.

HYPERVENTILATION—breathing at a very fast rate. Usually caused by stress, hyperventilation may cause major alterations in the body chemistry and should be avoided.

I

ICU—abbreviation for "Intensive Care Unit." A place in the hospital where very ill patients can receive close attention and treatment.

IMMUNE SYSTEM—the system in the body designed to fight infections.

IMMUNIZATIONS—treatments designed to protect the body from contagious diseases. Often injections of medications, actually made from the disease producing organisms, are required.

INFECTIONS—diseases produced by microorganisms that invade the body. Some of the microorganisms normally occur in or on the body in one place but can produce illness if they move to some other place in the body.

INFLAMMATION—the body's reaction to injury. Usually characterized by swelling, redness, heat and pain.

INTENSIVE CARE UNIT—a special place in the hospital where the very sickest patients can be cared for by highly trained staff and with the most sophisticated equipment.

INTESTINE—that part of the digestive tract from the end of the stomach to the anus, it's two main parts are the small intestine and large intestine.

J

JAUNDICE—yellow skin due to bile pigment deposition. This may indicate a serious illness that requires treatment.

JCAHO—an abbreviation for "Joint Commission on Accreditation of Health Organizations." An organization that inspects and approves hospitals based on predetermined standards.

K

KIDNEY—a bean shaped organ, usually paired, whose main function is to cleanse the body of waste products.

L

LENGTH OF STAY—a term used to describe the number of days a patient stays in the hospital.

LIFELINE—designed to be worn by a person, this device has a button that can be pressed to summon help in an emergency.

LIVING WILL—legally prepared instructions to your family, physicians and any one else, concerning how you want your medical care to proceed during periods when you are not able to give verbal instructions.

LVN—abbreviation for "Licensed Vocational Nurse."

M

M.D.—abbreviation for "Medical Doctor," the degree obtained following completion of a medical school program.

MAGNETIC RESONANCE IMAGING—a technique to visualize the internal organs of the body using very strong magnetic waves and very sophisticated computers.

MALIGNANCY—a cancerous tumor.

MAMMOGRAM—an x-ray examination of the breast particularly designed to evaluate the breast for tumors.

MEDICAID—a governmental health care program designed to provide health care assistance for low income individuals.

MEDICARE—a governmental health care program designed to provide health care assistance for elderly or disabled individuals.

METASTASES—spread of a disease process, usually referring to malignant diseases.

MICU—abbreviation for "Medical Intensive Care Unit" or "Mobile Intensive Care Unit" where very intensive care can be provided either in the hospital or en route to the hospital.

MRI—abbreviation for "Magnetic Resonance Imaging," a very sophisticated machine to evaluate the internal anatomy without the need for x-rays.

MYOCARDIAL INFARCTION—damage to the muscles of the heart due to loss of the blood supply. Also called a "heart attack."

N

NEOPLASM—literally a "new growth." It may be benign or malignant.

NOSOCOMIAL INFECTION—an infection acquired while in the hospital. Usually referring to those patients who are catheterized or have some predisposing factors that make infections develop more easily.

O

OR—abbreviation for "Operating Room." The highly specialized hospital unit where surgical procedures are performed.

OXYGEN—a chemical substance vital for the maintenance of life since all living tissues require oxygen to function.

P

PAP SMEAR–a test to evaluate the possibility of malignancy of the cervix or the vaginal part of the uterus.

PARAMEDICS–specially trained individuals who have the ability to render medical care, usually on an emergency basis and usually in a setting other than in the hospital.

PDR–abbreviation for "Physician's Desk Reference." A book listing the vast majority of drugs available for use by physicians. Also listed is a description of the drug, its side effects, complications and many other important facts about the medication.

PENICILLIN–an antibiotic designed to kill a variety of bacterial micro-organisms. Penicillin was one of the first antibiotics discovered.

PEPTIC ULCER–an ulcer in the stomach. Ulcers are open sores that may occur anywhere on the skin or in the internal organs. They are usually painful.

PHLEBOTOMIST–a health care worker specially trained in blood drawing techniques.

PHYSICAL THERAPIST–a health care provider specially trained in physical rehabilitation of patients after illness.

PICU–abbreviation for "Pediatric Intensive Care Unit." A special place in the hospital for the care of the seriously ill child.

PPO–abbreviation for "Preferred Provider Organization," an organization designed to provide health care at a reduced cost by limiting the number of participating doctors and negotiating reduced rates with them.

PREFERRED PROVIDER ORGANIZATION–an organization designed to provide health care at a reduced cost by limiting the number of participating doctors and negotiating reduced rates with them.

PRESCRIPTION–an order, by a physician, usually written and usually for some type of medication.

PROGNOSIS–a prediction of whether a patient will recover from an illness.

PROPHYLAXIS–prevention. Usually referring to the use of medications such as antibiotics to prevent the development of illness.

PROSTATE–a gland, about the size of a small egg, in the male that provides nutrients for the sperm.

PULSE–a rate or rhythm. Usually used in reference to the arterial blood vessels. The pulse can be counted and evaluated as to its character.

R

RADIATION–production and transmission of energy rays through the body. Radiation can be used to view the internal organs or treat some types of cancers.

REACH FOR RECOVERY–a support group designed to help women who have had major breast surgery.

RESUSCI-ANNIE–a "dummy" in the form of a human specifically designed as a method of learning cardio-pulmonary resuscitation.

RN–abbreviation for "Registered Nurse." A graduate from an approved nursing program who has passed a state licensure examination.

RR–abbreviation for "Recovery Room," a special area in the hospital to which patients are taken after their operations so that they may recover from the surgery and anesthetic sufficiently before they are taken back to their regular room.

RUPTURE–a breakage. Often used as the common term for a hernia.

S

SCUTWORK–a slang expression for the tasks performed by students and resident physicians in the hospital. The tasks, while important, are often menial.

SEIZURE–a sudden attack of pain. Usually used to describe epileptic seizure, produced by damage to the brain and resulting in convulsive activity.

SHOCK–an illness, usually an emergency, in which there is not enough blood returning to the heart for appropriate circulation. It may result from a variety of disease processes.

SINUSITIS—an inflammation or infection of the sinuses.

SKIN—the outer coverings of the body. Composed of several layers, the skin provides protection from the elements.

SPHYGMOMANOMETER—a machine to measure blood pressure.

SPLEEN—an abdominal organ found on the left side whose function is to filter, store and in some cases make blood.

STOMACH—an organ in the digestive tract that not only acts to hold food that has been eaten but also participates in the digestive process of that food.

STROKE—in medical terms usually referring to sudden loss of consciousness and paralysis. This is usually due to either bleeding into the brain or blockage of a blood vessel going to the brain.

STROKE CLUB—a support group designed to help people who have had strokes.

T

TARTAR—a hard material deposited around the teeth and gums that is produced by bacterial action in the mouth. It can be minimized by good tooth and gum care such as brushing and flossing.

THORAX—the chest. The lungs and heart are the major organs found in the thorax.

THYROID—a gland located in the neck that produces a hormone necessary to maintain bodily function.

TRACHEA—a tubular structure, in the neck and upper chest that conducts air to the lungs.

TRANSFUSION—the injection of blood into the bloodstream. This may vary from large quantities of blood to small quantities of blood products.

TRANSPLANTATION—the movement of an organ or tissue from one place to another. This may be in the same patient or from one individual to another.

TRAUMA CENTER—a special area in the hospital designed for the care of patients who have sustained some type of trauma or serious medical illness.

TRIAGE—a french word meaning "sorting." Triage is the determination made by health care workers as to who are the patients requiring most urgent care.

TUMOR—literally a swelling but usually used in regard to a neoplasm.

U

ULCER—an open sore that can occur on the skin or in internal organs.

ULTRASOUND—a device designed to allow the viewing of internal organs using sound waves, much like underwater sonar, to bounce off of the organs and create a picture on a screen.

UMBILICUS—also known as the "belly button," the umbilicus represents the place where the umbilical cord entered the body in the developing fetus. The umbilical cord carried the mother's blood to the placenta so that nutrients could be transferred to the baby.

URETER—a muscular tube connecting the kidney and the bladder through which urine passes.

URETHRA—a muscular tube that connects the bladder to the outside of the body through which urine passes. It goes directly through the prostate gland in the male.

UTERUS—an organ of female reproduction, the uterus is the site of the developing fetus or baby.

UTILIZATION REVIEW—a method to ensure the most effective and cost saving measures are used to diagnose and treat patients.

V

VARICOSE VEINS—dilated veins, usually appearing on the legs. The veins stretch and not only look unsightly but also produce pain.

VEIN—blood vessels that return blood to the heart after it passes through the various organs and tissues.

VITAMIN—a chemical substance vital to the normal bodily functions. Some are produced by the body and others must be eaten to be available for use.

W

WART—a growth, usually caused by viruses that occurs on the skin or other bodily coverings. Some are sexually transmitted.

X-Y-Z

X-RAY—a technique of producing special rays that can penetrate bodily tissues and can demonstrate internal anatomy on film.

Index

E

EAP   236
earache   143
ears   242
ECG   118
education   182
EEG   118
egional anesthetic   59
Egypt   74
EKG   118
elbow grease   35
elderly   1, 96
elective surgery   101
electrical outlet   21
electrical wiring   215
electricians   172
electronic devices   44
emergency   2, 7, 9, 44, 46,
    57, 102, 132, 138, 140, 213
emergency medical technician   46
emergency room   29, 50
endotracheal tubes   73
enema   74, 85
enemas   145
environment   12, 97
EPO   236
equipment   3
ER   118
estate taxes   9
ether   59
ethics   110
euthanasia   110
evaluations   53
exercise   190, 208, 218, 240, 248
expertise   106
exploratory operation   57
eyelids   244
eyes   79, 242

F

facial implants   226
faculty advisor   130
faith   83, 104
false name   16
family   58
family medicine   108, 150

family practitioner   105
fat   22, 201
FDA   161, 167
Federal Aviation Administration   49
fertility drugs   185
feverish   240
fiber   201
financial liability   1
fine china   22
fire department   48, 213
fire trucks   47
first aid   46, 211
flies   24
flowers   24, 41
flu   196
fluoroscope   69
fluoroscopy   70
food   24
Food and Drug Administra-
    tion   161, 226
food service   37
foreign country   199
foreign language   15
forms   14
freeways   49
funeral   9, 68

G

gall bladder   138
gall bladders   72
gastrointestinal tract   74
general anesthetic   59
general information   45
generators   172
generic drugs   165
gift shop   11
gift shops   31, 86
gifts   40
glaucoma testing   182
goat glands   161
gold   11
golden hour   48
good samaritan   211
government   1
government agency   229
governmental regulations   37
gown   133

gowns 75, 145
gravity 173
gray 250
groin 250
group therapy 231
guinea pig 63
gum disease 159
gums 244
gynecology 108

H

hair 240
handicapped 196
hazards 215
head 246
headaches 1, 240
health xi, 190
health care 1, 3, 11, 12,
    18, 93, 104, 131, 132
health care delivery system 146
health care system xi, 31, 235
health care team 37, 150
health clubs 218
health codes 4
health fairs 182
health insurance 50
health problem 112
health problems 189
hear 242
hearing impaired 196
heart 70, 71
heart attack 50, 52
heart attacks 46
heart surgery 109
helicopter 48
hematology 150
hepatitis 67
hernia 55, 56
high-rise buildings 49
highway 3
HIV 202
HIV virus 75
HMO 55, 103, 229, 235, 236
holidays 87
home 13
home care 100
honors 120

hospice 98, 192
hospital 2, 6, 9, 11, 12,
    18, 29, 132, 147, 179, 233
hospital costs 55
hospital food 22
hospital room 20, 24, 100
hospital stay 55
hospitalization 7
hospitals 4
hot dog 22
hotel 85, 97, 172, 199, 208
hotel reservation 20
house calls 131, 147, 174, 215
housekeepers 35, 37, 172
housing 2
HS 117
hurt 242
hygiene 35
hypertension 79, 108

I

I.V. 26, 46, 87, 118
ice cream 113
ICU 34, 118
identification 12
identification tag 90
illness 1
IM 117
immune system 91
immunizations 198
incision 63
incurable disease 98
indigent 110
infection control 92
infections 106
infectious diseases 89
insect bites 76
insects 24
insomnia 52, 91
inspection 4
institutions 2
instruments 174
insulin 164
insurance 175, 185
insurance company
    1, 7, 13, 17, 29, 101, 122, 229
intravenous fluids 187

menu 5, 23
microfilm 14
microsurgery 185
microwave ovens 215
military institutions 21
millionaire 114
ministry 83
mobile intensive care unit 46
moccasins 145
moles 203
money 11
monitor 26
monitors 12
motorbike 216
mouth 244, 246
movie stars 16
Mr. Yuk 170
MRI 70, 187
mucus 246
mud baths 207
muscle 113
music therapy 86

N

name tags 30
narcotic 111
Narcotics Anonymous 231
NASA 103
nasal tracheal tubes 73
neck 79, 246
needles 71
neurologist 108
neurosurgery 150
newspaper 17
newspapers 13, 110
next-of-kin 7
night 242
Nightingale, Florence 151
noise 26, 27
nonprofit organization 97
nose 73, 244
    stuffed 244
nose bleed 205
nosebleeds 240
nosocomial infections 91
notes 14
NPO 118

nurse call button 20
nurse practitioner 152
nurse-to-patient ratio 5
nurses 33, 37, 151
nursing home 96
nursing shortage 173
nutrition 65

O

O Positive 68
oat bran 230
occupational therapy 86
office visit 131
open heart surgery 56
operating room 58, 61, 188
operation 11, 147
opinion 90
OR 118, 147
oral sex 76
organ donation 9
orthopedic surgeon 108
ostrich syndrome 205
ounce of prevention is worth a pound
    of cure 156
outlets 172, 215
outside organizations 178
over-the-bed table 21
over-the-counter medicine 156
overhead 172
overweight 201, 230, 240
oxygen 21, 71, 73, 172, 205

P

PA 149
pagers 12, 139
pain 65, 113, 239
pain-free surgery 59
Painless Parker 156
pains 246, 250
Palmer, Arnold 194
PAP smears 201
paper trays 22
paramedic 46, 52
parathyroid glands 79
Pasteur, Louis 220
patches 240, 242
patient 14, 21, 42, 112

patient relations 78, 85
pauper 114
PDR 163
pediatrics 108, 130
penicillin 225
penile implants 226
per os Q.D. 117
periscope 63
permission for treatment 15
pests 24
pet 156
pharmacist 22, 117
pheasant 23
phlebotomist 30
PHO 236
phone call 41, 44
physical examinations 133, 149
physical therapists 14
physician-patient relationship 229
physician's assistant 149
PICU 118
pillows 246
pilot 48
pink ladies 31
plants 24
plastic surgery 56
pneumonia 65
poison 169
Poison Control Center 44, 169
Police 12
police department 48
polio vaccine 225
politicians 51
politics 83
pollen 135
POS 236
pounds 219
PPO 55, 103, 235, 236
prayer 41, 83
pre-certification 229
preferred provider 1
premium 1
preschooler 42
prescription 22, 52
prescriptions 40, 94
preventive maintenance 156
preventive medicine 201
primary care physician 108, 236

prison 7
privacy 17, 28, 34, 36, 85, 90
private nurse 33, 93
private room 5, 20, 77
PRN 117
profession of specialists 108
prognosis 125
prophylaxis 158
prostate 201
prostate gland 204
prostate screening 183
prostate surgery 56
psychiatrists 86, 209
psychiatry 130
psychologists 86, 209, 231
public funds 235
purses 11

Q

Q4H 117
questions 123
quiet 26, 42

R

radiation 172
radiation physicist 70
radiation therapist 70
radio control 21
radioactive material 92
radiologic technician 70
radiologist 70
radiology 70
records 14
records transfer 19
recovery 2, 23, 65
recovery room 58
recovery rooms 172
religion 83
remission 125
research 161, 189, 230
residency program 129
resolution 230
respirator 73
Resusci-Annie 213
rheumatologist 108
rich 147
right to die with dignity 110